Foundations
for a
Feminist Restructuring
of the Academic Disciplines

About the Editors

Michele Paludi, PhD, is Associate Professor of Psychology at Hunter College, in New York City. As a developmental psychologist, her research has focused on the sociopsychological and structural factors affecting women's achievement and the career pathways they follow. She is currently directing her research efforts toward the impact of role models and mentors on women's career development and sexual and gender harassment. She is also working on integrating the scholarship of women and individuals of color into the psychology curriculum. Dr. Paludi is the author of *Exploring/Teaching the Psychology of Women: A Manual of Resources*, editor of *Ivory Power: Gender and Sexual Harassment in the Academy,* and co-editor, with Florence Denmark, of the *Handbook of the Psychology of Women*.

Gertrude Steuernagel, PhD, is Associate Professor of Political Science and Coordinator of the Women's Studies Program at Kent State University, Kent, Ohio. She teaches an introductory women's studies course, as well as a class on women and politics. Her research interests include feminist theory and women and public policy, particularly questions related to women, work, and political participation. The author of *Political Philosophy as Therapy: Marcuse Reconsidered*, she has also written articles that have appeared in a number of professional journals.

Foundations for a Feminist Restructuring of the Academic Disciplines

Edited by
Michele A. Paludi
Gertrude A. Steuernagel

Harrington Park Press
New York • London

ISBN 0-918393-64-7

Published by

Harrington Park Press, 10 Alice Street, Binghamton, NY 13904-1580
EUROSPAN/Harrington, 3 Henrietta Street, London, WC2E 8LU England

Harrington Park Press, is a subsidiary of The Haworth Press, Inc., 10 Alice Street, Binghamton, New York 13904-1580.

Cover design by Marshall Andrews.

Library of Congress Cataloging-in-Publication Data

Foundations for a feminist restructuring of the academic disciplines / edited by
Michele A. Paludi, Gertrude A. Steuernagel.
    p.   cm.
   Includes bibliographical references and index.
   ISBN 0-918393-64-7
   1. Women's studies. 2. Education, Higher. 3. Feminism. I. Paludi, Michele Antoinette.
II. Steuernagel, Gertrude A.
HQ1180.F68 1990
   305.4'11—dc20

                                                 89-71663
                                                 CIP

To Antoinette—my mother—who taught Michael, Rosalie, Lucille, and me a valuable image of woman: STRENGTH.

M.A.P.

To Jessica, Abby, Kristen, and Joanna—my goddaughters and images of the future . . . and, to Scott—my love.

G.A.S.

CONTENTS

About the Contributors

Michele Paludi is a developmental psychologist whose research concerns the sociopsychological and structural factors affecting women's achievement and the career pathways they follow. Recently, she has focused her research efforts upon the impact of role models and mentors on women's career development and on sexual and gender harassment. She is also working on integrating the scholarship on women and individuals of color into the psychology curriculum. Michele is author of *Exploring/Teaching the Psychology of Women: A Manual of Resources*, editor of *Ivory Power: Gender and Sexual Harassment in the Academy*, and co-editor (with Florence Denmark) of the *Handbook of the Psychology of Women*. Recently, Michele organized a collective of educators for women of color. Together, they are writing *The Psychology of Women: Enhancing Sociocultural Awareness*.

Gertrude Steuernagel is an Associate Professor of Political Science and Coordinator of the Women's Studies Program at Kent State University. She teaches an introductory women's studies course as well as a class on women and politics. Her research interests include feminist theory, and women and public policy. She is particularly interested in questions related to women, work, and political participation. Her work has appeared in a number of journals, including, *Polity, Women and Politics*, and the *Journal of Popular Culture*. She is the author of *Political Philosophy as Therapy: Marcuse Reconsidered*.

Barbara Clements's research interests include women in the Communist Party in Russia and the Soviet Union, and women's experiences in the Russian Revolution. She teaches courses in Russian history and women's history at the University of Akron, in addition to women's studies, women in modern Europe, and women in the U.S. and the U.S.S.R. in the twentieth century. Barbara is the author of *Bolshevik Feminist: The Life of Aleksandra*

Kollontai. She has published her work on the impact of the civil war on women and family relations, Russian social-democracy and the woman question, and working class and peasant women in the Russian revolution.

Claire Etaugh is Professor of Psychology at Bradley University. Her research concerns sex-role development, psychology of women, and effects of material employment and day care. Claire has published her research on perceptions of women, effects of employment on children, demographic predictors of college students' attitudes toward working mothers, and gender differences in eating restraint and cognitive performance. Claire is an Associate Editor of the *Psychology of Women Quarterly* and is on the editorial board of *Sex Roles*. She teaches courses on the psychology of women, introduction to women's studies, and behavioral sex roles.

Judith E. Albino is Professor of Behavioral Sciences and Lisa A. Tedesco is Associate Professor of Fixed Prosthodontics and Behavioral Sciences at the School of Dental Medicine, the State University of New York at Buffalo, where they have collaborated on health behavior research for more than ten years. Their teaching in behavioral issues related to dentistry and in communication skills has provided an avenue for adapting dental professional education and practice to the needs and concerns of women patients and to a growing number of women dental students and dentists. Their research is not focused exclusively on women's issues nor on dentistry, but employs a feminist perspective in analyzing a variety of issues related to health behavior. Their research team provides a rich and supportive training ground for undergraduate, graduate, and postdoctoral students interested in developing their research skills in a health behavior setting. Both Judith and Lisa have research grants funded by the National Institute of Dental Research, and both are active in the American Association for Dental Research and the American Psychological Association. Judith has served for three years as Associate Provost at the State University of New York at Buffalo and currently is Interim Dean of the School of Architecture and Environmental Design. Judith consults widely on issues related to dental education and is president elect of the Educational Research/Development and Curriculum Section of the American Association of Dental Schools.

Cheryl Shenkle is currently Director of the Division of Applied Research at the School of Management, State University of New York at Buffalo. As of the writing of her chapter for this volume, Cheryl was a research associate with Judith Albino and Lisa Tedesco on a five-year orthodontic behavior study. Cheryl has over ten years of research experience, which includes areas of management-related applied research and health behavior research conducted as a member of the Judith Albino and Lisa Tedesco research team.

Barbara Burnell is an Associate Professor of Economics at the College of Wooster in Wooster, Ohio. During 1985 she was a Visiting Scholar at The Urban Institute in Washington, DC. Her research interests include federal tax reform, government structure in metropolitan areas, state and local public finance, economics and philosophy, and women and technological change. Barbara has taught courses on principles of economics, economic statistics, women in the economy, introduction to women's studies, and women and work.

Elizabeth Langland is an Associate Professor of English at the University of Florida. She is the author of *Society in the Novel* and co-editor of *The Voyage In: Fictions of Female Development* and *A Feminist Perspective in the Academy: The Difference It Makes*. She teaches images of women in literature and religion as well as women and literature.

Judith Worell is a Professor and Director of Training in Counseling Psychology, University of Kentucky. She teaches courses in sex-role development and counseling women in addition to her regular teaching assignments in ethics, cognitive-behavioral counseling, and social development. Current research interests focus on women's close relationships, including friendship and romantic partners, and explorations in loneliness. She regards herself as a feminist therapist, is recent Past-President of the Clinical Psychology of Women section of the American Psychological Association, and is completing a text on counseling women. She is also the editor of the *Psychology of Women Quarterly*, a journal of theory and research on feminist psychology. Recent publications include "Single Mothers: From Problems to Policies" (*Women & Therapy*, 7(4)

1988, pp. 3-14) and "Support and Satisfaction in Women's Close Relationships" (*Clinical Psychology Review*, in press).

Vivian P. Makosky was Executive Director for Educational and Public Affairs at the American Psychological Association. She was Professor of Psychology at St. Lawrence University, where she was also chairperson of the department until her position at the American Psychological Association in 1985. Vivian's research concerns interpersonal relationships and attraction, achievement among women, and life stress and mental health of low-income mothers. Vivian has taught courses in social psychology, group dynamics, and social research. In addition, she taught the first course in the women's studies program at St. Lawrence: Psychology of Women. Vivian also co-taught Images of Women with colleagues from the English and Fine Arts departments. She is a member of several divisions of the American Psychological Association, including psychology of women, teaching of psychology, and ethnic minority issues. Vivian is also a participant of the Task Force on Women and Depression sponsored by the American Psychological Association.

Dorothy O. Helly is a historian of Victorian England. She is a Professor of History at Hunter College, and has been an Associate Dean and Coordinator of Women's Studies.

Foreword

Women's studies as a field is entering its third decade; integrating the new scholarship on women, first called "mainstreaming," is entering its second. Now referred to as balancing the curriculum for gender, race, ethnicity, and social class, this process of curricular transformation has been bringing about an academic revolution. Today, using gender as a category of analysis has become part of theoretical and practical studies everywhere on the frontiers of knowledge in the fields of the social sciences and the humanities and is making inroads into the arts and the natural sciences. Today's university classroom not only reflects a changing demography in American higher education, it also reflects the site of today's academic revolution. The changes in perspective and knowledge wrought by feminist approaches to scholarship have left no part of the academic world immune: from the organization and administration of the university itself to its staffing, its recruitment policies, its student support facilities, its faculty advancement policies, and not least, the classroom itself.

The editors of this book are to be congratulated for taking the issues raised by this academic revolution and exploring them for those who would like to understand what is happening today in the disciplines. This is contested ground. No longer are our towers ivory and secluded or our pronouncements of limited interest to the world: we are struggling with the shape of who we are, where we have come from, and where we are going. Too long has that shape simply been expected to follow the form of the privileged white male of the Western past without asking who the rest of us have been and how our experiences have differed and whether we view the priorities for the future in another light. We are concerned not to label as "universal" the ideas and reactions of a small strata of one gender who held the power to pass on their views successfully. We now listen to all our different voices, past and present, telling us how various and cross-grained our lives have been, are still, and may continue to be. These voices are in our classrooms. It is critical that we learn how to listen carefully to them.

The wonderful part, which this book shares with you, is just how exciting this academic revolution is. We are finding out more about all ourselves, forming new hypotheses about matters long thought incontestable, and sharing this adventure with our students. We have all become learners; we all help each other to learn. This book invites you to join in and discover this new world. Michele Paludi and Gertrude Steuernagel are to be congratulated on making these essays available to us all.

Dorothy O. Helly
Professor of History and Women's Studies
Hunter College CUNY

Preface

Efforts to integrate feminist scholarship into the curriculum of colleges and universities received an impetus from an unexpected quarter, the Chicago-based political philosopher, Allan Bloom. The publication of his *Closing of the American Mind* (1987) was greeted by the public with an amazing degree of receptivity. Bloom's criticisms of the American system of higher education included an attack on feminism and what it has done to that system. He took particular care to attack what the present volume attempts to do, that is, to integrate feminist scholarship into the curriculum. For Bloom, feminists are akin to hero slayers. "But," he says of the feminist position concerning Great Books, "never, never must a student be attracted to those old ways and take them as models for him or herself" (Bloom, 1987, p. 69). The monolithic, destructive role Bloom attributes to feminist scholarship is as dangerous as it is erroneous. The essays in this volume serve as an engaging and provocative response to this attack.

This volume comes out of the experiences of women who are intimately involved with feminist pedagogy and curriculum transformation. All contributors to this volume have described a variety of educational environments feminists have established in the academy. As pointed out by the contributors to this volume, the impact of feminist scholarship on the substance of the academy is illusive. Women's studies as a discipline is now in its third decade of life. There are abundant opportunities for students to obtain majors or minors in women's studies or to sample courses with a feminist perspective. Faculty members now frequently hold joint positions with women's studies programs and indeed, some universities even have tenure track positions in women's studies. Women's studies scholarship has found avenues through respected journals such as *Signs* and *Feminist Studies*, and scholars have found forums for their feminist work in journals in their discipline, for example,

Women & Politics and *Psychology of Women Quarterly*. To what extent, however, has feminist scholarship impacted the basic curriculum of the academy? The success of women's studies programs has been a mixed blessing. Too often, the tendency has been for feminist scholarship to be contained within the boundaries of women's studies courses and journals. The initial revolutionary thrust of women's studies is threatened by the growing acceptance and recognition of women's studies as a legitimate academic enterprise. What is happening to women's studies, however, is tantamount to what happens to many areas of learning once they gain status within colleges and universities. They become the prerogative of the practitioners. Psychologists don't do physics, historians don't do chemistry, and only women's studies people do women's studies. Feminist scholarship, consequently, becomes contained within the boundaries of women's studies programs, faculty, and students. Initially, feminist scholarship was directed at the very roots of the academy. Conceived as a clarion call to eliminate gender bias in knowledge and ways of knowing, it has become the unwitting victim of the forces of institutionalization.

This is the realization that inspired us to compile this book. From its inception, it has been intended for an audience not familiar with feminist scholarship. As planned, this volume is meant to be shared with faculty and students who have not "gone the women's studies route" in their professional lives but who are interested in what feminist scholarship has to say. The articles in this book have not appeared elsewhere. They were specifically written with the goals of this project in mind. All of the contributors have had experience with teaching and scholarship in women's studies as well as their "home" disciplines. None of the contributors make any assumptions about the backgrounds of the readers. Each of the chapters is constructed so as to be accessible to the reader unfamiliar with feminist scholarship or the discipline under study. As such, this book is intended to supplement and complement many of the fine works currently utilized in women's studies courses. It is not intended to replace them.

Ideally, this volume will be received as an integral part of an emerging tapestry of feminist scholarship directed at transforming the curriculum. As such it is an extension of the vision offered in earlier works such as Elizabeth Langland (a contributor to this volume) and Walter Gove's edited book, *A Feminist Perspective in the Academy* (1981) and Elizabeth Abel and Emily Abel's edited *Signs* reader, *Women, Gender, and Scholarship* (1983). Readers interested in an overview of the theory and methods for transforming the curriculum are urged to consult *Feminist Visions*, edited by Diane Fowlkes and Charlotte McClure (1984). An excellent update of current projects is available in an edition of the *Chronicle of Higher Education* (1987).

The chapters in this volume reflect various disciplines in the academy. We were interested primarily in assuring representation for major fields within the traditional liberal arts curriculum. Even the most cursory glance at the table of contents will reveal serious omissions, but we feel that the decisions we made have resulted in a useful and illustrative guide to those interested in the impact of feminist scholarship on traditional academic disciplines. We readily admit the deficiencies, and hope that there will be sufficient interest in our approach to warrant a second volume.

Most of the work for this volume was completed during Michele Paludi's two years as a Visiting Associate Professor of Women's Studies and Psychology at Hunter College in Manhattan, New York. A great deal of the impetus for this volume came from three major works published by faculty at Hunter College: (1) the Hunter College Women's Studies Collective's text, *Women's Realities, Women's Choices: An Introduction to Women's Studies* (1983); (2) the *Report on a Project to Integrate Scholarship on Women into the Introductory Courses at Hunter College* (edited by Denmark, Helly, & Lees, 1986); and (3) the *Report on a Project to Integrate Scholarship on Women into the Professional Curriculum at Hunter College* (edited by Abramowitz & Helly, 1987).

We are grateful to members of Hunter College's Women's Studies Program who offered suggestions and support: Dorothy O. Helly, Florence Denmark, Sue Rosenberg Zalk, Joan Tronto, Susan Tolliver, Ros Petchesky, Anya Soskin, and Susan Lees. We would also like to thank our colleagues and friends who have contributed to our own feminist education and teaching: Louise Fitzgerald, Darlene DeFour, Richard Barickman, Rhoda Unger, Marcia Darling, Margaret Matlin, Patricia Rozee-Koker, Kathryn Quina,

Nancy Betz, Judy Frankel, Virginia O'Leary, Barbara Wallston, Sandy Shullman, Mary Koss, Laurel Wilcox, Nancy Benham, Virginia Harvey, Linda Rinker, Susan Barnard, Kathe Davis, Jeannette Reuter, Helga Kaplan, Peggy Conway, and David Ahern.

We also commend Bill Cohen at The Haworth Press for understanding that feminist scholarship thrives in an atmosphere of sharing and cooperation and for not insisting that the publishing world needs to harken to a territorial imperative. We especially thank Don Reisman who encouraged us to pursue publication with The Haworth Press. Margaret Anderson, Linda Cohen, Ellen Cole, and Esther Rothblum deserve recognition for their helpful suggestions. We thank you!

We would also like to thank participants in the introductory courses on women's studies at Hunter College and Kent State University for their insight, encouragement, and sage advice. Michele Paludi would like especially to thank the participants in her introductory course in women's studies in the fall, 1987 semester at Hunter College for their comments on various drafts of this volume. They each deserve recognition: Gayle DeWindt, Sandra Texidor, Mary Greer, Diana Torres, Donnie Tuen, Annie Jih, Christine Melenhausen, Hilary Knepper, Mary Ciecierski, Isabella Scapini, Theresa Alessi, Diane Rungu, Gladys Moreno, Angie Mendez, Elsie Jacques, Deborah Silberberg, Judith Ortiz, Mary Robinson, Liz Cruz Chavarro, Wendy Mathis, Rita Walton, Josephine Torres, Maria Hohlahakis, Sandra Petersen, Cynthia Kaplan, Linda Brassell, Jennifer Mancia, and Yonetta Sha Hart.

Finally, we would like to thank each of the women who contributed to this volume: Vivian Makosky, Judith Worell, Claire Etaugh, Judith Albino, Linda Tedesco, Cheryl Shenkle, Barbara Burnell, Barbara Clements, and Elizabeth Langland. Feminism and women's studies remain viable enterprises at the institutions where these women participate because of their dedication to integrating feminism into their professional and personal lives. While they wrote on a variety of images of women in the academy, they agree all women shared some common beliefs: that scholarship on women of color needs to be integrated into the disciplines in the academy, and that the integration of the scholarship on women and women scholars into any one discipline in the academy affects *all* of the academy. The feminist images of women in the academy offered by the contributors to this volume empowered us. We hope you also feel inspired by reading this volume.

Michele A. Paludi and Gertrude A. Steuernagel

Feminism and Women's Studies in the Academy

Vivian P. Makosky
Michele A. Paludi

It seemed pure waste of time to consult those gentlemen who specialise in woman and her effect on whatever it may be — politics, children, wages, morality — numerous and learned as they are. One might as well leave their books unopened.

Virginia Woolf wrote these words fifty-seven years ago when describing British universities. Since that time, many feminists have added their voices to the chorus asserting that the academy has played handmaiden to social values which have been androcentric, focusing on men and coming from a male perspective. As Catherine Stimpson (1971) noted, with regard to women, there have been three kinds of problems in the curriculum: omission, distortions, and trivializations.

Feminists (rightly enough) have identified, protested, lamented, and criticized the sorts of problems defined by Stimpson. What is seldom discussed is the fact that the status of women and women's studies in the academy is not an isolated deviation in an otherwise pure history of the search for academic and scientific "truth." The sciences, particularly, have an aura of being objective and value-free, but as Stanovich has pointed out (1986, p. 14), this has never been the case:

> Each science has gone through a phase when there was resistance to its development. Hypatia of Alexandria, the last scholar to work in the great library, was murdered by members of the early Christian church because her interest in science and learning was associated with paganism. Learned contemporaries of Galileo refused to look into his new telescope be-

1

cause the existence of the moons of Jupiter would have violated their philosophical and theological beliefs. For centuries, the understanding of human anatomy progressed only haltingly because of lay and ecclesiastical prohibitions against the dissection of dead human bodies. Darwin was denounced by the Bishop of Oxford and, of course, by countless others. Broca's Society of Anthropology was opposed in France because knowledge about human beings was thought to be subversive to the state.

Such resistances are not all in the past, as witnessed by the current opposition to the teaching of evolutionary biology in the public schools. When a field with such a long and convincing record of scientific support can still engender such opposition, the resistance to feminist scholarship is placed in a context which makes it seem less unique, albeit no less crippling and offensive.

THE DESIRABILITY OF VALUES IN THE ACADEMY

There is no denying that feminism is an educational value, but it is only one of many. There is no such thing as value-free education. Upon examination, we find so many constraints on the objectivity of scholarly research that we should ". . . view the findings . . . as demonstrating not what necessarily occurs in the world, but what is *possible* if human beings were considered from a particular perspective" (Howard, 1985, p. 261). Even when feminism is not the issue, some scholars today are beginning to advocate that we stop denying the role of values and instead recognize that scholarship which is not concerned with the larger society cannot deal with much of reality. For example, Bellah (1985, p. 38) states:

> Social science as public philosophy cannot be "value free." It accepts the canons of critical, disciplined research, but it does not imagine that such research exists in a moral vacuum. . . . The analysts are part of the whole they are analyzing. In framing their problems and interpreting their results, they draw on their own experience and their membership in a community of research that is in turn located within specific traditions and institutions.

Critics often maintain that women's studies are overtly value-laden, while not seeing the role of values in their own approaches. The academy itself and each discipline within it has a deeply rooted set of traditions. Scholarship is not a disembodied intellectual exercise. The real issue is that they don't like work that is laden with the values of women (Shaw, in McMillen, 1986). Those who maintain that the feminist perspective is the best alternative are stating their value judgments much more explicitly than is typically the case in the academy.

THE ROLE OF ACADEMIC NORMS AND VALUES IN SHAPING SCHOLARSHIP AND EDUCATION

Most academics are not aware of the extent to which their beliefs and values influence their work as scholars and teachers. Most view themselves as objective, if not actually neutral, and certainly they see themselves as fair in their evaluations of students and colleagues. There is little recognition of the extent to which their beliefs and values have been determined by cultural and academic socialization. The reality is that beliefs and values are such an integral part of the self that they are indistinguishable from absolute truth or fact.

The classic goal of scholarship is the search for "truth." This goal is typically accompanied by the implicit belief that there is only one such truth available at a particular point in time (Unger, 1982). Both this goal and criteria used to evaluate whether a piece of work moves us closer to this goal constitute values that are seldom recognized as such. For example, Howard (1985) concludes that scientific theory-appraisal is a sophisticated form of value judgment: When making their appraisals, individual scientists emphasize different subsets of such research values as predictive accuracy, internal coherence, external consistency, unifying power, fertility, simplicity, and testability. Stated more broadly, the point is that values determine which evidence will be weighed more heavily. Indeed, investigations which prove current theories incorrect do not necessarily change them (Unger, 1982), for there are numerous ways in which scholars' values, institutional norms and values, and societal norms and values unobtrusively affect the academy.

The Effects of the Individual Scholars' Values

Finding Topics Worthy of Study

Individuals' values affect every aspect of the scholarly enterprise, beginning with the choice of topic to be studied. Those who choose to present a "standard overview" of 19th century history are implicitly valuing the standard perspective over others. Indeed, the values inherent in conformity are seldom noticed, and disapproval, by definition, is less likely. It is the values inherent in *deviation* that attract attention and condemnation. For example, as Caplan and Nelson ask,

> Why do we constantly study the poor rather than the nonpoor in order to understand the origins of poverty? Why do we study nonachievement among minority group members and undesirable behavior, but do not study exaggerated profit motive among "successful" businessmen [sic] as a form of deviance? Why do we study the use of marijuana as a "drug problem," but not Federal government involvement in the drugging of "minimal brain dysfunction" (MBD) children in our grammar schools? (1973, p. 207)

Feminist scholars have found clearly different topics worthy of study. Feminism has provided answers to a set of research problems that did not come to light in traditional disciplines and could not be solved by the androcentric paradigm (e.g., androgyny, rape, sexual harassment, battered women, and sexism in psychotherapy). Feminist research and scholarship is often generated by examining the disparities between individual experiences and perceptions and existing theory.

Choosing Who Will Be Studied

In the several sciences in which people are studied, the values of the researcher affect not only the selection of topic, but also the participants to be studied. Kelman (1972) points out that much research deals with college students in participant pools, military recruits, children, people on welfare, or institutionalized problem populations, and that all these groups suffer a power deficiency *vis à vis* the researcher. This situation creates "bad science": typically, research is not conducted from the perspective of the disadvantaged groups who are so often the object of study, and the results may range from being irrelevant to being detrimental to the interests of the groups studied.

The biases in the selection of populations for study have been pervasive and long-standing. When Prescott (1978) asked a sample of psychology researchers why they had used single-sex designs for their studies, she received answers ranging from the scientific (e.g., sex differences in this area are already well-documented) through the practical (e.g., availability of only one sex for participation) to the "extrascientific" (e.g., the researcher just didn't want to deal with the other sex). However, none of these individual types of answers would account for the systematic exclusion or inclusion of women in entire fields of study. For example, the classic theories and research on morality and achievement motivation were based on males only (Kohlberg, 1966; McClelland, Atkinson, Clark, & Lowell, 1953). In addition, in research on aggression, nearly 50% of the studies were conducted using male participants only, 10% using females only, and 40% using both sexes. This 50% is higher than the percentage of male-only research in psychology in general (McKenna & Kessler, 1977), supporting the conclusion that when scientists investigate a stereotyped "masculine" behavior, they are less likely to include female participants. The strong historical bias excluding women, old people, and the impoverished from the population samples in stressful life events research has been documented (Makosky, 1980). Thus, the questions a scientist asks are shaped not only by a theoretical model but also by social and gender-role stereotypes. It has taken feminist scholars to identify the biases regarding women and to question the values underlying not only the omissions, but also the over-inclusions. Omissions such as those in research on aggression were noticed more quickly. Blechman (1984) points out that when she sampled three prominent behavioral journals in 1979, in 80% of the articles concerned with intervention, women were all or the majority of clients, but that authors neither examined nor discussed sex or gender effects. It has taken feminists to ask questions about the extent to which the different social worlds of women and men make them more or less responsive to particular therapeutic interventions. Feminism has thus addressed whether research and theorizing on males is indicative of people in general and whether males are more worthy of investigation than females. Women's studies has been a direct response to the failure of the academy to present a comprehensive, inclusive, and affirmative investigation of human behavior.

What's in a Name?

Values are reflected in the labels put on things and the examples chosen for illustration. The classic rule of grammar that says that the masculine pronouns can be used both for the masculine cases and for the generic cases is a good illustration. Grammarians could define such words any way they pleased, but the evidence from research is clear in demonstrating that the reader or hearer was comprehending the masculine, not the generic. For example, when Schneider and Hacker (1973) showed subjects an outline for a purported textbook with chapter titles such as "Urban Man" and "Social Man" for one group and the same outlines labeled "Urban Life" and "Society" for another, those in the former condition chose significantly more "appropriate illustrations" containing only males. Using the traditional forms and examples carry messages which may be unintended, but they are powerful. Linguistic invisibility leads to conceptual invisibility (Harrison, 1975). Knowing this and refusing to change represents a value statement. (It may well be that the more general acceptance of the term "women's studies" rather than "feminist studies" is another example of the importance of labeling, with the former connoting more of the traditional academic "objectivity.")

Defining "Appropriate" Methods of Study

Students in traditional courses seldom realize that the scholars' values have shaped the method of investigation, the analysis of findings, and the choice of explanatory variables selected for examination. In psychology, people have long been making the case for participatory research patterns (Kelman, 1972) and for increased flexibility in research design in general (Schneider, 1974), but it has been primarily feminist scholars who have put such methods into practice.

At the same time, many scholars maintain that although there is a feminist *philosophy* of scholarship, there is no one *method* that is inherently feminist. Such scholars support the importance of a variety of methods in developing a comprehensive view of a topic. For example, Denmark (1983, p. 46) maintains, "Our theories and the questions we researchers ask, as well as the interpretations of our data, can be feminist. However, the methods we use should be appropriate to our questions."

What Does It All Mean?

One of the most powerful ways in which scholars' values affect science and education is through their interpretation of facts and events. Again, interpretations which deviate from the standard or accepted assumptions are likely to be questioned or labeled as value-laden, but those that conform to the norm are not. In the United States, we have strong cultural values emphasizing independence, the effectiveness of individual striving, and the control of individuals over their own lives. These values have strong effects on scholarly interpretations in the academy. For example Caplan and Nelson (1973) discuss the fact that research relating to social problems exhibits a causal attribution bias, favoring explanations that focus on the personal characteristics of those who have the problem to the exclusion of environmental factors. These authors further point out several outcomes of the person-blame interpretations of social problems that society might construe as advantageous. Two outcomes are that these interpretations free the government and other social institutions of blame for the problem, and therefore of responsibility for the solution; and they reinforce generally held beliefs about one's control over his/her fate, thus justifying public complacency about people who have problems. This tendency toward "blaming the victim" is apparent among those who resist a feminist revamping of the curriculum by statements to the effect that if women scholars had done anything worthy of inclusion in textbooks, etc., they would have been included.

Social values and stereotypes affect both the implicit and the explicit interpretations of facts. For example, there is a strong tendency to assume that it's bad that boys from father-absent homes are less masculine than boys from father-present homes. Scales of masculinity and femininity are constructed of test items to which the majority of women and men respond differently. The items themselves are not chosen because they reflect particularly desirable traits or behaviors, so the assumption that it is "better" for males to be masculine is simply a reflection of what that means! And of course the same has held for females and femininity, even though in that case, the content of the assumptions about what constitutes femininity actually has included things that are undesirable in the abstract (Broverman, Broverman, Clarkson, Rosenkrantz, & Vogel, 1970). Masculinity and femininity are value-laden terms, but they have been used as though they are objective. Scholars have often talked about what *is* without examining the implications for what is right or appropriate or desirable, without examining the values base assumed.

The Role of Institutional Norms and Values

The stereotype is of the academy as a place where new ideas, approaches, and views are welcome. Although educational institutions may be more liberal than society at large, the fact remains that they are strong pressed toward conformity to the status quo operating in the academy. This norm is strongly entrenched and serves to support the continuation of the other existing norms and values. For this reason, this implicit conservatism is perhaps the most basic of the unexamined academic norms.

Valuing Objectivity

In the academy there is a traditional norm favoring "objectivity" in teaching and learning processes and in the operation of the evaluation system. It is assumed that one's work is judged only on its merits, for both students and faculty. Richardson (1982) has characterized this norm of objectivity as giving primary importance to cognitive/impersonal processes knowledge acquisition while discrediting or even disallowing emotional/personal modes of learning. Feminist scholars are, by definition, social activists, and this brings them into conflict with peers who have been socialized to believe that advocacy and scholarship are incompatible (Unger, 1982). It is also a source of internal conflict for some.

Valuing Cumulative Over Revisionist Approaches

A third norm operating in the academy is the expectation that a field of study will be based on a substantive, solid, and accumulating body of knowledge which will determine which models and theories will be accepted as valid (Unger, 1982). This expectation has been a hindrance to women's studies (in which the field is constantly being revised) as well as to more traditional fields of study such as developmental and social psychology (Richardson, 1982).

Expertise and Power

A fourth norm in the traditional academy states that the teacher is an expert in the course being taught and, based upon this expertise, accords power in the teacher-student roles primarily to the teacher (Richardson, 1982). Thus, the teacher typically determines not only course content but also (either implicitly or explicitly) how learning will take place. Women's studies teachers typically embrace the feminist philosophy of shared power and responsibility in the classroom, deviating markedly from this norm.

The Superiority of Pure Over Applied Anything

A fifth pervasive norm (which is sometimes explicitly stated, particularly in "liberal arts" contexts) is the one which assigns intellectual superiority and status to "theoretical" or "pure" courses and programs, and defines "applied" or "practical" areas as inferior or derivative (Fisher, 1982). This attitude is apparent in the status of anything "vocational." Given that many of the things that women have learned about the world are based on practical experience and that they have often been concentrated in the "applied" areas in the academy, the existence of this norm has constituted a disproportionate burden on women.

Clearly, there are numerous ways in which academic norms affecting the classroom experience are usually left unexamined—or at least not made explicit to students. These and other institutional norms and values affect academic scholarship as well. One issue is that institutional values, as represented by decision-making groups or individuals, determine what receives funding and/or other types of support. There are few if any situations in which "anything goes," and deans and department chairs frequently make judgments of relative worth when deciding the distribution of funds for travel to scholarly meetings, the allocation of research space, the approval and scheduling of new courses, etc.

State and Federal Funds

Peer review panels rate the worthiness of applications made to outside agencies. As the amount of money available has declined relative to the number and size of the requests made, competition has increased, and with competition, conservatism: when it is necessary to receive a perfect or nearly perfect score in order to qualify for funding, a proposal that offends or appears trivial to even one reviewer is doomed. Funding tends to go to mainstream ideas and already-established scholars. The funding of gender-related research projects declined dramatically between 1980 and 1984 (Rubin, 1985).

Publication

Having access to resources greatly eases the burden of scholarly productivity, which is often operationally defined as publishing. Publishing has been documented as the single most important factor in hiring, promoting, and tenuring academics (Astin & Bayer, 1979). As a result of a strong buyers market since 1970, all types of campuses have moved to upgrade the importance of scholarly productivity as a criterion for promotion and tenure (Schuster & Bowen, 1985).

Although women academics often subscribe to the same belief in hard work and publishing in "top" journals as a means to get ahead, the fact is that there is a much smaller relationship between productivity and promotion for women than for men (O'Connell, Alpert, Richardson, Rotter, Ruble, & Unger, 1978). Feminist research (which is not always acceptable to traditional reviewers) is often published in more specialized "women's studies" outlets (Denmark, 1983), which are typically less prestigious across the academy than more "mainstream" journals. "In summary, even after controlling for differences between academic men and women for degrees, fields, productivity, continuous employment, and so forth — all primary criteria for rewards in the present system — sex differences in rank and salary were still obtained" (Astin & Bayer, 1979, p. 217).

Institutional Values and Career Advancement

Not all types of work will advance one's career. As already discussed, scholarship has more weight than other faculty activities. In addition, the same principle of competition that applies to the review of funding proposals applies to the review of faculty: when there are more academicians than there are academic openings, faculty members must be more acceptable to more people in order to be retained. The academic marketplace has been increasingly tight since 1970 (Schuster & Bowen, 1985). This press toward conservatism has effects across the academy: in English departments, British literature is more prestigious than American literature, which is in turn more prestigious than popular culture or any other more recent upstart. In general, work which appears more objective and less value-based is higher in prestige. Feminist research and women's studies courses have generally been considered to be political rather than scholarly, peripheral rather than central to the academic enterprise.

Joan Wallach Scott is only the second woman invited to join the faculty of the Institute for Advanced Study since its inception in 1930 (Hinds, 1985), and as she points out, ". . . universities have a much easier time hiring and tenuring mediocre men than mediocre women. Women could indeed get through if they were good enough — and being good enough always meant they were *absolutely* better than anyone else" (Hinds, 1985, p. 53).

Joint appointments and divided responsibilities often work against the retention and advancement of newer faculty. At the same time being — or being perceived as — the token woman in a department undermines one's feelings of professional accomplishment: being told that one has been chosen for a particular office, tenured, or promoted "because you are a woman" reinforces the stereotype that men succeed because of what they do whereas women succeed based on what they are.

Some authors (e.g., Fisher, 1982) have discussed the issues relating to competition in the academy. One of the major issues of concern is the extent to which women academics have succumbed to individual careerism and the exploitive use of opportunities provided by women's studies programs.

Societal Values Reflected in the Academy

The Value of Specialists

Individual and institutional values do not stand in isolation from broader societal values (e.g., Spence, 1983). An avalanche of information and technological advances have contributed to making us a society of specialists. "Esoteric and highly refined methodologies with corresponding specialized knowledge frequently characterize traditionally defined specialty areas" (Boxer, 1983, pp. 46-47). The highest levels of prestige and pay are often reserved for those in the most specialized fields. This is one of the implicit academic norms from which women's studies faculty deviate: Women's studies is, by definition, broad and interdisciplinary. Approximately 1% of doctoral degrees conferred in 1981-82 were in interdisciplinary studies (Weis, 1985) and nationwide, women make up little more than 25% of all tenured professors (McMillen, 1986). This means that most women working in women's studies are not only reviewed primarily by male faculty, they also come up for tenure in traditional departments. This puts them at a clear disadvantage, according to Annette Kolodny (quoted in McMillen, 1986, p. 24); "Most faculty members are not acquainted with the scholarship in women's studies. They don't read it, so they don't know what it is or even how to evaluate it." There is still great debate about the extent to which scholars working in women's studies have gained acceptance and are viewed as legitimate (McMillen, 1986).

The Power of Public Thinking

New information is not sufficient to change or discard a theory. There is clear documentation in the philosophy and history of science that the perceived truth or validity of scientific facts depends on the beliefs of the society in which the research is done (Payer, 1977). When scholarship runs counter to societal values and beliefs, the result is likely to be benign neglect of the work, if not ridicule of the scholar. Both social institutions and individuals often deal with deviance by ignoring it (Unger, 1979). One example of the way in which this benign neglect operates is offered by Denmark (1983): although introductory psychology textbooks give extensive coverage to male and female sexuality, much of the research cited has long been superceded by more recent work. Facts which don't fit popular conceptions are often omitted altogether — e.g., the fact of women's much greater orgasmic capacity, which is contrary to the stereotype of men as more sexual.

At the present time, it is difficult to disentangle the reasons for the lack of academic and scholarly legitimacy suffered by women's studies: we do not know whether it is because it is done by women, because it is about women, or because it is a new and revisionist perspective (Unger, 1982). In discussing the psychology of women, Unger (1982, p. 14) said, "Authority can be consensual; it can be conferred by historical precedent; or it may come from institutional fiat. Thus far, the field lacks all of these bases of authority. Others define us." The same is true of women's studies in general.

Valuing Individuality and Competition

American society has a long history of valuing individual achievement and success in competition. These values are reflected in the academy in the emphasis on individual work (e.g., valuing single-authored publications more than coauthorship). Competition for whatever economic and status rewards an institution has to offer is a fact of life that affects feminist academics as well as non-feminists (Fisher, 1982) while running counter to the feminist ethic on cooperation and support. ". . . [B]oth higher education and liberal feminism reflect the dominant social order, with its creed of equal opportunity and its acceptance of interest group politics" (Fisher, 1982, p. 65). While subscribing to these same overarching social norms, there is great variability among feminists in their beliefs about the most effective means of promoting social change and the purpose of a feminist education. Some of the main variations on the role of education include education as an instrument or weapon, education as truth telling, education to mobilize women for political action, education with an emphasis on study and critique of theory, and education for the purpose of recovering and developing specifically feminine traditions of knowing and learning (Fisher, 1982). Such differences contribute to the stress and conflict feminist academics face within their support circle as well as across the institution.

DESIRABILITY OF FEMINISM IN THE ACADEMY

What is feminist education, why is it important, and how does it differ from a more traditional education? A feminist education is defined by the values reflected in the questions asked. Although Lerner (1979) made the following points concerning women's history, they are valid across the curriculum: Who were the women scholars? What did they contribute by the standards established by men? What would the discipline be like if it were viewed through the eyes of women and ordered by values they define? At the present time, women's studies is primarily concerned with the compensatory and contributory perspectives reflected in the first two questions, but we are making beginnings on the "new order": we are beginning to look critically at the way society has supplied definitions. Feminists, through writings and instruction in women's issues, have counteracted the neglect and misrepresentations of women in the academy.

Boneparth (1977) summarized the criteria used by the women's studies program at San Jose State University. Women's studies courses need to look at new and old research about women, raise new questions that are relevant to women, question the silence of traditional disciplines about women, question the androcentric bias of traditional fields, raise questions about gender-role relationships, question basic assumptions about society, and encourage students and faculty to do research on women and to share it with others.

Feminism has changed the way the academy has thought about a variety of important issues: politics, children, pay equity, psychopathology, morality, and career development. Feminist scholarship and programs have helped shift viewing the world from revolving around men to revolving around men and women jointly. Women's studies propose the rules of the academy be changed in order to correct the omissions, distortions, and trivializations of women and women's lives. Feminism has broken down and reorganized disciplinary boundaries. It does not merely consist of a set of political biases; rather, advocates see feminism as a method which seeks to inquire into the evaluation of concepts such as power, division of labor, and mental health which divide our world into two.

It is rare for scholars to question whether or how the mathematics department, psychology department, English department, or the American studies program impacts on an institution. Of course one questions how well these programs are maintaining their teaching and research functions but not whether they should be departments at all. The value of their existence is assumed. This is not the case with new departments or programs. The questions raised by the academy about women's studies have been asked by feminists about the institution as traditionally constituted. In short, feminism and women's studies rock the boat in the academy. On a broader level, Howe presented five reasons why women's studies is particularly compatible with the goals of a liberal education: "It is interdisciplinary and unifying, it teaches skills in critical analysis, it assumes a problem-solving stance, it clarifies the issue of value judgment in education, and it promotes socially useful ends" (in Boxer, 1982, pp. 681-682).

As feminist scholarship has developed, academic women's studies has shifted focus somewhat so that there is now less emphasis on strategies for institutional change and more emphasis on attacking sexist scholarship and teaching (Boxer, 1982). Nevertheless, women's studies is the academic arm of the women's liberation movement. Although the emphasis has shifted somewhat, and recommended methods of achieving goals differ, there is still a ". . . consensus that women's studies in the long run implies profound change in the structure of knowledge, the university, and society" (Boxer, 1982, p. 677).

TRANSLATION OF FEMINIST VALUES
INTO EDUCATIONAL PRAXIS

Women's studies courses have always been the academic arm of the women's liberation movement. As such, their goals have been both academic and political. Such courses are often expected to meet a wide range of student and faculty needs, many of which are left unarticulated (Billingham, 1982). Lord (1982) suggests feminist academics should choose a teaching-learning model that fosters desired student behavior, and contains assumptions consistent with our learning objectives, our assumptions about how learning occurs, and our philosophy of optimal female development. In Table 1 we have presented Lord's set of assumptions guiding her own teaching which reflect many of the beliefs and values inherent in feminist teaching strategies and techniques.

Incorporating Emotional/Personal Learning

Students participate in courses on women's studies with a variety of expectations and interests. The majority want the opportunity to interpret and discuss the authenticity of their experiences as women and men. In the traditional academy, this emphasis on emotional/personal knowledge acquisition has taken definitely second place to the more typical cognitive/impersonal mode of learning (Richardson, 1982). The emotional/personal modes are often recognized as "strengths buried in women's reality" (Richardson, 1982), and this makes them especially appropriate for women's studies courses. This is particularly true in the context of the topics which are common in women's studies courses.

Several scholars have offered advice to assist faculty in meeting the goals of emotional/personal learning for their students. Recommendations have ranged from having students conduct empirical research on a topic of their own choice (Riger, 1978; 1979), to instructors adopting a non-hierarchical strategy in which the instructor is a facilitator of discussion, not an authority (Freedman, Golub, & Krauss, 1982; Howe, 1975), to dividing the class into same-sex discussion groups (Piliavin & Martin in Deaux, 1976; Thorne & Henley, 1975), to evaluating book authors' feminist positions (Sholley, 1986). One of the difficulties of these techniques is achieving the appropriate balance and integration of experiential and content segments of the course.

Table 1.   Assumptions guiding the development of a feminist teaching-learning model, taken from Lord's 1982 discussion of the psychology of women and modified to be applicable to other women's studies courses.

1.   The course should be a laboratory of feminist principles.

2.   The traditional patriarchal teaching-learning model Is dysfunctional In the development of healthy women (and men).

3.   Every individual in the class is a potential teaching resource.

4.   Integration is imperative for the development of healthy, whole women (and men). Therefore the course should foster mind/body integration as well as the integration of ideas and behavior, and thoughts and feelings.

5.   Effective human behavior In social Interactions and within social systems Is related to understanding the relationship between the personal and political.

6.   A women's studies course should deal with women only and treat women as the norm.

7.   If at all possible, the primary coordinators of the course should be women.

8.   The subjective, personal experience of women (and men) Is valid and important.

9.   The student should ultimately assume responsibility for her or his own learning and growth.

10. Cooperation among students In pursuing learning objectives creates a more positive learning climate than does competition; cooperative learning Is fostered through the use of criterion-referenced rather than a norm-referenced evaluation system.

TABLE 1 (continued)

11. Providing vehicles outside the class through which students can deal with personal feelings and frustrations (such as journals, dyads, assertiveness training, and growth groups) enhances the quality of class discussion.

12. The generic use of terms such as woman and the female pronouns to refer to humans is an effective teaching-learning tool.

13. Both men and women should be exposed to and have an understanding of the course material. However, a structure must be provided which allows women to meet with women and men with men for a significant portion of the time.

Teaching Traditional Students

A common problem reported by instructors of courses in the psychology of gender roles who have tried to incorporate emotional/personal techniques into their courses concerns students' beliefs that problems of inequality in politics, business, law, salary, and attitudes have all been solved (e.g., Belle, 1985; Hunt, 1985). Recently Paludi (1986a) has found this reluctance to accept the presence of discrimination and bias in the family, work, and education to relate to life events adolescent and early adulthood students have not yet dealt with or mastered, e.g., menopause, pregnancy, parenthood, dual-career marriages, widowhood. Reentry students, on the other hand, typically have an understanding of these issues because many have had these experiences. Paludi has offered suggestions for designing material relevant to students' life stage that serve to maintain high levels of interest as well as to illustrate the continued bias and discriminatory practices. Exercises and topics for discussion can draw from personal experience as well as new observation to encourage the assimilation of information about women's studies. Taking into account students' life stage brings concepts from the class under the close scrutiny of their own experiences and evaluation. Paludi suggests this provides a way of adding their own analysis to the concepts of the course.

The majority of students who participate in courses on women's studies (as well as in other college courses) are in a transitional phase of their development in which they are preoccupied with questions about their essential character and wish to satisfy their longing for self-definition (Erikson, 1959; Newman & Newman, 1984). The central process through which individuals resolve this issue is role experimentation or psychosocial moratorium (Erikson, 1959). This process may take several forms (e.g., part-time jobs, changing the college major, extensive reading, developing a point of view about feminism) and results in the individuals' personal conceptions of how they can fit into society.

One way the psychosocial moratorium has been incorporated into courses on the psychology of women has been by devising experiential exercises and topics for discussion that draw from personal experiences (Paludi, 1986a). Another effective translation of the psychosocial moratorium concerns providing students with a team of instructors who teach the material. Exposure to a variety of women who know the topics is an important ingredient in students' growth, self-concept development, self-definition in terms of feminism, and pursuit of career options (Faunce, 1985). Feminist instructors have considerable ability to empathize with women students because of shared experiences of being a woman in the culture as well as increased sensitivity to women's issues. Furthermore, team-teaching women's studies courses emphasizes the "personal-is-political" concept: that women's experiences are shared by many and are therefore political. Team-teaching can also provide students with validation of their own experiences, learning new interactional skills, and affirming individual perceptions of experience (Paludi, 1986b). An interdisciplinary perspective also challenges the emphasis on specialized knowledge in a speciality area.

Some feminist scholars (e.g., Boxer, 1982) have commented on the changes in the composition of the student body, maintaining that since the late '70s, fewer are likely to identify themselves as feminists or to understand sexism, often subscribing again to traditional sex-roles. Such students may well be less receptive to experiential learning techniques.

In addition to students' developmental stage and the possibility of political conservatism as potential issues in students' resistance to women's studies courses as designed by feminist faculty, Fisher (1982) suggests another source of tension and conflict between students and faculty: she identifies several parallels between women's studies faculty and human service workers, and notes that faculty "providers" and student "clients" differ in background, perspectives, and the results hoped for (or feared) from the "service" being offered/forced on them. The greater the differences between teachers and students in life chances, class, race, sexual preferences, or "social fate," the greater the potential for conflict.

Because experiential components of learning are typically not recognized as legitimate, courses which incorporate them are likely to be criticized for lacking standards, being "easy" and/or having no "content." In order to avoid such criticisms, many teachers of women's studies courses have gone to the other extreme, demanding exceptionally large amounts of reading and project work.

Women of Color and Lesbian Women

The feminist goal for education is that it be about and for all women, not only free from sexism, but also from prejudice and discrimination based on race, class, age, sexual preference, and other oppressive biases (e.g., Boxer, 1982).

> The frequent complaint that the women's movement and women's studies courses are permeated by a white middle-class bias takes on added cogency under the impetus of this analysis [that sexism, racism, and classism are interacting and interstructured rather than simply analagous]. Moreover, for the receptive instructor, these views cast into doubt the validity of substantial portions of what might be considered the basic course content. . . . Moreover, the full implications of this perspective cannot be dealt with adequately by special topic sessions on black women or working-class women, for example. (Richardson, 1982, p. 48)

This revisionist perspective calls for a constant reexamination of all generalizations and abstractions about women. The challenges these issues raise for feminist scholars and teachers are often as painful as the challenges feminism has raised for the traditional academy.

Disagreements over the political and academic goals of women's studies courses, and dissatisfaction with the treatment of women of color, lesbians, and radical feminism have been sources of conflict since the early 1970s, and continue to plague women's studies programs today. Although black women have fared somewhat better than other women of color, all women of color have been largely neglected in courses, materials, programs, and conferences (Boxer, 1982).

In the discipline of the psychology of women, Brown, Goodwin, Hall, and Jackson-Lowman (1985) noted that in their review of 28 textbooks on the psychology of women, 18 offered either minor or no reference to Afro-American women. Asian women, Native American women, and Hispanic women received even less attention. Brown et al. identified four definitive steps to be followed to rectify this problem in the field:

1. Psychology of women writers must confront the racism, ethnocentrism, and classism manifested in the exclusion and limited treatment throughout their works of Third World, non middle-class women.
2. In-depth research and study must be undertaken, as well as research programs that specifically seek to reveal the impact of culture, race, and social class on the psychological development of Third World Women.
3. Course offerings on Afro-American, Native American, Hispanic, Asian-American, and other Third World Women must be added to the curriculum of Women's Studies and given the same status as other required psychology of women courses.
4. Efforts to develop a comprehensive and integrative study of the psychology of women must be pursued. Model construc-

tion and theory development must reflect the importance of culture, racial, and social-class variables on female development. (p. 37)

Recently, DeFour and Paludi (1988) have described procedures for integrating the scholarship on women of color into the psychology of women course and the introductory course in women's studies. They have made three recommendations. First, it is important to avoid the use of value-laden references so as not to legitimize negative stereotypes of women of color. Second, women's experiences are extremely diverse, yet most researchers describe women of color collectively. This approach engenders the same error that occurs when one collectively describes any group: women of color are as varied and differ as much among themselves as do white women. Third, the use of the term women of color should also address socioeconomic class stratification. Thus, disciplines within the academe, including women's studies, need to develop a perspective on the dialectics of sex, gender role, race, class, and ethnicity.

The feminist decision to include freedom of sexual preference as a major goal was relatively recent, with the result that there is relatively little on lesbianism, bisexuality, and heterosexual privilege in the literature and curriculum (Boxer, 1982). This has again created conflict among feminists, but many have expressed willingness to include consideration of lesbian experiences and perspectives in women's studies courses. The recent text by the Boston Lesbian Psychologies Collective (1987) should prove useful for integrating the information on lesbianism into women's studies courses.

Power in the Classroom

The double purpose of women's studies—to expose and redress the oppression of women—was reflected in widespread attempts to restructure the classroom experience of students and faculty. Circular arrangement of chairs, periodic small-group sessions, use of first names for instructors as well as students, assignments that required journal keeping, "reflection papers," cooperative projects, and collective modes of teaching with student participation all sought to transfer to women's studies the contemporary feminist criticism of authority and the validation of every woman's experience. (Boxer, 1982, p. 667)

These new modes of teaching created two problems for instructors. One was how to manage the appropriate inclusion of these experiences related to power in the classroom without the instructor's abdicating responsibility for the class (Richardson, 1982). In addition, being receptive to students' suggestions for content and structure can be disruptive and create extreme disorganization. Students whose values and priorities differ might come into conflict with other students, as well as with the instructor. Paludi (1986b) describes a course structure and techniques useful in minimizing power issues in the classroom.

Team-teaching

Paludi (1986b) suggests that there is tremendous support value in having co-facilitators; this serves to ease the isolation that may occur when only one individual teaches these courses (Carmen & Driver, 1982). The team-teaching approach encourages experimentation with different expressions of feminism for the co-facilitators as well as the other participants. When taught by several co-facilitators, courses in women's studies allow individuals the freedom from the expectations for role performance. Their experimentation with new feminist roles, values, and belief systems may result in a personal conception of how they fit into feminist aspects of the culture. Consequently, Paludi suggests that they maximize their strengths and gain recognition and support from their community.

Boxer (1982) discusses several problems and criticisms associated with the implementation of teaching techniques aimed at the achievement of feminist goals, among them Freeman's demonstration that "structurelessness" can lead to the development of informal power networks based on friendship and elitism.

The relationship between women's studies and the feminist movement and the appropriate balance between activist and academic goals continue to promote debate, but this source of conflict also stimulates and enriches women's studies (Boxer, 1982). Even with the protection of tenure, it is impossible for faculty to totally ignore the traditional values and demands of the institutions employing them (Richardson, 1982). As Richardson notes further, "On yet another level, total rejection of the traditional values and related knowledge may blind us to potentially valid and valuable tools and methods for understanding human behavior" (p. 52). Faculty in women's studies programs are continuing to struggle with the task of turning the tension of this conflict into creative tension.

Further, several issues in women's studies (e.g., lesbian relationships, racial and ethnic distinctiveness) may create class sessions that are emotionally charged arenas (Paludi, 1988). Many of the students who participate in these courses have never encountered feminist philosophy in prior courses. They may have no one at home or in their dorm with whom to discuss the class content; they may be seen as rocking the boat and may be laughed at and/or called derogatory names because of their association with women's studies and feminism. The classroom, therefore, needs to become a place where women can feel good about themselves and other women without the fear of being laughed at or considered "unfeminine." Paludi (1989) offers some pedagogical techniques to help replace women's self-doubt with certainty, low self-esteem with self-respect and caring. Most of these techniques concern working with women to express the anger they feel because they do not live their lives according to feminist principles or because they believe their voice isn't being heard. Paludi reports that permitting the anger and directing the energy tied into the anger toward individual and social change have been useful.

In addition, Paludi points out that a great deal of anger is directed toward the feminist facilitator of the course. She writes:

> In the last few years I have felt I have been the bearer of bad news: subtle discrimination in the workplace, the myth of the Superwoman concept and having it all, etc. I do believe it is my responsibility to tell students (emotionally and intellectually) the truth and not to protect them from awful realities. I want women to know that when discrimination occurs to them they are not at fault; that the onus for change is not on themselves. I hope this sharing of the emotional impact on women will help them to trust their own experiences and not impose

self-silence and shame. I also believe it is important for women to see how other women have handled their anger and victimization and have become survivors. It is this developmental process I believe will ensure women connecting and continuing to work for social change.

Even those who approve the goals of women's studies often disagree on what is the best next step. Boxer (1982) presents women's studies as the educational success story of the 1970s. Clear signs of the increasing importance of feminism in the academy are a growing number of expert faculty, courses in women's issues, departments of women's studies, and an impressive coverage in textbooks and scientific journals, also illustrated by the chapters in this volume. Several national and regional organizations concerned with issues devoted to feminism in the academy have been established in fields such as anthropology, adult education, economics, statistics, biophysics, geoscience, psychology, and history.

Priorities of these courses, publications, and organizations have centered on the need to make up for the deficiencies in information about and for women. Women's studies has definitely brought the feminist paradigm into the academy.

But has it made a substantial difference in the traditional curriculum? Most of the writers in this volume have recognized that the change is coming slowly. Many have observed that women are entering traditionally "masculine" fields in increasing numbers, yet not all of them have brought a feminist perspective into their disciplines. Furthermore, those women who have taken a feminist perspective have found themselves to be isolated since many disciplines still consign feminism and women's studies to the peripheries of the academy. Thus, interpretations of these individuals' importance as scholars analyzing their disciplines remain biased and unfavorable. While it is typically recognized that there is considerable potential to transform the academy, women's studies has not yet met this potential. It is clear from the chapters in this volume that women's studies must continue to restructure disciplines within the academy so that women's drive for true equality in the university will be successful.

Those whose implicit (or explicit) goal has been to succeed and get rid of ourselves—i.e., to have a feminist perspective and feminist research so integrated into every course that students are getting a comprehensive education—maintain that the time may have come to phase out women's studies courses. There is no doubt that the number of women earning doctorates is higher than ever before. Those who argue for a continuation of "separatism" typically agree on the facts, but disagree on the inferences and conclusions. It can be argued that the presence of women on campuses in greater numbers does not automatically lead to curricular change, even in the departments in which they are represented (Walsh, 1985). The increase in women is uneven across campuses and across departments: women are more likely to be at smaller, less prestigious schools and in the humanities rather than the sciences. And textbooks have lagged behind in presenting adequate coverage of women scholars and feminist points of view. (Again, the sciences are most likely to believe that they are gender free, in spite of evidence to the contrary.)

Kahn and Jean (1983) described three positions relating to whether the psychology of women should be mainstreamed into the curriculum: integration and elimination; integration following equality; and separation and self-definition. We see aspects of these positions as relevant to whether women's studies should be mainstreamed into the curriculum, and if so, when.

Immediate Integration into Traditional Courses

As the label implies, proponents of this position advocate integrating scholarship by and about women into all courses as quickly as possible. Basic general education courses (preferably required ones) need to be redefined and expanded. This position has as its ultimate goal the elimination of special women's studies courses and programs. True mainstreaming would allow us to drop out minority identity. In addition, in this system, information about women would reach a larger number of people and would inform their general education. It may well be that students who would not take a course designated as a women's studies course would benefit particularly from an exposure to feminist scholarship. By integration, proponents of this position do not simply mean that chapters on women should be added to the general texts for the course (e.g., Denmark, 1983). Such chapters could easily be omitted, and their very existence testifies to the fact that "women's issues" are really not an integral part of the topic under study.

Denmark, Helly, and Lees (1986) have reported their extensive project to integrate scholarship on women into the introductory courses at Hunter college. Abramovitz and Helly (1987) have reported a similar project with the professional curriculum at Hunter college. So Denmark, Helly, and Lees (1986) summarize:

The plan was simple. We invited one member from every department in the college that offered an undergraduate major to spend a semester in a workshop to revise the introductory-level course or courses required by that department. The object was not to invent a new course which would be an elective; it was to redesign the existing required course(s) to integrate or reflect recent scholarship on women in its content and pedagogy or both. In exchange for time in and preparing for the weekly workshop, each faculty participant would be released from teaching one course during that semester. To keep the workshops a manageable size, the selected faculty were divided into two groups. Faculty in the Social Sciences, Sciences, and Mathematics met in the spring 1983; those in the Humanities, the Arts, and Education met in the fall 1983. The three faculty coordinators, who received released time to plan these workshops, attended both.

Workshops met for two hours once a week. Participants read and discussed materials raising general issues and volunteered to lead discussions of materials of both general and specific interest to their fields. Four outside consultants entered this process at important points. Elizabeth Minnich, a philosopher who has been active in this work over several years, addressed the first workshop before they began their formal meeting and came back to talk with the second workshop during their working semester. Bonnie Spanier, then directing a major integration project at Wheaton college, spoke about women and science; Anne Fausto-Sterling, a biologist at Brown University, discussed the historical context of scientific ideas and her own course on the biology of women; and Barbara Wright of the University of Connecticut at Storrs told the second workshop of her work with the introductory German language course. Workshop participants were asked to present their recommendations for course revisions to their colleagues in written form and, where appropriate, to lead departmental discussions on them. The reports compiled here, in 1984-1985, reflect their efforts. (pp. 1-11)

One of the basic beliefs underlying the total integration position is that changing traditional perspectives of disciplines requires that women's studies "be of them, in them, and about them" (Boxer, 1982) and thus the proper goal is to become part of the fundamental structure and content of the universities. In addition, as Boxer (1982, p. 681) points out:

The failure of affirmative action to add women to existing faculties, the limited prospects for growth expected in the coming decade, and the spreading appeal of "back to basics" all suggest that fundamental change in educational institutions will come only after feminist academics insinuate women's studies into the traditional, and especially the required or general education, curriculum.

As Kahn and Jean (1983) point out, there are significant differences between those who wish to proceed with the elimination of special courses and programs immediately and those who feel that "as soon as possible" is not yet: they labeled the second group as advocating "integration follows equality." Nevertheless, goals, methods, and "vision" are very similar, and the primary differences are on the basis of assessing progress to date.

The main criticism of immediate integration (Kahn & Jean, 1983) is that sexism is so deeply imbedded in the traditional content and methods of disciplines that feminism would not stand a chance and would simply be absorbed and disappear. Feminism would no longer be able to foster alternative values in the field.

The main criticisms of integration following equality are much more fundamental: integration rests on the assumptions that the same terms, methods, and theories are applicable to both women and men. It is assumed that differences between women and men can be reconciled and presented in complimentary if not identical fashion. Critics question these basic assumptions, maintaining that integration would destroy feminists' ability to promote alternative values in the academy (Kahn & Jean, 1983). Furthermore, some feminists ". . . question whether content can be abstracted from a feminist framework or taught by faculty at large without sacrificing essential goals" (Boxer, 1982, p. 682). Another "logistical" criticism is that an integrated curriculum requires great coordination and the support of most of the faculty, making such an approach impractical as well as raising issues of academic freedom (Billingham, 1982). Rather than true integration, research/scholarship by and about women might be presented in such a way that it seems shallow and/or seems to be "tacked-on" to existing course content.

Separate Departments and Self-Definition

Proponents of this approach are, of course, the critics of the integration position. Proponents see a separate department for women's studies as a source of identity, generating research, and providing independence in choosing faculty and establishing a curriculum (e.g., Williams, 1974). On a more basic, philosophical level, separationists maintain that women and men are fundamentally and irreconcilably different and, therefore, that it is impossible to have a successful merging of scholarship to create discipline applicable to both women and men, to scholarly products created by both women and men, to art and literature created by both, etc. The primary criticism of this position is that it may be creating false dichotomies and functioning to maintain differences that are socially based and that need to be eliminated for equality to be realized. Some feminists reject the concept of disciplinarity as a male mode of analysis, fragmenting social experience (Boxer, 1982). Furthermore, integrationists often question the methodological validity and rigor in the work of the separationists (Kahn & Jean, 1983). Non-feminists frequently see the separationists as exceptionally "fringey" and radical.

Citing home economics and black studies departments as precedents, some feminists believe that women's studies departments would be co-opted by the university, turning into female ghettos with little impact on most education (Boxer, 1982). Furthermore, there is a concern that in times of economic retrenchment, such departments would be particularly vulnerable.

Interdepartmental Programs

The third position that needs discussion states that both separate women's studies programs *and* mainstreaming are indispensible.

Some Definitions: Programs vs. Courses

Courses about women in various disciplines in the academy should be distinguished from women's studies programs, majors, and departments (Howe & Lauter, 1980). Courses in women's issues (e.g., history of women, women and politics, women and literature) are offered at most of the 3,000 campuses in this country. Women's studies programs, however, are found on 330 college and university campuses in the United States.

The majority of women's studies programs are quite similar in organizational structure (Howe & Lauter, 1980): (1) networks involving faculty whose major disciplines are in more traditional departments; and (2) a small number of staff whose appointments have been in women's studies. In terms of the curriculum of the majority of programs in women's studies, students initially take an overview course, interdisciplinary in nature, which has as its goal the continuity and coherence of images about women through history. The major premise of this initial course is that beliefs about the relations of women to their bodies, to men, to children, and about their role in society have influenced the ways in which women have been treated. This initial course is usually team taught. One of the main difficulties with such survey courses is the amount of information which needs to be included, as well as the coordination of team teaching. A common student complaint is that such courses lack coherence. In addition, there may be limits on how far interdisciplinary courses can be developed without encountering insurmountable problems related to competing commitments stemming from the differing theoretical orientations of the disciplines themselves (Fisher, 1982).

The next level of the structure of women's studies curricula involves departmentally based women's studies courses, e.g., The Psychology of Women. Although these courses are more manageable in many ways than are the interdisciplinary overview courses, there is still concern about voluminous material, course emphasis, and variable quality (Billingham, 1982). (Perhaps it should be pointed out that the same issues of course content and emphasis apply to *all* introductory survey courses, and that this lament is just as likely from the teacher of the Survey of American Literature as from anyone else). Occasionally departments will offer several courses on women, so that, for example, students could take not only a survey course on women's history, but also a course on women in the 19th century labor movement. Frequently women's studies programs will have a selection of courses within an academic discipline that students are encouraged to take because of the women's issues topics discussed, e.g., social psychology, marriage and the family, parent-child relationships. Such courses are typically "cross-listed" and can be taken either for women's studies credit or for departmental credit. Many programs have also developed an advanced project or thesis in women's issues.

Women's studies programs (whether they offer a major, a minor, or a certificate) differ from women's studies courses in their structured and organized curricula. Students in such programs have the opportunity to share information and attend colloquia offered by feminist scholars. In addition, they often have the option of participating in women's studies musical events, art exhibits, etc.

Because equality has not yet been achieved for women, either in society or in the academy, we still need descriptive and compensatory courses. In addition, the very existence of separate courses and programs is an aid to mainstreaming. Walsh (1985) cites three reasons for establishing or maintaining separate courses on women within departments: (1) a separate course serves as leverage, resulting in increased exposure to new research on women, with material developed for the separate course being mainstreamed into appropriate sections of the teacher's "regular" courses; (2) one course can serve as a continuing catalyst for change, including the development of other new courses; and (3) teaching a separate course may stimulate research and publication, including new textbooks. All of these efforts serve to legitimize the claims of a discipline that many see as still emerging. Thus, Walsh maintains that there is a direct connection between teaching a course on women and mainstreaming this new material into the rest of the curriculum.

Those who believe in the goals of both the integrationists and the separationists are essentially asking for the best of both worlds: reaching the largest possible number of people, replacing old male-centered theories with new gender-neutral conceptualization, methodological and theoretical innovation, recognizing women and their works as legitimate specialties within disciplines.

The major problem with this approach is the danger of burn-out. Feminists who are meeting the demands and standards of their disciplines in an already-existing content area and who wish to participate in women's studies may find themselves with two distinct bodies of literature to master and two sets of professional associations to which to contribute. These feminists may find themselves fragmented, confused, and exhausted (Kahn & Jean, 1983).

On the other hand, proponents argue that feminism is a value system leading to a particular approach to scholarly and academic issues: in and of itself, it is not a content area. Thus, the ultimate goal is to promote this value system and this approach throughout the academy, leading inevitably to integration. Although some early feminist writers questioned whether women's studies could succeed at all in male-defined and dominated universities, fearing isolation and tokenism, this concern has largely been put aside now (Boxer, 1982).

The future of women's studies in the curriculum must be considered in the context of the changing student body. Frieze (1984) asserts that many college women are now career oriented while maintaining traditional role values and McPherson (1985) reports a move toward a more politically conservative climate on campus. These conditions create new tasks for feminist scholars. As the needs of the student body change or as the status of women in society changes, not only will the content of women's studies change, but the methods of presenting the material will change as well.

KEY ISSUES AND RESEARCH ON WOMEN'S STUDIES

Although women's studies teachers and students often anecdotally report many profound changes in attitudes and perceptions, a review of the literature by Porter and Elleenchild (1980) found no clear evidence of this. These authors made several suggestions for additional variables to be considered, including sex of instructor and student, instructor's political goals, and classroom structure.

Boxer (1982) suggests that one promising technique for measuring the outcome of women's studies courses might be a technique developed by Guttentag, involving measuring the impact of the course on the basis of the goals identified by the participants themselves, students as well as teachers.

Johnson (1982) summarizes the status of research on psychology of women courses. Her conclusion supports Porter and Elleenchild (1980) that there is no clear evidence that students' attitudes are changed in predicted ways. Furthermore, she points out that the original impetus for such research was three-fold: to measure attitude change, to provide academic value, and to demonstrate political potency. She then argues that (1) these courses are now an integral enough part of the psychology curriculum that the focus of research no longer needs to be the demonstration of academic value; and (2) the scholarly work of feminist psychologists is the best example of political potency. Therefore, research on these courses needs to focus on attitude change in the larger context of attitudinal research. Johnson (1982) recommends: comparative studies of the effects of psychology of women courses versus other related psychology courses (e.g., developmental, social); psychology of women courses versus other related experiences (e.g., consciousness-raising, feminist therapy); studies that use follow-up measures in addition to end-of-course measures; and research that uses behavioral measures rather than paper-and-pencil attitude scales only.

The same approaches would prove valuable in other women's studies courses as well. The basic issue is to treat such research as a scholarly speciality rather than as a defense against the criticisms of detractors.

CONCLUSION

Women's studies has emerged in idiosyncratic ways, in all types of academic settings. Although emphasizing feminism as a value and theoretical perspective, the focus often shifts among women as scholars, as teachers, as students, and as a content area. The forms they take reflect the beliefs, energies, and personalities of the faculty involved, as well as the characteristics of the institution and the surrounding community (Williams, 1974).

Deciding whether women's studies should be mainstreamed into the curriculum and/or maintained as a separate program in a women's studies department is a values decision made in the context of the history and mission of a particular institution and of the faculty involved. There are dangers in establishing a single model for women's studies, similar to the danger in having a single strain of corn: with uniformity, you have uniform susceptibility and weakness. We have already seen that the strengths of mainstreaming are often the weaknesses of separationism, and vice versa. Stimson (1973) discusses the diversity in educational, social, and political circumstances that have given rise to the diversity of styles, methods, and goals in women's studies and concludes that all programs must work out their own destiny, and that all women's studies programs need to be seen as a multiplicity of intersecting activities.

REFERENCES

Abramovitz, M., & Helly, D.O. (1987). *Report on a project to integrate scholarship on women in the professional curriculum at Hunter College*. New York: Women's Studies Program of Hunter College.

Astin, H.S., & Bayer, A.E. (1979). Pervasive sex differences in the academic reward system: Scholarship, marriage, and what else? In D.R. Lewis and W.E. Becker (Eds.), *Academic rewards in higher education*. Cambridge, MA: Ballinger.

Bellah, R.N. (1985, March/April). Creating a new framework for new realities: Social science as public philosophy. *Change*, 35-39.

Belle, D. (1985, October). Teaching the new psychology of women. Conversation Hour Program, Research on Women and Education, Boston, MA.

Billingham, K.A. (1982). Building a course on the psychology of women: Methods and resources. *Psychology of Women Quarterly*, 7, 32-41.

Blechman, E. (Ed.) (1984). *Behavior modification and women*. New York: Guilford.

Boneparth, E. (1977). Evaluating women's studies: Academic theory and practice. *The Social Science Journal*, *14*, 23-31.

Boston Lesbian Psychologies Collective (Eds.) (1987). *Lesbian psychologies: Explorations and challenges*. Champaign, IL: University of Illinois Press.

Boxer, M.J. (1982). For and about women: The theory and practice of women's studies in the U.S. *Signs*, 7, 661-695.

Broverman, I., Broverman, D., Clarkson, F., Rosenkrantz, P., & Vogel, S.

(1970). Sex roles stereotypes and clinical judgments of mental health. *Journal of Consulting and Clinical Psychology, 34*, 1-7.

Brown, A., Goodwin, B.J., Hall, B.A., & Jackson-Lowman, H. (1985). A review of psychology of women textbooks: Focus on the Afro-American women. *Psychology of Women Quarterly, 9*, 29-38.

Caplan, N., & Nelson, S.D. (1973). On being useful: The nature and consequences of psychological research on social problems. *American Psychologist, 28*, 199-211.

Carmen, E., & Driver, F. (1982). Teaching women's studies: Values in conflict. *Psychology of Women Quarterly, 7*, 81-95.

Deaux, K. (1976). *The behavior of women and men*. Monterey, CA: Brooks/Cole.

DeFour, D.C., & Paludi, M.A. (1988, March). Integrating the scholarship on women of color and ethnicity into the psychology of women course. Workshop presented at the Association for Women in Psychology, Bethesda, MD.

Denmark, F.L. (1983). Integrating the psychology of women into introductory psychology. In C.J. Scheirer and A.M. Rogers (Eds.), *The G. Stanley Hall Lecture Series, vol. 3*. Washington, DC: The American Psychological Association.

Denmark, F.L., Helly, D.O., & Lees, S.H. (1986). *Report on a project to integrate scholarship on women into the introductory courses at Hunter College: 1982-1986*. New York: Women's Studies Program of Hunter College.

Erikson, E. (1959). The problem of ego identity. *Psychological Issues, 1*, 101-164.

Faunce, P. (1985). Teaching feminist therapies: Integrating feminist therapy, pedagogy, and scholarship. In L.B. Rosewater & L.E.A. Walker (Eds.). *Handbook of feminist therapy: Women's issues in psychotherapy* (pp. 309-322). New York: Springer.

Fisher, B.M. (1982). Professing feminism: Feminist academics and the women's movement. *Psychology of Women Quarterly, 7*, 55-69.

Freedman, R.J., Golub, S., & Krauss, B. (1982). Mainstreaming the psychology of women into the core curriculum. *Teaching of Psychology, 9*, 165-168.

Frieze, I.H. (1984, Spring). Teaching psychology of women in the 1980s. *Division 35 Newsletter*, p. 1.

Harrison, L. (1975). Cro-magnon women—In eclipse. *Science Teacher, 42*, 8-11.

Hinds, K. (1985, July/August). Joan Wallach Scott: Breaking new ground for women. *Change*, 48-53.

Howard, G.S. (1985). The role of values in the science of psychology. *American Psychologist, 40*, 255-265.

Howe, F. (Ed.) (1975). *Women and the power to change*. New York: McGraw-Hill.

Howe, F., & Lauter, P. (1980). *The impact of women's studies on the campus and the disciplines*. Washington, DC: National Institute of Education, Department of Health, Education, and Welfare.

Hunt, L. (1985, October). An interdisciplinary approach at a two-year college.

Paper presented at the North Central Women's Studies Association, Oxford, OH.

Johnson, M. (1982). Research on teaching the psychology of women. *Psychology of Women Quarterly, 7,* 96-104.

Kahn, A.S., & Jean, P.J. (1983). Integration and elimination or separation and redefinition: The future of the psychology of women. *Signs, 8,* 659-671.

Kelman, H. (1972). The rights of the subject in social research: An analysis in terms of relative power and legitimacy. *American Psychologist, 27,* 989-1016.

Kohlberg, L. (1966). A cognitive-developmental analysis of children's sex-role concepts and attitudes. In E.E. Maccoby (Ed.). *The development of sex differences.* Stanford: Stanford University Press.

Lerner, G. (1979). *The majority finds its past: Placing women in history.* New York: Oxford University Press.

Lord, S.B. (1982). Teaching the psychology of women: Examination of a teaching-learning model. *Psychology of Women Quarterly, 7,* 70-80.

Makosky, V.P. (1980). Stress and the mental health of women: A discussion of research and issues. In M. Guttentag, S. Salasin, & D. Belle (Eds.), *The mental health of women.* New York: Academic Press.

McClelland, D.C., Atkinson, J.W., Clark, R.A., & Lowell, E.L. (1953). *The achievement motive.* New York: Appleton-Century-Crofts.

McKenna, W., & Kessler, S. (1977). Experimental design as a source of sex bias in social psychology. *Sex Roles, 3,* 117-128.

McMillen, L. (1986, April). Legal experts eye two sex bias lawsuits brought by women's studies scholars. *The Chronicle of Higher Education,* 23-25.

McPherson, M. (1985). The younger generation: What's it coming to? *Change, 17,* 62.

Newman, B.M., & Newman, P.R. (1984). *Development through life.* Homewood, IL: Dorsey.

O'Connell, A., Alpert, J.L., Richardson, M.S., Rotter, N.G., Ruble, D.N., & Unger, R.K. (1978). Gender-specific barriers to research in psychology. *JSAS Catalogue of Selected Documents in Psychology, 8,* 80 (MS. No. 1753).

Paludi, M.A. (1986a). Teaching the psychology of gender roles: Some life-stage considerations. *Teaching of Psychology, 13,* 133-138.

Paludi, M.A. (1986b). Teaching the psychology of women: Integrating feminist pedagogy, scholarship, and politics. Paper presented at the Conference on Research on Women and Education, Washington, DC.

Paludi, M.A. (1989). *Exploring/teaching the psychology of women.* Albany: SUNY Press.

Payer, M.E. (1977). Is traditional scholarship value free? Conference Proceedings: The Scholar and the Feminist. New York: Barnard College.

Porter, N., & Elleenchild, M.T. (1980). *The effectiveness of women's studies.* The Women's Studies Monograph Series, Washington, DC: National Institute of Education.

Prescott, S. (1978). Why researchers don't study women: The responses of 62 researchers. *Sex Roles, 4,* 899-905.

Richardson, M.S. (1982). Sources of tension in teaching the psychology of women. *Psychology of Women Quarterly*, 7, 45-54.

Riger, S. (1978). A technique for teaching the psychology of women: Content analysis. *Teaching of Psychology*, 5, 221-223.

Riger, S. (1979). On teaching the psychology of women. *Teaching of Psychology*, 6, 113-114.

Rubin, M. (1985). A declining federal commitment of research about women: 1980-1984. Manuscript available from the National Council for Research on Women, 47-49 E. 65th St., New York, NY 10021.

Schneider, J.W., & Hacker, S.L. (1973). Sex role imagery and the use of the generic "man" in introductory texts: A case in the sociology of sociology. *The American Sociologist*, 8, 12-18.

Schneider, S.F. (1974). Training for research, Part II: Issues, problems, prospects for the future. Unpublished manuscript, National Institute of Mental Health, Rockville, MD.

Schuster, J.H., & Bowen, H.R. (1985, September/October). The faculty at risk. *Change, 17*, 13-21.

Sholley, B. (1986). Value of good discussions in a psychology of women course. *Teaching of Psychology*, 13, 151-153.

Spence, J.T. (Ed.) (1983). Introduction. *Achievement and achievement motives: Psychological and sociological approaches* (pp. 1-5). San Francisco: Freeman.

Stanovich, K.E. (1986). *How to think straight about psychology*. Glenview, IL: Scott, Foresman.

Stimpson, C. (1971). Thy neighbor's wife, they neighbor's servants: Women's liberation and black civil rights. In V. Gornick & B.K. Moran (Eds.), *Woman in sexist society: Studies in power and powerlessness*. New York: Basic Books.

Stimpson, C. (1973, September). The new feminism and women's studies. *Change*, 5, 43-48.

Thorne, B., & Henley, N. (1975). *Language and sex: Difference and dominance*. Rowley, MA: Newbury House.

Unger, R.K. (1979). *Female and male: Psychological perspectives*. New York: Harper & Row.

Unger, R.K. (1982). Advocacy versus scholarship revisited: Issues in the psychology of women. *Psychology of Women Quarterly*, 7, 5-17.

Walsh, M.R. (1985). The psychology of women course: A continuing catalyst for change. *Teaching of Psychology*, 12, 198-202.

Weis, L. (1985, November/December). Progress but no parity: Women in higher education. *Academe*, 29-33.

Williams, J. (1974, Summer). Administering a women's studies program. *Women's Studies Newsletter*, 2, 5, 11-12.

Women's Lives:
Images and Realities

Claire Etaugh

Images of women—including both the ways they view them
selves and the ways in which others perceive them—form a changing kaleidoscope as women proceed through the adult years.

Changes in women's lives during adulthood may be viewed in
one of two perspectives. One theoretical framework sees these
changes as tied to chronological age; the other views them as related
to social roles or role transitions (Reinke, Holmes, & Harris, 1985).
Advocates of age-based theories conceptualize the adult life cycle
as a series of stages, each associated with its own tasks, events, and
problems (e.g., Erikson, 1980; Gould, 1978; Levinson, 1978). This
life-stage perspective is based almost exclusively on experiences of
men, however, and may not be very useful in understanding the
adult lives of women.

Theories based on social roles and role transitions place more
emphasis on the intertwining of various roles—such as those of
spouse, parent, and worker—which change in importance throughout the adult years and have a great impact on each other (Evans,
1985). Several writers (e.g., George, 1980; Giele, 1982; Rossi,
1980) believe that this role perspective is particularly applicable to
women's lives. In this chapter, I will examine the traditional roles
which women have played in American society, the ways in which
these roles are changing, and some of the forces which have led to
these changes.

The author wishes to thank the following individuals for providing valuable
comments on earlier drafts of this paper: Andrea Etaugh, Patricia Hall, Jacqueline
Kandyba, Harold Rosenberg, Bonnie Spiller, and William Wilsen.

SOCIAL ROLES

First of all, what exactly is a role? A *role* may be defined as "the functions a person performs when occupying a particular position within a particular social context" (Shaw & Costanzo, 1982, p. 296). When we interact with people who are in a particular role, we assume that they will act in certain ways. These assumptions are called *role expectations* (Deaux & Wrightsman, 1984). Since we all occupy a number of different roles at the same time, and since each role contains a different set of expectations, the potential exists for a situation called *role conflict*.

Role Conflict

Role conflict is said to occur when a person occupies several positions which have incompatible demands (Deaux & Wrightsman, 1984). In a situation involving role conflict, difficulties are created because all the role expectations cannot be satisfied simultaneously. For example, a woman business executive finds that her child's school play occurs at the same time as a scheduled meeting with important clients. If she cannot reschedule the meeting, she must choose between fulfilling her role as a mother or her role as a professional.

White women are more likely than black women to view the roles of wife and mother as incompatible with the role of paid worker (Murray & Mednick, 1977). Hyde (1986), however, suggests that the black woman is more likely to experience other role conflicts stemming from the differences between the values of the dominant white culture and her own black culture. One example involves perceived conflict between support for women's rights and support for black rights. Another potential conflict revolves around child-bearing decisions. The black professional woman's choice to limit family size (Epstein, 1973) is viewed by some black leaders as a form of racial genocide and disloyalty (Hyde, 1986).

Role Overload

Role overload occurs when several roles simultaneously make extensive time demands on an individual, whether or not the various activities are inherently incompatible with each other (Frieze,

Parsons, Johnson, Ruble, & Zellman, 1977). A college student, for example, may have to choose between studying for an exam and writing a paper which is due the next day. Women who are attempting to combine a number of roles, such as those of wife, mother, and student or employee, will frequently experience both role overload and role conflict at the same time. A number of strategies are used by women to cope with role overload. These include establishing priorities, performing several tasks at once, and not carrying out certain tasks (Katz, 1975). It would seem that an effective way to handle role overload would be to reallocate various responsibilities. For example, an employed mother could request that her husband and children take on greater homemaking responsibilities or she could arrange to pay someone to perform various childcare or household tasks. Many women, however, are reluctant to do this. For one thing, family members may feel threatened by the working mother's nontraditional role behavior and by the request that they take on additional responsibilities. In addition, the employed wife and mother may feel guilty about not performing the traditional feminine domestic and childrearing tasks (Etaugh, 1984). She may even overcompensate by insisting on doing all of her own housework, entertaining lavishly, and cooking gourmet meals in addition to pursuing a career (Stein & Bailey, 1973). One may question the advisability of pursuing such a physically and psychologically demanding "superwoman" lifestyle.

Role Changes

As a rule, women undergo a greater number of role changes during their adult lives than do men. Men typically assume both work and family roles in their twenties which remain in force throughout their adult years (e.g., Levinson, 1978). Women, on the other hand, are more likely to change back and forth from work roles to family roles to work roles. In addition, many more women than men undergo the role transition from marriage to widowhood in late life. Women not only switch roles with greater frequency than men, but they also show a greater variety of role change patterns. In her book *Passages*, Gail Sheehy (1976) describes four major life patterns for married women: the caregiver, the nurturer who defers achievement, the achiever who defers nurturance, and the integrator. In the caregiver pattern, which has been the traditional one for women, the woman typically gives up the role of student or employee once she marries or has children. While she has no plans to resume these roles in the future, she may indeed do so once her children are in school or after they are grown. The nurturer who defers achievement follows a pattern similar to that of the caregiver, with the exception that she *intends* to resume extrafamilial roles at a later time. The achiever who defers nurturance postpones the role of mother and sometimes that of wife in order to pursue a professional role. She may give up her work role when her children are small, but return to it later. Finally, the integrator attempts to combine marriage, motherhood, and career simultaneously.

Changing roles involves learning new skills and behavioral expectations. To the extent that the old and new roles contain incompatible demands, the individual will experience *role conflict*, described previously. Often, however, role transitions can be eased by *anticipatory socialization* (Brim & Ryff, 1980). This is a process in which individuals are prepared for entry into new roles through information or training received prior to assuming the new status. Parenting classes and apprenticeship courses are examples of anticipatory socialization experiences. Anticipating socialization into a new role is most likely to occur when the role is adopted at a time in the life cycle when many others also are assuming that role (Brim & Ryff, 1980). The fact that many life events tend to occur at certain fairly predictable periods during the adult years has led to the concept of the *social clock*.

The Social Clock

The *social clock*, first proposed by Bernice Neugarten and her colleagues (1968), consists of societally based norms which describe the roles women and men should assume at different stages of adulthood. A 1965 study of middle-aged adults found strong agreement, within social classes, on the expected timing of such events as marriage, birth of the first child, first job, and grandparenthood (Neugarten, 1968). Those who perceive themselves as being "off-time," that is, as deviating from the social clock, may experience both internal and external pressures to conform. Women who are not married by the age of thirty, married women of thirty-five without children, or women returning to school in their forties are likely to be viewed as being "off-time." More recently, however, Neugarten (1981) has stated that the social clock is becoming less important as a regulator of behavior. As indicators of the increasingly fluid life cycle, she points to the growing rates of divorce and remarriage, the increasing number of women entering, leaving, and re-entering both institutions of higher education and the labor force, and the greater incidence of mid-life career changes for women and men.

TRADITIONAL AND CHANGING ROLES OF WOMEN

The roles of women in American society have always included those of wife, homemaker, mother, student, and member of the labor force. Each of these roles has changed over time, however. Until recently, the traditional path followed by women emphasized the roles of wife, homemaker, and mother. In the late nineteenth century, for example, fewer than 20 percent of females were in the labor force. Typically, these workers were young single women who worked for only a few years between the time they finished their schooling and the time they got married (Bernard, 1981). Although more women are employed today than ever before, including married women with children, the primary social role assigned to women in American society still is that of wife (O'Leary, 1977).

Wife

For most women and men, marriage is viewed as the most natural and desirable marital status (Duberman, 1974). Fully 94 percent of all American women marry at some time in their lives (U.S. Bureau of the Census, 1984).

The average age at first marriage for women has changed during the last century, declining from 22.0 in 1890 to 20.2 in 1955 (Bernard, 1981). Since 1955, this trend has reversed. By 1980, the average age at first marriage for women was 22.1 years (Bianchi & Spain, 1983). Moveover, in the age group in which women and men have typically married (20-24 years old), the percentage of never-married women increased sharply from 36 percent in 1970 to 56 percent in 1983. Over the same period of time, the percentage of never-married women of ages 30-34 increased from 7 percent to 13 percent (U.S. Bureau of the Census, 1984). These trends suggest that women not only are postponing marriage, but that an increasing number of them may never marry.

What are the reasons for this change in marriage patterns? One explanation is that the growth of educational opportunities for women has given them alternatives to the traditional life pattern, and that more women are delaying their roles as wife (and mother) in order to pursue educational and career goals. Another factor is the greater incidence and acceptance of unmarried couples living together (Van Dusen & Sheldon, 1976).

Marital satisfaction typically is high for women in the early years of marriage (Campbell, Converse, & Rogers, 1976). By middle age, however, men appear to be more satisfied with their marriages than women (Lowenthal, Thurnher, & Chiriboga, 1975; Veroff & Feld, 1970). Jessie Bernard (1972) has suggested that marriage may be more beneficial to men than to women. In support of her claim, it has been found that mental illness rates are higher for married women than for married men (Gove, 1972; Gove & Geerken, 1977). Similarly, married women report more depression than do married men (Radloff, 1975). By contrast, unmarried women (including the never-married, divorced, and widowed) have better mental health than their male counterparts (Gove, 1972). What are some of the stresses that might lead to higher rates of mental illness in married women? For one thing, marriage entails a greater loss of autonomy and independence for women than for men (Frieze et al., 1977). Gove (1977) suggests several other factors. First, a married man has two primary sources of gratification—his family and his work. A married woman who does not work, however, may have no alternative source of gratification to turn to if her family roles are unfulfilling. Second, even if she is employed, she may well be a victim of sex discrimination in the workplace and find herself in a menial, low-paying job. Furthermore, the employed married woman still performs most of the household and child care tasks, a situation which can produce considerable role conflict and over-load, as we saw earlier. Finally, those women who are full-time homemakers may be frustrated by various aspects of the housewife role. Let us explore this last point in greater detail by turning now to an examination of another traditional role of women, the home-maker.

Homemaker

In terms of sheer numbers, the occupation of homemaker or housewife claims more women than any other. Married women in the labor force are homemakers at least part-time, and nearly half of all married women those who are not employed are full time homemakers (Bernard, 1981). Historically, domestic skills were greatly valued in young women, and the housewife role was emphasized as a major one for women until the 1970s (Williams, 1983). The traditional role of full-time housewife-mother was more characteristic of white middle-class women than black women, however, because of economic necessity (Hyde, 1985).

The relatively high status of homemaker was reflected in the attitudes of women themselves. For example, in a study of both employed and nonemployed women conducted in the late 1960s, the majority of the women stated that the most important roles of a woman were those of mother, wife, and housewife (Lopata, 1971).

During the last 10 or 15 years, however, the social status of the housewife has declined dramatically and many women who are full-time homemakers have become defensive about being "just a housewife" (Bernard, 1981). The decline in status of the housewife role has been accompanied by a decrease in the amount of work required to run a household. The availability of labor-saving appliances, convenience foods, and wash-and-wear clothing has lightened the housewife's load. Families live in smaller dwellings, have fewer children, and are less likely to care for elderly parents in the home.

As Williams (1983) notes, the role of housewife is very different from that of occupational roles performed outside the home. For one thing, there are no "admissions" requirements or prerequisite skill levels, and therefore anyone can become a housewife. In addition, society does not provide any formal training for the job, and there are no objective tests of good performance. Furthermore, the role of housewife is relatively unstructured, invisible, and ambiguous, which may be a source of stress and frustration (Gove, 1972).

Ann Oakley (1974) interviewed 40 London housewives and found that 70 percent were dissatisfied with housework. Major reasons given for dissatisfaction were monotony, loneliness, lack of structure, and long hours. The most frequently mentioned positive aspect of the housewife role was autonomy—having the ability to structure one's own time. Those women who had previously held high-status jobs outside the home expressed the greatest dissatisfaction with housework.

With the rise of the women's movement and the influx of married women into the labor force in recent years, are husbands now more likely to participate in the household chores traditionally assigned to women? According to most research, women who are employed full-time get more help from their husbands with housework than do women who are full-time housewives (Beckman & Houser, 1979; Ericksen, Yancy, & Ericksen, 1979; Weingarten, 1978). This is even more likely to happen when the couple has more than one child (Walker & Woods, 1976).

Nevertheless, women still do most of the child care and housework, whether they are employed or not (Barnett, 1983; Nyquist, Slivken, Spence, & Helmreich, 1985; Robinson, 1977; Walker & Wood, 1976). A recent study of middle-class couples, for example, found that men did no more than one-third of the child-care and household tasks even if their wives worked. In fact, 70 percent of the men reported that they had *no* child care responsibilities. Women, on the other hand, performed about 80 percent of all child care tasks (Barnett, 1983).

With our attention focused on child care, it is appropriate that we turn now to a discussion of another major traditional role of women, the role of mother.

Mother

The fertility rate (that is, the average number of births a woman will have in her lifetime based on present birth rates) declined in the United States throughout the early twentieth century, reaching a low point of 2.2 births during the Depression years of the late 1930s. The baby boom following World War II peaked in the late 1950s, when the fertility rate reached 3.7. After that, the fertility rate gradually dropped to 1.8 in the mid 1970s, where it has remained since (U.S. Bureau of the Census, 1983).

Women not only are having fewer children, but they also are having them later. Between 1960 and 1983, the percentage of never-married women between 20 and 24 years of age with no children grew from 24 percent to 40 percent. For 25 to 29-year-old never-married women, the percentage who were childless grew during this period from 13 percent to 27 percent. Even among 30 to 34-year-olds, who are approaching the end of their childbearing years, 16 percent had no children in 1983, compared with only 8 percent in 1970 (U.S. Bureau of the Census, 1975, 1984). As in the case of delayed marriage, this trend may indicate that many women have decided not only to postpone motherhood, but to remain childless.

Why are more women choosing to have no children? Career and income factors often are key considerations in making this decision (Silka & Kiesler, 1977). In some instances, having grown up in a less-than-ideal family environment also may be involved. One study, for example, found that women who decided early (even before marriage) not to have children reported more psychological distance and incompatibility between themselves and their parents and less warmth in their families when they were growing up (Houseknect, 1979).

Despite the fact that more women are deciding not to have children, the majority do become mothers. In 1980, for example, 94 percent of all never-married American women between the ages of 40 and 44 had had at least one child (Bianchi & Spain, 1983). Motherhood still is considered to be a central component of a woman's life, a concept that has been labelled "the motherhood mandate" (Russo, 1979). This mandate is so powerful that couples who choose to remain child-free are often seen as selfish, immature, poorly adjusted, and unhappy (Peterson, 1983; Veevers, 1973).

Motherhood can be extremely fulfilling, although it is often stressful as well. In a recent study, 90 percent of parents said that if they could relive their lives, they would have children again (Yankelovich, 1981). Yet the birth of the first child can create considerable strain. The new mother is expected to be the infant's primary caretaker, a time-consuming and exhausting job for which she usually has no formal preparation. The new child places an added economic burden on the couple as well, and to some extent disrupts the husband-wife relationship. Indeed, married couples without children report greater happiness and marital satisfaction than do married couples with children (Campbell et al., 1976). Studies of marital satisfaction over the life span indicate that satisfaction is highest for young married couples with no children. Satisfaction drops after the birth of the first child and is at its lowest during the years when children are preschoolers. As children get older, marital happiness begins to increase again. It continues to grow after the children have left home, almost reaching the peak level of the early "honeymoon" years (Renne, 1976).

Working Mothers

We have seen that a powerful "motherhood mandate" exists in American society. According to this mandate, not only should a woman bear children, but she also should be responsible for their care (Russo, 1979). Popular articles and books on child care have perpetrated the belief that a woman must stay home with her child in the early years in order to ensure the child's optimal development (Etaugh, 1980). Despite such attitudes, mothers of children of all ages have been entering the work force in ever-increasing numbers. In 1984, 65 percent of married mothers of 6 to 17-year-old children were employed, as were 52 percent of married mothers of children under 6. For divorced mothers, the comparable figures were 84 percent and 68 percent (U.S. Bureau of the Census, 1984). Even mothers with infants under one year of age are participating in the labor force in unprecedented numbers: nearly half of them were employed in 1984 (Select Committee, 1984). Black women with children under 18 are more likely to be employed than white or Hispanic women with children (National Commission, 1986).

What are the effects of maternal employment on children? This is a rather complex question. The answer depends upon a number of factors: the age and sex of the child, various conditions of maternal employment (for example, full-time versus part-time employment, length of employment, type of occupation), specific conditions and features of child care arrangements, and the mother's satisfaction with her various roles.

Nearly 70 percent of children under 5 with employed mothers are cared for either in someone else's home or in their own homes by someone other than their mother. Another 19 percent are cared for in group day care centers (Select Committee, 1984). Research indicates that good quality care received in any of these settings does not have adverse effects on the infant's and preschool child's social, emotional, or intellectual development (Belsky, 1984; Clarke-Stewart & Fein, 1983; Etaugh, 1980). Similarly, children of elementary school age appear to develop equally well whether or not their mothers are employed (Etaugh, 1984; Hoffman, 1979). Hoffman (1979) has suggested that maternal employment may benefit school-age children by fostering greater independence and encouraging responsibility and competence. These benefits continue into adolescence, when the need for independence becomes even greater. The effects of maternal employment seem to be particularly beneficial for adolescent girls. Adolescent daughters of employed women often show better personality adjustment, greater academic achievement, and higher educational and career aspirations than daughters of nonemployed women (Etaugh, 1984; Hoffman, 1979). It is important to note that whatever the age and sex of the child, mothers who are satisfied with their lives—whether they are employed or not—tend to have the best-adjusted children (Etaugh, 1984).

Divorce

An increasing number of American women and men are experiencing divorce, single parenting, and remarriage (Hetherington & Camara, 1984). The ratio of divorced to married people increased from 47 per 1000 in 1970 to 114 per 1000 in 1983 (U.S. Bureau of the Census, 1984). The divorce rate for black families is approximately twice that of white families (McNett, Taylor & Scott, 1985). It is estimated that if this trend continues, about half of all marriages begun in the mid 1970s will end in divorce (Cherlin, 1981). The rising divorce rate has been largely responsible for an increase in the number of one-parent households, 90 percent of which are headed by the mother. In 1984, 44 percent of black families, 23 percent of Hispanic families, and 13 percent of white families were headed by women (National Commission, 1986). Between 1970 and 1982, the percentage of children living with only one parent nearly doubled from 12 percent to 22 percent. In 1982, 13 percent of children under the age of 18 were living with a divorced or separated mother, and nearly 2 percent with a divorced or separated father. The comparable figures for 1970 were 7 percent and less than 1 percent (U.S. Bureau of the Census, 1983). Most individuals who divorce – about 75 percent of women and nearly 85 percent of men – remarry, with approximately half of those remarriages occurring within 3 years after the divorce (Cherlin, 1981).

Because both divorce and widowhood involve a rupture of the attachment bond to a spouse and a return to the role of unmarried person, these two life events may be viewed as involving a period of grieving and transition (Brown, Feldberg, Fox, & Kohen, 1976; Weiss, 1976). Coping with the change in role from that of married to divorced person is more difficult for women who are more dependent, more traditionally oriented, and older (Brown & Manela, 1978; Chiriboga, 1982; Chiriboga, Roberts, & Stein, 1978; Granvold, Pedler, & Schellie, 1979; Hetherington, Cox, & Cox, 1982).

Divorced women experience stress in several areas. For one thing, divorced persons in our society are perceived in an unflattering light: they are considered to be less stable, responsible, reliable, satisfied, and well-adjusted than married individuals (Etaugh & Malstrom, 1981; Etaugh & Petroski, 1985; Etaugh & Stern, 1984). Divorced women (and men) do, in fact, frequently experience emotional upheaval in the year following divorce. They report feeling more anxious, depressed, angry, rejected, and incompetent (Hetherington et al., 1982).

There are practical problems for divorced women as well. Financial burdens are increased, as are the responsibilities of running a household (Brown et al., 1976; Hetherington et al., 1982; Weiss, 1979). Since the mother usually is the custodial parent, she must take on not only the major responsibilities of raising her children and supporting them financially, but also any household responsibilities which her husband formerly carried out. Role overload consequently is a frequent problem (Hetherington et al., 1982). In addition, social life often is curtailed. Mothers may feel isolated from adult contacts, especially if they are not employed. Problems in parent-child relationships also may occur initially. Hetherington and her colleagues (1982) found that in the year following divorce, parents communicated less well with their children, were less affectionate, and were more inconsistent in discipline than were married parents. Mothers of sons experienced more problems than mothers of daughters. By the end of the second year following the divorce, however, the various emotional, economic, household, social, and parent-child stresses had diminished, and most parents and children had adapted reasonably well to their lives.

Support from family and friends is important in helping both women and men adjust to divorce (Colletta, 1979; Hetherington et al., 1982; Weiss, 1975). Having a supportive intimate relationship also enhances feelings of life-satisfaction in the years following divorce (Spanier & Furstenberg, in press).

Widowhood

Despite the increasing divorce rate, most marriages are terminated not by divorce, but by the death of a spouse. Women are much more likely to become widowed than are men, since women not only have a longer life expectancy but also tend to marry men older than themselves. As of 1983, there were 10.9 million widows but only 1.9 million widowers in this country, a ratio of greater than five to one. About 67 percent of women over the age of 75, but only 22 percent of men the same age, are widowed (U.S. Bureau of the Census, 1984). Remarriage rates are much higher for widowers than for widows. Widowed men over 65, for example, are eight times more likely to remarry than are widows of the same age (Carter & Glick, 1976). One reason for the higher remarriage rate of widowers is that unmarried older women greatly outnumber unmarried older men. In 1982, for instance, there were 23 unmarried men aged 65 and over for every 100 unmarried women in that age category (U.S. Bureau of the Census, 1983). Furthermore, since men tend to marry women younger than themselves, the pool of potential mates expands for an older man but shrinks for an older woman.

Following the death of a spouse, the widow or widower undergoes a period of grieving. According to Parkes and his colleagues

(Parkes, 1972; Parkes & Weiss, 1983), grieving for a spouse typically consists of four overlapping stages: numbness, yearning and
protest, disorganization and despair, and reorganization.

Numbness or shock is the typical initial reaction to the death of a
spouse, usually lasting for about a week. The next stage consists of
two reactions: yearning and protest. Yearning involves intense preoccupation with thoughts of the dead spouse, "searching" for the
lost person, and frequent crying. Guilt is a common response, as the
surviving spouse wonders what could have been done to prevent the
spouse's death. These feelings alternate with feelings of anger and
protest directed toward relatives, physicians, clergy, or the de-
ceased spouse for leaving the survivor alone. Parkes (1972) found
that the intensity of yearning and protest diminishes by the end of
the second month, and is replaced by depression and apathy. In this
stage, the widows interviewed by Parkes expressed little interest in
planning for the future. During the process of reorganization or recovery, the survivor gradually comes to accept the loss both intellectually and emotionally, and reorganizes his or her self-concept
(Parkes & Weiss, 1983). While this process usually begins within a
year, recovery may take two or three years.

A woman's reaction to widowhood depends on many factors including her age, the degree of forewarning of the spouse's death,
and her personal, social, and financial resources. Compared to the
young widow, the older widow is more likely to be financially secure, to have no child care responsibilities, to have friends in similar circumstances, and to be more psychologically prepared for the
death of herself and her spouse (Treas, 1983). Studies comparing
the mental and physical health of older widows and older married
women generally have not found any differences between these
groups (e.g., Heyman & Gianturco, 1973; Pihlblad & Adams,
1972). Younger widows, however, appear to experience greater
difficulties than older widows in coping with their situation
(O'Leary, 1977). In addition to the reasons mentioned above, one
reason for the greater distress experienced by young widows may be
the greater likelihood that the husband's death was unexpected. In a
longitudinal study of widows and widowers younger than 45 years
of age, Parkes and Weiss (1983) found that those persons whose
spouses died with little or no forewarning had greater difficulty ac-

cepting the reality of the death, and felt more anger and guilt than those who had knowledge of the impending death.

The importance of social, personal, and economic resources in a woman's adaptation to widowhood has been shown in a series of studies by Helene Lopata (1973, 1975, 1979). She classified widows in terms of their degree of re-engagement into social involvement. At one extreme was the active engaged woman, who initiated changes and retained control of her life after her spouse's death. She was likely to have a greater income, a higher educational level, and more friends than other groups of widows. Another type of widow lived in an essentially sex-segregated world, often in an ethnic community. She often continued to remain involved with her neighbors, relatives, and church group. At the other extreme was the widow who became a social isolate. She often had a low educational level, and had married a man of similar status upon whom she became quite dependent. With marginal financial resources, and often lacking skills to successfully re-engage into society after her husband's death, she became withdrawn and isolated.

It is important to note that our knowledge of widows has been obtained primarily from older women, most of whom have had traditional marriages. When the young women of today become widows, they will be more likely to have had a college education and occupational experience than the current population of widows, and they may therefore be better prepared to make the adjustment to widowhood (Perlmutter & Hall, 1985).

Singlehood

As we noted earlier, more women are delaying marriage and it is likely that an increasing number of them will never marry. Society's attitudes toward those who remain single is changing as well. In 1957, 80 percent of Americans labeled those who do not marry as "sick," "neurotic," or "immoral"; by 1981, only 25 percent felt this way (Yankelovich, 1981). Negative stereotypes still persist, however. Middle-aged people who have never married are perceived as less sociable, likable, attractive, and well-adjusted than middle-aged married individuals (Etaugh & Malstrom, 1981; Etaugh & Petroski, 1985; Etaugh & Stern, 1984).

To be sure, there are some disadvantages to the single life. American society is couples-oriented and the single person may feel left out and lonely (Cargan & Melko, 1982; Parlee, 1979).

There are a number of advantages to being single, however. These include personal freedom, opportunities for career development, and the availability of privacy (Edward, 1977; Stein, 1975). Another frequently mentioned advantage of being a single woman is a sense of self-sufficiency and competency (Donelson, 1977).

Singlehood appears to be a more advantageous state for women than for men. Compared to single men, single women are happier (Campbell, 1975) and have better mental health (Gove, 1972). Furthermore, single women have higher levels of education, occupational status, and earnings than do married women, whereas this pattern is reversed for men (Hudis, 1976; Treiman & Terrell, 1975). Among single women themselves, life satisfaction is associated with being healthy, not being lonely, living with a female housemate, having some intimate and many casual friendships, and being highly involved with work (Loewenstein et al., 1981).

About 5 percent of all adults over the age of 65 have never been married (U.S. Bureau of the Census, 1983). They are not especially lonely in old age, and their life satisfaction is similar to that of older married adults. They are more positive than older widowed or divorced adults, who have undergone the experience of losing a spouse (Gubrium, 1974). In this sense, being single in old age may be advantageous.

Women in Higher Education

We have seen that women are marrying later, delaying childbearing, and having fewer children. In other words, they are spending less time in traditional family roles. At the same time, women are becoming more involved in roles outside the family, particularly the roles of student and paid worker (Van Dusen & Sheldon, 1976). Let us first examine women's increasing participation in higher education.

Historically, women have been less likely to enroll in college and to complete degrees than men, but the difference between the sexes has been decreasing since 1950 (Bianchi & Spain, 1983). Women's enrollments in higher education have increased at a faster rate than men's since the 1970s, and by 1979, just over half of all college students were women (National Center for Education Statistics, 1983). Much of the enrollment increase for women has occurred in the older age groups, particularly age 25 and older (Randour, Strasburg, & Lipman-Blumen, 1982). Approximately one-third of the college population is now older than age 25, and two-thirds of these older students are women (Saslaw, 1981). Since the 1960s, minority women have improved their educational attainments. Asian American women have the highest college graduation rates, followed by whites, blacks, and Hispanic and American Indian women (Daniel, 1987).

There are several possible explanations for women's greater participation in higher education in recent years. Young women of traditional college age (18 to 24) are marrying and having children later, and so have more time to attend school or work before marriage and childbearing (Bianchi & Spain, 1983). Older returning women students may resume their education for a variety of reasons depending on their marital and family status, occupational status, and financial needs. The re-entry woman may be a middle-class woman taking courses for personal fulfillment, but she is increasingly likely to be a lower-income single parent seeking to better support her family, or a single woman preparing for career advancement (Holliday, 1985).

More women are not only enrolling in institutions of higher education, but more of them are completing degrees at every level. In 1982, half of all bachelor's and master's degrees and 32 percent of all doctoral degrees were earned by women ("Earned Degrees Conferred," 1984).

Certain majors remain popular with women students: home economics, library science, health professions, education, foreign languages, and fine and applied arts. More than half of the master's degrees and over one-third of the doctoral degrees earned by women are in the field of education (Randour et al., 1982). Still, more women have been moving into traditionally male fields. Between 1971 and 1982, the percentage of bachelor's degrees awarded to women increased in agriculture from 4 to 31 percent; in architecture, from 12 to 29 percent; in biological sciences, from 29 to 45 percent; in business and management, from 9 to 40 percent; in computer and information sciences, from 14 to 35 percent; in engineering, from less than 1 to 11 percent; and in physical sciences, from 14 to 25 percent ("Earned Degrees Conferred," 1984; Randour et al., 1982). Women have made inroads into the traditionally male-dominated professional fields of law, medicine, and dentistry, as well (Bianchi & Spain, 1983). In 1982, 33 percent of all law degrees were earned by women, compared to only 5 percent in 1970. During the same period of time, the proportion of medical degrees awarded to women increased from 8 to 25 percent, and the percentage of dentistry degrees from less than 1 to 15 percent (Bianchi & Spain, 1983; "Earned Degrees Conferred," 1984).

Women in the Labor Force

Women's participation in the labor force has increased dramatically during this century. In 1900, only 20 percent of women were in the labor force (Bernard, 1981). By 1984, this figure had risen to 54 percent, and women constituted 43 percent of the labor force (U.S. Bureau of the Census, 1984). Employment rates are higher among black women than white women, with Hispanic and American Indian women having the lowest rates (Almquist & Wehrle-Einhorn, 1978; Nieva & Gutek, 1981).

Certain factors increase the likelihood that a woman will work. One factor is financial need: women with no husbands or with husbands who are unemployed or have low incomes are more likely to work than are women who have husbands with high earnings. A second factor is the age of a woman's children: women with school-age children are more likely to be employed than those with pre-schoolers (Smith, 1979).

Recent statistics illustrate how these marital and family characteristics influence labor force participation in women. In 1984, 66 percent of 35 to 44-year-old married women with husbands present were in the labor force, compared with 83 percent of women who had never married and 80 percent of divorced and widowed women. And, as we saw earlier, two-thirds of married mothers with 6 to 17-year-old children are working, as compared to about half of married mothers with preschoolers (U.S. Bureau of the Census, 1984).

Since the 1960s, the largest increase in women's labor force participation has been among 25 to 34-year-olds, the age range when most women are bearing and rearing young children. Historically, women were least likely to work during these years (Van Dusen & Sheldon, 1976). In 1960, 36 percent of women 25-34 years old were in the labor force; by 1983, this figure had risen to 69 percent (U.S. Bureau of the Census, 1984; U.S. Department of Labor, 1983).

What are the reasons for women's increasing participation in the labor force? Rising educational levels of women have given them access to more attractive, higher paying jobs. In addition, service occupations expanded after World War II. These jobs — including those of teacher, nurse, librarian, social worker, and clerical worker — have traditionally attracted a high proportion of female workers. The supply of young, single women who had filled these positions in the past was not large enough to keep up with the growing demand for female labor, and married women were increasingly drawn into the work force. Other factors leading to women's greater labor force participation include rising divorce rates, declining birthrates, the lessening of housework demands, and changing sex-role attitudes which made it more socially acceptable for married women and those with children to work (Nieva & Gutek, 1981; Smith, 1979; Van Dusen & Sheldon, 1979). It is not always easy to tell whether a particular factor is a *cause* of increased employment, or an *effect* of it, however. For example, employed women have fewer children than women who are not employed (Moore & Hofferth, 1979). Is this because women with fewer children are more likely to decide to work, or because working women decide to have fewer children? Both factors appear to be involved.

Not only are women majoring in traditionally male fields and joining the work force in increasing numbers, but they are moving into occupations traditionally dominated by men. From 1962 to 1982, the percentage of women bartenders grew from 11 to 50 percent and the percentage driving buses rose from 12 to 47 percent. Other jobs showing an increase in the proportion of women during this period include: engineers, from 1 to 6 percent; mail carriers, from 3 to 17 percent; physicians, from 6 to 15 percent; and insurance agents, from 10 to 26 percent (Serrin, 1984).

Nevertheless, most women work in jobs that are highly sex-segregated (that is, dominated by members of their own sex). Of 420 different occupations listed by the U.S. Department of Labor, 80 percent of all women work in only 25 of them (Ferraro, 1984). In 1983, women comprised 99 percent of all secretaries; 97 percent of child-care workers; 96 percent of registered nurses and domestic workers; 88 percent of clerks, cashiers, and waiters/waitresses; 87 percent of librarians; and 83 percent of elementary school teachers (Gest, 1984). About half of all women were in clerical and service occupations (including private household work) in 1985. Black women were somewhat more likely to hold such jobs (55 percent of black women workers) than were Hispanic women (51 percent) or white women (47 percent; National Commission, 1986).

One reason for occupational segregation may be "initial assignment segregation," in which women and men with equal entry-level skills are channeled into different jobs based on their sex (Ferraro, 1984). For example, although women are more likely than men to take so-called white-collar jobs, men's white collar jobs tend to be the better-paying and higher status professional, administrative, or scientific occupations. Women's white collar jobs, on the other hand, are more likely to be lower-paying, dead-end clerical positions (Kahl, 1983).

Women who work full-time earn only about 64 percent of the income of men. This figure has changed relatively little since 1960 (Barrett, 1979; Bianchi & Spain, 1983; National Commission, 1986; Serrin, 1984). Minority women earn 10 to 16 percent less than white women (National Commission, 1986). Hard as it is to believe, the average female college graduate earns less than the average male high-school dropout. These discrepancies are not just due to the fact that women are concentrated in lower-paying jobs. Even after statistically adjusting for male-female differences in age, education, type of occupation, and prior work experience, approximately half of the wage gap between the sexes remains, suggesting the presence of sex discrimination (Bianchi & Spain, 1983; Ferraro, 1984).

Although the Equal Pay Act of 1963 outlawed separate pay scales for women and men doing the same work, some employers got around the law simply by reclassifying certain jobs (Barrett, 1979).

More recently, the issue of "equal pay for equal work" has been replaced by the concept of "equal pay for *comparable* work." Supporters of "comparable worth," also known as "pay equity," believe that women and men should receive comparable salaries for jobs that require equivalent overall effort, skill, responsibility, and working conditions. Some recent court decisions and state laws have supported efforts to adopt comparable worth policies. For example, in 1987 the state legislatures of Connecticut and Oregon and the city of San Francisco appropriated 11, 22.6, and 35 million dollars, respectively, for pay equity adjustments ("Pay Equity," 1987).

Earlier we examined the effects of a woman's working on her children. Another frequently asked question concerns the effects of working on women themselves. Specifically, are working women more satisfied with their lives than full-time homemakers? The answer to this question is not clear. Some studies have found that working women have better psychological health than nonworking women (Ferree, 1976; Gove & Geerken, 1977; Kessler & McCrae, 1981; Northcott, 1981; Welch & Booth, 1977). Others, however, find no differences in psychological well-being between the two groups (Aneshensel, Frerichs, & Clark, 1981; Newberry, Weissman, & Myers, 1979; Wright, 1978). A major reason for the apparent contradiction in research findings is that a woman's well-being depends not just on her employment status but, as we have seen, on many other factors such as her marital status and the presence of children in the home. For single women with no children at home, a clear association has been found between employment and better mental health (Warr & Parry, 1982), probably because employment is a major source of role satisfaction for such women (Gove, 1972). For married women with children at home, however, life satisfaction and happiness is no greater for the employed woman than for the full-time homemaker (Warr & Parry, 1982). It may be that the psychological and social rewards provided by outside employment are offset by the strains of role overload and role conflict for women who are involved in juggling the multiple roles of wife, mother, and worker (Shehan, 1984). As women move into middle-age and approach the "empty nest" period of life when children leave home, women who work outside the home once again are found to have better mental health and higher levels of self-esteem than home-makers (Baruch, Barnett, & Rivers, 1983; Birnbaum, 1975; Coleman & Antonucci, 1983; Powell, 1977). Employment at this time in a woman's life may be beneficial because it directs attention away from concerns about physical health, marital dissatisfaction, and the launching of children (Coleman & Antonucci, 1983).

Retirement

Retirement is one of the two major role transitions which occur in later life, the other one being widowhood. Much of what we know about the effects of retirement is based on studies of men. One reason for this is that, until recently, a relatively small proportion of women spent their adult lives in the labor force. In addition, it has been assumed that retirement is a less critical event for women than for men because of women's greater involvement in family roles. Recent research, however, indicates that female retirees were just as committed to their work as were male retirees (Atchley, 1976; Streib & Schneider, 1971), and that retirement from the labor force has important consequences for women (George, Fillenbaum, & Palmore, 1984; Szinovacz, 1982).

Both sexes typically adjust well to retirement (Gratton & Haug, 1983), although women may take longer to become used to retirement (Atchley, 1976). Retirement has both negative and positive effects for women and men. Negative effects include increased psychosomatic symptoms and decreased income (George et al., 1984). Retired women are more likely than retired men to report that their incomes are inadequate (Atchley, 1976). This reflects the fact that women's retirement income typically is only about one-half that of men's (Bentsen, 1984). Women's concentration in low-paying jobs and their often interrupted or delayed work careers result in smaller retirement benefits. In addition, women are less likely than men to be covered by private pension plans (O'Rand & Henretta, 1982; Sheppard, 1976).

On the positive side, retired women and men spend more time in personal hobbies and increase their interactions with friends (George et al., 1984; Holahan, 1981). Retired women, particularly unmarried ones, are more involved with friends and neighbors than are retired men or lifelong housewives (Depner & Ingersoll, 1982; Fox, 1977). For both sexes, a high level of life satisfaction in retirement generally is associated with having good health, adequate income, and a high activity level (Atchley, 1982).

CONCLUSION

We have examined many images of women—wife, homemaker, mother, widow, divorcee, single woman, student, worker, retiree. These images—these roles—have been changing rapidly over the past century and even more rapidly during the past 25 years. Women are delaying entry into traditional family roles and they are spending less time in these roles (Van Dusen & Sheldon, 1976). Increasing numbers of women are choosing nontraditional family roles: they are staying single, getting divorced, or if married, remaining child-free. More women than ever are getting a college education and majoring in traditionally male areas. Labor force participation is now a fact of life for the majority of women. These rapid social changes have resulted in changing and often conflicting role expectations for women (Evans, 1985). The challenges facing today's women are great; the opportunities are tremendous.

REFERENCES

Almquist, E. M., & Wehrle-Einhorn, J. L. (1978). The doubly-disadvantaged: Minority women in the labor force. In A. H. Stromberg & S. Harkess (Eds.), *Women working* (pp. 63-88). Palo Alto, CA: Mayfield.

Aneshensel, C., Frerichs, R., & Clark, V. (1981). Family roles and sex differences in depression. *Journal of Health and Social Behavior, 22,* 379-393.

Atchley, R. C. (1976). Selected psychological and social differences among men and women in later life. *Journal of Gerontology, 31,* 204-211.

Atchley, R. C. (1982). The process of retirement: Comparing women and men. In M. Szinovacz (Ed.), *Women's retirement* (pp. 153-168). Beverly Hills, CA: Sage.

Barnett, R. C. (1983, August). Determinants of father participation in child care. In P. Bronstein (Chair), *Fatherhood in the 1980s: Men's changing family roles.* Symposium conducted at the meeting of the American Psychological Association, Anaheim, CA.

Barrett, N. S. (1979). Women in the job market: Occupations, earnings and career opportunities. In R. E. Smith (Ed.), *The subtle revolution: Women at work* (pp. 32-61). Washington, DC: Urban Institute.

Baruch, G., Barnett, R., & Rivers, C. (1983). *Life prints: New patterns of love and work for today's women*. New York: McGraw Hill.

Beckman, L. J., & Houser, B. B. (1979). The more you have, the more you do: The relationship between wife's employment, sex-role attitudes, and household behavior. *Psychology of Women Quarterly, 4*, 160-174.

Belsky, J. (1984). Two waves of day care research: Developmental effects and conditions of quality. In R. C. Ainslie (Ed.), *The child and the day care setting* (pp. 1-34). New York: Praeger.

Bentsen, S. K. (1984). Old age financial security — Or insecurity? In *Women, work and age: Policy challenges*. Ann Arbor, MI: University of Michigan, Institute of Gerontology.

Bernard, J. (1972). *The future of marriage*. New York: World.

Bernard, J. (1981). *The female world*. New York: Free Press.

Bianchi, S. M., & Spain, D. (1983). *American women: Three decades of change* (Report No. CDS-80-8). Washington, DC: Bureau of the Census.

Birnbaum, J. A. (1975). Life patterns and self-esteem in gifted family oriented and career committed women. In M.T.S. Mednick, S. S. Tangri, & L. W. Hoffman (Eds.), *Women and achievement: Social and motivational analyses* (pp. 396-419). New York: Halsted Press.

Brim, O. G., & Ryff, C. (1980). On the properties of life events. In P. B. Baltes & O. G. Brim (Eds.), *Life-span development and behavior* (Vol. 3, pp. 367-388). New York: Academic Press.

Brown, C. A., Feldberg, R., Fox, E. M., & Kohen, J. (1976). Divorce: Chance of a new lifetime. *Journal of Social Issues, 32*, 119-133.

Brown, P., & Manela, R. (1978). Changing family roles: Women and divorce. *Journal of Divorce, 4*, 315-328.

Campbell, A. (1975, May). The American way of mating: Marriage si, children only maybe. *Psychology Today*, pp. 39-42.

Campbell, A., Converse, P. E., & Rodgers, W. L. (1976). *The quality of American life*. New York: Russell Sage.

Cargan, L., & Melko, M. (1982). *Singles: Myths and realities*. Beverly Hills, CA: Sage.

Carter, H., & Glick, P. C. (1976). *Marriage and divorce: A social and economic study* (rev. ed.). Cambridge, MA: Harvard University Press.

Cherlin, A. J. (1981). *Marriage, divorce, and remarriage*. Cambridge, MA: Harvard University Press, 1981.

Chiriboga, D. A. (1982). Adaptation to marital separation in later and earlier life. *Journal of Gerontology, 37*, 109-114.

Chiriboga, D. A., Roberts, J., & Stein, J. A. (1978). Psychological well-being during marital separation. *Journal of Divorce, 2*, 21-36.

Clarke-Stewart, K. A., & Fein, G. G. (1983). Early childhood programs. In P. H. Mussen (Ed.), *Handbook of child psychology* (Vol. 2, pp. 917-999). New York: Wiley.

Coleman, L. M., & Antonucci, T. C. (1983). Impact of work on women at midlife. *Developmental Psychology, 19,* 290-294.

Colletta, M. D. (1979). Support systems after divorce: Incidence and impact. *Journal of Marriage and the Family, 41,* 837-846.

Daniel, R. L. (1987). *American woman in the 20th century.* San Diego, CA: Harcourt Brace Jovanovich.

Deaux, K., & Wrightsman, L. S. (1984). *Social psychology in the 80s* (4th ed.). Monterey, CA: Brooks/Cole.

Depner, C., & Ingersoll, B. (1982). Employment status and social support: The experience of the mature woman. In M. Szinovacz (Ed.), *Women's retirement* (pp. 61-76). Beverly Hills, CA: Sage.

Donelson, E. (1977). Becoming a single woman. In E. Donelson & J. Gullahorn (Eds.), *Women: A psychological perspective* (pp. 228-246). New York. Wiley.

Duberman, L. (1974). *Marriage and its alternatives.* New York: Praeger.

Earned degrees conferred in 1981-82 by U.S. colleges and universities (1984, January 11). *The Chronicle of Higher Education,* p. 18.

Edwards, M. (1977). Coupling and recoupling vs. the challenge of being single. *Personnel and Guidance Journal, 55,* 542-545.

Epstein, C. F. (1973, August). Black and female: The double whammy. *Psychology Today, 7* (3), 57.

Ericksen, J. A., Yancy, W. L., & Ericksen, E. P. (1979). The division of family roles. *Journal of Marriage and the Family, 49,* 301-313.

Erikson, E. H. (1980). *Identity and the life cycle.* New York: Norton.

Etaugh, C. (1980). Effects of nonmaternal care on children: Research evidence and popular views. *American Psychologist, 35,* 309-319.

Etaugh, C. (1984). Effects of maternal employment on children: Implications for the family therapist. In S. H. Cramer (Ed.), *Family therapy collections: Vol. 10. Perspectives on work and the family* (pp. 16-39). Rockville, MD: Aspen Systems.

Etaugh, C., & Malstrom, J. (1981). The effect of marital status on person perception. *Journal of Marriage and the Family, 43,* 801-805.

Etaugh, C., & Petroski, B. (1985). Perceptions of women: Effects of employment status and marital status. *Sex Roles, 12,* 329-339.

Etaugh, C., & Stern, J. (1984). Person perception: Effects of sex, marital status and sex-typed occupation. *Sex Roles, 11,* 413-424.

Evans, N. J. (1985). Women's development across the life span. In N. J. Evans (Ed.), *Facilitating the development of women* (pp. 9-27). San Francisco: Jossey-Bass.

Ferraro, G. A. (1984). Bridging the wage gap. *American Psychologist, 39,* 1166-1170.

Ferree, M. (1976). Working class jobs: Housework and paid work as sources of satisfaction. *Social Problems, 23,* 431-441.

Fox, J. H. (1977). Effects of retirement and former work life on women's adaptation in old age. *Journal of Gerontology, 32,* 196-202.

Frieze, I. H., Parsons, J. E., Johnson, P. B., Ruble, D. N., & Zellman, G. L.

(1977). *Women and sex roles: A social psychological perspective*. New York: W. W. Norton.

George, L. K. (1980). *Role transitions in later life*. Monterey, CA: Brooks/Cole.

George, L. K., Fillenbaum, G. G., & Palmore, E. (1984). Sex differences in the antecedents and consequences of retirement. *Journal of Gerontology, 39*, 364-371.

Gest, T. (1984, February 20). Battle of the sexes over comparable worth. *U.S. News & World Report*. pp. 73-74.

Giele, J. Z. (Ed.). (1982). *Women in the middle years*. New York: Wiley.

Gould, R. L. (1978). *Transformations: Growth and change in adult life*. New York: Simon & Schuster.

Gove, W. R. (1972). The relationship between sex roles, marital status and mental illness. *Social Forces, 51*, 34-44.

Gove, W. R., & Geerken, M. R. (1977). The effect of children and employment on the mental health of married men and women. *Social Forces, 56*, 66-76.

Granvold, D. K., Pedler, L. M., & Schellie, S. G. (1979). A study of sex role expectancy and female postdivorce adjustment. *Journal of Divorce, 2*, 383-393.

Gratton, B., & Haug, M. R. (1983). Decision and adaptation: Research on female retirement. *Research on Aging, 5*, 59-76.

Gubrium, J. F. (1974). Marital desolation and the valuation of everyday life in old age. *Journal of Marriage and the Family, 35*, 107-113.

Hetherington, E. M., & Camara, K. A. (1984). Families in transition: The processes of dissolution and reconstitution. In R. D. Parke (Ed.), *Review of child development research: Vol 7. The family* (pp. 398-439). Chicago: University of Chicago Press.

Hetherington, E. M., Cox, M., & Cox, R. (1982). Effects of divorce on parents and children. In M. Lamb (Ed.), *Nontraditional families* (pp. 233-288). Hillsdale, NJ: Erlbaum.

Heyman, D. K., & Gianturco, D. T. (1973). Long-term adaptation by the elderly to bereavement. *Journal of Gerontology, 28*, 359-362.

Hoffman, L. W. (1979). Maternal employment: 1979. *American Psychologist, 34*, 859-865.

Hoffman, L. W. (1984). Maternal employment and the young child. In M. Perlmutter (Ed.), *The Minnesota Symposia on Child Psychology: Vol. 17. Parent-child interactions and parent-child relations* (pp. 101-127). Hillsdale, NJ: Erlbaum.

Holahan, C. K. (1981, August). *Activity involvement in aging women: Career pattern and retirement*. Paper presented at the meeting of the American Psychological Association, Los Angeles.

Holliday, G. (1985). Addressing the concerns of returning women students. In N. J. Evans (Ed.), *Facilitating the development of women* (pp. 61-73). San Francisco: Jossey-Bass.

Houseknect, S. K. (1979). Timing of the decision to remain voluntarily childless:

Evidence for continuous socialization. *Psychology of Women Quarterly, 4*, 81-96.

Hudis, P. M. (1976). Commitment to work and family: Marital status differences in women's earnings. *Journal of Marriage and the Family, 38*, 267-278.

Hyde, J. S. (1986). *Half the human experience: The psychology of women* (3rd ed.). Lexington, MA: Heath.

Kahl, A. (1983). Characteristics of job entrants in 1980-1981. *Occupational Outlook Quarterly, 27*, 18-26.

Katz, M. (1975, August). *Sex role training and coping behavior in a role conflict situation: Homemaking-career conflicts*. Paper presented at the meeting of the American Psychological Association, Chicago.

Kessler, R., & McCrae, J. (1981). Trends in the relationship between sex and psychological distress: 1957-1976. *American Sociological Review, 46*, 443-452.

Levinson, D. J. (1978). *The seasons of a man's life*. New York: Knopf.

Loewenstein, S. F., Bloch, N. E., Campion, J., Epstein, J. S., Gale, P., & Salvatore, M. (1981). A study of satisfactions and stresses of single women in midlife. *Sex Roles, 11*, 1127-1141.

Lopata, H. (1971). *Occupation: Housewife*. New York: Oxford University Press.

Lopata, H. (1973). *Widowhood in an American city*. Cambridge, MA: Schenkman.

Lopata, H. Z. (1975). Widowhood: Societal factors in life-span disruption and alternatives. In N. Datan & L. H. Ginsberg (Eds.), *Life-span developmental psychology: Normative crises* (pp. 217-234). New York: Academic Press.

Lopata, H. Z. (1979). *Women as widows: Support systems*. New York: Elsevier-North Holland.

Lowenthal, M. F., Thurnher, M., & Chiriboga, D. (1975). *Four stages of life*. San Francisco: Jossey-Bass.

McNett, I., Taylor, L., & Scott, L. (1985). Minority women: Doubly disadvantaged. In A. G. Sargent (Ed.), *Beyond sex roles* (2nd ed., pp. 226-232). St. Paul, MN: West.

Moore, K. A., & Hofferth, S. L. (1979). Woman and their children. In R. E. Smith (Ed.), *The subtle revolution: Women at work* (pp. 125-157). Washington, DC: Urban Institute.

Murray, S. R., & Mednick, Martha T. S. (1977). Black women's achievement orientation: Motivational and cognitive factors. *Psychology of Women Quarterly, 1*, 247-259.

National Center for Education Statistics (1983). *The condition of education, 1983 statistical report*. Washington, DC: U.S. Government Printing Office.

National Commission on Working Women and Wider Opportunity for Women (1986). *An overview of minority women in the work force*. Washington, DC: Author.

Neugarten, B. (Ed.). (1968). *Middle age and aging*. Chicago: University of Chicago Press.

Neugarten, B. (1981). The aging society. *National Forum, 61*, 3.

Newberry, P., Weissman, M. M., & Myers, J. K. (1979). Working wives and housewives: Do they differ in mental status and social adjustment? *American Journal of Orthopsychiatry*, *49*, 282-291.

Nieva, V. F., & Gutek, B. A. (1981). *Women and work: A psychological perspective*. New York: Praeger.

Northcott, H. (1981). Women, work, health and happiness. *International Journal of Women's Studies*, *4*, 268-276.

Nyquist, L., Slivken, K., Spence, J. T., & Helmreich, R. L. (1985). Household responsibilities in middle-class couples: The contribution of demographic and personality variables. *Sex Roles*, *12*, 15-34.

Oakley, A. (1974). *The sociology of housework*. Bath, England: Pitman.

O'Leary, V. (1977). *Toward understanding women*. Monterey, CA: Brooks/Cole.

O'Rand, A., & Henretta, J. C. (1982). Midlife work history and retirement income. In M. Szinovacz (Ed.), *Women's retirement* (pp. 25-44). Beverly Hills, CA: Sage.

Parkes, C. M. (1972). *Bereavement: Studies of grief in adult life*. New York: International Universities Press.

Parkes, C. M., & Weiss, R. S. (1983). *Recovery from bereavement*. New York: Basic Books.

Parlee, M. B. (1979, October). The friendship bond. *Psychology Today*, pp. 43-54.

Pay equity victories (1987, Summer). *Pay Equity Newsnotes*, p. 1.

Perlmutter, M., & Hall, E. (1985). *Adult development and aging*. New York: Wiley.

Peterson, R. A. (1983). Attitudes toward the childless spouse. *Sex Roles*, *9*, 321-332.

Pihlblad, T., & Adams, C. (1972). Widowhood, social participation and life satisfaction. *Aging and Human Development*, *3*, 323-330.

Powell, B. (1977). The empty nest, employment, and psychiatric symptoms in college-educated women. *Psychology of Women Quarterly*, *2*, 35-43.

Radloff, L. (1975). Sex differences in depression: The effects of occupation and marital status. *Sex Roles*, *1*, 249-265.

Randour, M. L., Strasburg, G. L., & Lipman-Blumen, J. (1982). Women in higher education: Trends in enrollments and degrees earned. *Harvard Educational Review*, *52*, 189-202.

Reinke, B. J., Holmes, D. S., & Harris, R. L. (1985). The timing of psychosocial changes in women's lives: The years 25 to 45. *Journal of Personality and Social Psychology*, *48*, 1353-1364.

Renne, K. S. (1976). Childlessness, health, and marital satisfaction. *Social Biology*, *23*, 183-197.

Robinson, J. P. (1977). *How Americans use time*. New York: Praeger.

Rollins, B. C., & Galligan, R. (1978). The developing child and marital satisfaction of parents. In R. M. Lerner & G. B. Spanier (Eds.), *Child influences on marital and family interaction* (pp. 71-105). New York: Academic Press.

Rossi, A. S. (1980). Life-span theories and women's lives. *Signs*, *6*, 4-32.

Russo, N. F. (1979). Overview: Sex roles, fertility, and the motherhood mandate. *Psychology of Women Quarterly*, *4*, 7-15.

Saslaw, R. W. (1981). A new student for the eighties: The mature woman. *Educational Horizons*, *69*, 41-46.

Schaie, K. W., & Geiwitz, J. (1982). *Adult development and aging*. Boston: Little, Brown.

Select Committee on Children, Youth, and Families (1984). *Families and child care: Improving the options*. Washington, DC: U.S. Government Printing Office.

Serrin, W. (1984, November 25). Experts say job bias against women persists *New York Times*, pp. 1, 18.

Shaw, M. E., & Costanzo, P. R. (1982). *Theories of social psychology* (2nd ed.). New York: McGraw-Hill.

Sheehy, G. (1976). *Passages*. New York: E. P. Dutton.

Shehan, C. L. (1984). Wives' work and psychological well-being: An extension of Gove's social role theory of depression. *Sex Roles*, *11*, 881-899.

Sheppard, H. (1976). Work and retirement. In R. H. Binstock & E. Shanas (Eds.), *Handbook of aging and the social sciences* (pp. 286-309) New York: Van Nostrand Reinhold.

Silka, L., & Kiesler, S. (1977). Couples who choose to remain childless. *Family Planning Perspective*, *9*, 16-25.

Smith, R. E. (1979). The movement of women into the labor force. In R. E. Smith (Ed.), *The subtle revolution: Women at work* (pp. 1-29). Washington, DC: Urban Institute.

Spanier, G. B., & Furstenberg, F. F. (in press). Remarriage and reconstituted families. In M. B. Sussman & M. Steinmetz (Eds.), *Handbook of marriage and the family*. New York: Plenum.

Spreitzer, E., Snyder, E., & Larson, D. (1975). Age, marital status and labor force participation as related to life satisfaction. *Sex Roles*, *1*, 235-247.

Stein, A. H., & Bailey, M. M. (1973). The socialization of achievement orientation in females. *Psychological Bulletin*, *80*, 345-366.

Stein, P. (1975). Singlehood: An alternative to marriage. *Family Coordinator*, *24*, 489-505.

Streib, G. F., & Schneider, C. J. (1971). *Retirement in American society: Impact and process*. Ithaca, NY: Cornell University Press.

Szinovacz, M. (1982). Introduction: Research on women's retirement. In M. Szinovacz (Ed.), *Women's retirement* (pp. 13-21). Beverly Hills, CA: Sage.

Treas, J. (1983). Aging and the family. In D. S. Woodruff & J. E. Birren (Eds.), *Aging: Scientific perspectives and social issues* (2nd ed.) (pp. 94-109). Monterey, CA: Brooks/Cole.

Treiman, D. J., & Terrell, K. (1975). Sex and the process of status attainment: A comparison of working men and women. *American Sociological Review*, *40*, 174-200.

U.S. Bureau of the Census (1975). *Fertility expectations of American women*:

June 1974. (Current Population Reports, Series P-20, No. 271). Washington, DC: U.S. Government Printing Office.

U.S. Bureau of the Census (1983). *Population profile of the United States: 1982*. (Current Population Reports, Series P-23, No.130). Washington, DC: U.S. Government Printing Office.

U.S. Bureau of the Census (1984). *Statistical abstract of the United States: 1985* (105th ed.). Washington, DC: U.S. Government Printing Office.

U.S. Department of Labor (1983). *Time of change: 1983 handbook on women workers*. (Bulletin 298). Washington, DC: U.S. Government Printing Office.

Van Dusen, R. A., & Sheldon, E. B. (1976). The changing status of American women: A life cycle perspective. *American Psychologist, 31*, 106-116.

Veevers, J. E. (1973). Voluntarily childless wives: An exploratory study. *Sociology and Social Research, 57*, 356-366.

Veroff, J., & Feld, S. (1970). *Marriage and work in America: A study of motives and roles*. New York: Van Nostrand Reinhold.

Walker, K. E., & Woods, M. E. (1976). *Time use: A measure of household production of family goods and services*. Washington, DC: American Home Economics Association.

Warr, P., & Parry, G. (1982). Paid employment and women's psychological well-being. *Psychological Bulletin, 91*, 498-516.

Weingarten, K. (1978). The employment pattern of professional couples and their distribution of involvement in the family. *Psychology of Women Quarterly, 3*, 43-52.

Weiss, R. S. (1975). *Marital separation*. New York: Basic Books.

Weiss, R. S. (1976). The emotional impact of marital separation. *Journal of Social Issues, 32*, 135-145.

Weiss, R. S. (1979). *Going it alone: The family life and social situation of the single parent*. New York: Basic Books.

Welch, S., & Booth, A. (1977). Employment and health among married women with children. *Sex Roles, 3*, 385-397.

Williams, J. H. (1983). Psychology of women: *Behavior in a biosocial context* (2nd ed.). New York: W. W. Norton.

Wright, J. D. (1978). Are working women really more satisfied? Evidence from several national surveys. *Journal of Marriage and the Family, 40*, 301-313.

Yankelovich, D. (1981). *New rules*. New York: Random House.

Images of Women:
A Literature Perspective

Elizabeth Langland

... How little can a man know even of [a woman's life] when
he observes it through the black or rosy spectacles which sex
puts upon his nose. Hence, perhaps, the peculiar nature of
woman in fiction; the astonishing extremes of her beauty and
horror; her alternations between heavenly goodness and hellish
depravity—for so a lover would see her as his love rose or
sank, was prosperous or unhappy.

Virginia Woolf, *A Room of One's Own*

Woman as angel, woman as demon, selfless, selfish, sexual,
frigid, young virgin, old maid: dichotomies abound in images of
women. She is a fragmented creature, at one extreme or another,
missing the complexity that normally gives shape to human existence. Virginia Woolf's statement which opens this chapter suggests a source of those dichotomies; woman has been seen almost
exclusively in light of men and their needs. She takes her blunt
coloring—black or white—from her ability and willingness to meet
those needs. As a person in her own right, with integrity and will,
she is little known. She has been the subject of literature written by
men; only relatively recently has woman had a substantial literature
of her own.

The inevitable differences between images of women in literature
by women and in literature by men provides a basic organization for
this chapter. It does not, however, lead to easy generalizations and
conclusions. There are men who have written about women with
great subtlety; nonetheless, we can agree with Virginia Woolf, that
even those men are "terribly hampered and partial in [their] knowl-

69

edge of women, as a woman in her knowledge of men" (p. 87). The division, then, serves as a heuristic device, a way of proceeding to make intelligible the complexity that confronts us.

First we shall look at these common images of women in literature by men (the mother, wife, mistress, and old maid), but, in assessing and describing them, we shall also consider women writers' revisions of these traditional images. The second part of this chapter will concentrate on women as they have seen themselves, the additional images that emerge when women writers represent themselves and their experience. The first part naturally focuses on roles — the *functions* women have played *vis à vis* their men. The second part focuses less on the visible role and more on inner conflict, on the images and metaphors through which the writer seeks to make palpable her dilemmas and disenfranchisement in a patriarchal society.

THE MOTHER

The image of the mother takes us back to the Bible and myth. The Judeo-Christian tradition gives us two figures: Eve and Mary. Eve is our first mother, credited with our expulsion from the Garden of Eden. It was she who listened to the serpent's temptation and ate first of the apple from the tree. It was she who made us fully human, heir to the frailties and temptations of the flesh. As mother her image is ambivalent. She gave us life, and she also brought us mortality or death. She is thus a figure of praise and blame.

The Eve figure finds her echo in Greek myth in the person of Pandora, a name meaning "all gifts." Pandora was the first woman on earth, created on Zeus' orders in revenge for Prometheus' theft of fire. Pandora was to be an evil being whom all men would desire. Each of the major goddesses bequeathed to her irresistible qualities: knowledge in the arts, beauty, and cunning. She brought with her to earth a box which the gods warned her never to open. But her curiosity, like Eve's in the Garden of Eden, led her to ignore the warnings and thus to let loose all the world's vices, sins, and diseases.

Recent psychoanalytic studies of mothers and mothering support this same ambivalence inherent in the Biblical story and in myth. Dorothy Dinnerstein's book *The Mermaid and the Minotaur* develops the thesis that, because we are so dependent on our mothers in infancy, we develop a complex response of love and hatred: love for the nurturing, hatred for the failures at nurturing and for the very dependency that provides a base for the mother-infant relationship. In adulthood, these deep ambivalences culminate in a distrust of women and conviction of female inferiority and evil.[1]

Eve, however, is only part of the story. The Virgin Mary embodies the opposite of the temptations of the flesh represented in Eve. Conceived herself without sin according to the doctrine of Immaculate Conception, Mary is pure spirit and, as mother of Jesus, is imaged as the source of redemption. Her divinity seems to reside partly in her absolute submission. Where Eve is rebellious, Mary presents a model of obedience beautifully captured in her response to Archangel Gabriel who brings her tidings that she will bear God's child: "I am thy handmaiden, Lord." Mary has no will or desire of her own. She is servant in thought and deed to patriarchal authority, which finds its most magnificent expression in the Godhead.

Mary is echoed in early story in the person of patient Griselda. Boccaccio tells her tale in *The Decameron*; Chaucer retells it in *The Canterbury Tales*. Briefly, Griselda is a peasant girl wed by a noble, who demands absolute submission from her. To test her obedience, her husband evolves several trials, the most severe of which is his demand that she give up her children to their deaths. Griselda uncomplainingly complies and, after enduring repeated indignities, is rewarded for her submission by the restoration of all she has believed lost or dead.

The Mary and Griselda figures, although approved by patriarchal authority as the essence of goodness and pure womanhood, contain ambivalences equivalent to those we found to characterize Eve and Pandora. In this case the mother, the supreme protectress of her children, gives up their lives on the command of patriarchal authority. Mary submits to Christ's crucifixion, albeit on the command of divinity. Griselda yields only to a husband's tyranny, not a heavenly plan for humankind's redemption. But in yielding to a male, she abdicates her supreme duty as protector to her children.

Literature has picked up and developed all of the ambiguities implicit in these roles: source of gratification and denial, pleasure and punishment, life and death. Mother is depicted as protector and betrayer, goddess and witch, deity and monster. *How* she appears depends partly on point of view. Literature has given us two radically different perspectives on the mother: the child's and the mother's view of herself.

For children, mothers become reflections of their conflicts, particularly their need to be independent and their simultaneous clinging to the comforts of dependency. Logically, a mother can never be adequate to this conflict. In *Fear of Flying*, Erica Jong's heroine, Isadora Wing, splits her mother into two selves, good and bad, but comments that "Neither my good mother nor my bad mother could help me out of this dilemma" (p. 157). A mother must ultimately be ineffectual because of the contradictory demands made upon her.

While the word "mother" has positive connotations for most individuals—we think of motherhood, apple pie, and the American flag—the *roles* and stereotypes associated with motherhood are invariably negative: mother-in-law, Jewish mother, stepmother. All imply a suffocating protectiveness or a vicious jealousy of the child. The queen in "Snow White," metamorphized into the witch, is perhaps the most memorable stepmother jealous of a beautiful daughter. Mother-in-law jokes capture effectively the hostility toward this often innocuous figure.

The surrogate mother, or the Nanny, is a common image in the novels of contemporary black women writers, an image that expresses another kind of ambivalence. She often represents warmth and refuge to the white children for whom she cares; their natural mother remains aloof and cold. But to her own children, she is distant and harsh. In Toni Morrison's *The Bluest Eye*, class and race intersect to generate tensions that alienate Pecola from her mother who fondles her white, blond surrogate child, in whose home she finds "beauty, order, cleanliness, and praise" (p. 101). She jealously guards that world for herself and "never introduced it . . . to her children. Them she bent toward respectability, and in so doing taught them fear. . . . Into her son she beat a loud desire to run away, and into her daughter she beat a fear of growing up, fear of other people, fear of life" (pp. 101-102). Pecola Breedlove, denied her mother and denied by her mother, ultimately cannot preserve her sanity.

When we shift from the child's to the mother's point of view, the image becomes more subtle, less absolute. The mother's love for her child extends naturally into a desire to protect, to screen. Yet she is also acutely aware of her child's need for independence and separation, and she therefore must painfully accept the poignant irony that if she does her job well, her child no longer needs her in an intimate and immediate way. As the child grows, there is regret for the loss of the early simplicity, a regret expressed in a line from Adrienne Rich's poem "Her Waking": "If milk flowed from my breast again."[2] Tillie Olsen's "Tell Me a Riddle" defines motherhood as being "forced to move to the rhythms of others" (p. 76). But having submitted to the child-love—to "the passion of tending"—the mother finds herself "when the need was done" nearly consumed by the "painful damming back and drying up of what still surged, but had nowhere to go" (p. 92-93). For the mother who is asked to give herself up for her children, the difficulties are twofold: when the children are gone, she has no self left; or, if a core of self remains, she must rechannel her energies. The children want them no more.

WIVES

Mary and Eve are clearly dominant models for the images we have of mothers. They are also models for other images of women, for example, images of wives. Literature depicts two stereotypes of wives: the submissive wife modelled on Mary and the dominating wife, modelled on Eve. The submissive wife is obviously obedient, passive, unassuming. The dominating wife is aggressive, disobedient, and presumptuous. She seeks to control her husband rather than be controlled by him.

The most extreme form of the dominating wife is figured in the person of Lilith, the Hebrew she-demon, part of mystical religious belief since 2500 B.C. Lilith's story, a history traced by Lisa Masciello, is told in an alternative tale of Creation to the one handed down in Genesis. "According to this legend, Lilith was the first wife of Adam, created like him from the dust of the earth. For some unexplained reason, however, God used filth and sediment to mold her, while Adam was formed from clean dust (p. 2). A whole misogynist tradition is apparent in the characterization of this figure. She refuses submission and insists on equality with Adam. After quarrelling with Adam, she flew away to the Red Sea where she mated with demons. When Adam tried to reclaim her, she refused to return and threatened to "destroy any progeny that might be born to Adam by a second wife" (p. 2). Obviously a dangerous and destructive individual, she serves as warning to women who reject their proper submission. Part of her danger, of course, lies in her licentiousness which admits no curb.

In realistic literature, it is rare for such pure demons to make an appearance. Her closest analogue might be fairy tale's witch or the wife transformed into witch as in "Snow White." In more realistic representations, perhaps Chaucer's Wife of Bath is a close approximation. She is not openly vengeful, but she seems to use up husbands with regularity, and, when we meet her, she has married her fifth. The tale she tells—in which a Knight is asked to choose between a young, beautiful, and potentially unfaithful wife and an old, ugly, yet faithful wife—enforces a lesson that women should be given the rein in marriage. The Knight is applauded for allowing the choice to be made *for him*.

John Milton's *Paradise Lost* gives us a tempered portrait of Eve as dominating wife. Adam, as the uxorious husband, is faulted for not asserting his authority. Indeed, when the dominating wife makes her appearance, she is often accompanied by her complement, the doting or henpecked husband. Her behavior is seen, at least in part, as a consequence of his failed mastery. The dominating wife, then, is an expression of a failed relationship. Ernest Hemingway's "The Short Happy Life of Francis Macomber" presents just such a daughter of Eve. Margot Macomber is hard, cold, cruel—an emasculating wife who humiliates her husband by sleeping with other men and flouting the fact. But he has shown himself to be a "coward" on safari and thus deserves the infidelity. When he asserts his courage, we are to recognize that the infidelities will end. In our last picture of the formerly dominating wife, Margot, she is pleading submissively, "Please, please, please stop" (Ferguson, p. 203).

This narrative movement from dominance to submission often characterizes the fate of daughters of Eve. They are finally taught a lesson. Shakespeare's *The Taming of the Shrew* (a story retold in the contemporary musical *Kiss Me Kate*) presents a classic and famous picture to this pattern. Kate, the shrew, is brought to proper submission by Petruchio so that she is willing to belie her own senses and call the moon and sun if he so wills it: "What you will have it named, even that it is,/And so it shall be still for Katherine" (IV, v, 11, p. 21-22).

At the end of the play Petruchio wins his wager that his tamed shrew will surpass the other wives in showing "more sign of her obedience,/Her new-built virtue and obedience" (p. 109). Kate speaks the moral for all wives, "Thy husband is thy lord, thy life, thy keeper,/Thy head, thy sovereign". . . . who "craves no other tribute at thy hands/But love, fair looks, and true obedience" (p. 113).

Rebellious Eve has become submissive Mary. When we looked at the image of Mary as mother, we remarked her absolute, unquestioning obedience: "I am thy handmaiden, Lord." But absolute submission to patriarchal authority is relatively rare. Griselda presents the extreme instance, which we have already examined under the image of mother. The instance is extreme because in its pure form, submission demands that a woman be without opinion, mind, or will of her own. It demands, in fact, that she have no identity, that she be literally self-less. It is ironic that becoming a nonentity should be woman's ideal *self* realization.

Obviously such submission is not a state to which most women can bring themselves; the self must urge some claims. In its more attractive forms, the ideal of submission becomes an ideal of loyalty to the husband. The legendary paragon of female fidelity is *The Odyssey*'s Penelope who, beset with importunate suitors during her husband's long absence at the Trojan Wars, showed resourcefulness and strategy in outwitting their determined advances.

Penelope represents the ideal of submission in a positive manifestation. More commonly, the pressure of the ideal as negative model afflicts women. Virginia Woolf has given articulate expression to this expectation of submission and service in her essay "Professions for Women." She chooses to tell her own story, "a simple one," about her desire to write and her discovery that she must write *about* something and that something is supposed to be a review of a "novel by a famous man." She is continually obstructed by what she terms "The Angel in the House," the image of ideal womanhood:

> She was intensely sympathetic. She was immensely charming. She was utterly unselfish. She excelled in the difficult arts of family life. She sacrificed herself daily. If there was chicken, she took the leg; if there was a draught she sat in it—in short she was so constituted that she never had a mind or a wish of her own, but preferred to sympathize always with the minds and wishes of others. Above all—I need not say it—she was pure." (p. 237)

Woolf confesses that "I did my best to kill her. . . . Had I not killed her she would have killed me" (pp. 237-238). Of course, the consequence of absolute submission is death.

We might focus, too, on Woolf's assertion of the purity of the Angel of the House. Obviously, actual sexual purity was impossible for any wife—she could not be conceived without sin as was the Virgin Mary and she could not abstain from sexual relations. When the ideal of sexual purity became particularly insistent in the Victorian era, the daughter became important in the myth of the family. She was considered the ornament of the family, and she could embody the ideals of submission and purity without contradiction.[3]

Virginia Woolf felt an expressed need to kill the image of submission, the Angel of the House, before she could become a successful writer. In literature, female characters have learned to manipulate the role to their advantage. Submission becomes a game by which women gain their wishes without appearing to do so. Charlotte Brontë's Jane Eyre charms Rochester in the early stages of their engagement by this apparent submission. Rochester praises her: "I never met your likeness. Jane: you please me, and you master me—you seem to submit, and I like the sense of pliancy you impart . . . I am influenced—conquered; and the influence is sweeter than I can express" (p. 229). Margaret Schlegel, in E.M. Forster's *Howards End* enjoys a similar triumph over her husband, Henry, but she is fully aware of the ambiguities and shamefulness of her tactics:

> [His acquiescence] was the reward of her tact and devotion
> through the day. Now she understood why some women prefer
> influence to rights. Mrs. Plynlimmon, when condemning suf-
> fragettes, had said: "The woman who can't influence her hus-
> band to vote the way she wants ought to be ashamed of her-
> self." Margaret had winced, but she was influencing Henry
> now, and though pleased at her little victory, she knew that she
> had won it by the methods of the harem. (p. 230)

Ironically, the dominant wife, seemingly determined to have her
way at all costs, often fails utterly to achieve her ends, while the
submissive wife, ostensibly so acquiescent, employs subtle arts to
enact her purposes, making her husband believe they are his.

MISTRESSES

We have traced the influence of Eve and Mary on images of
mothers and wives; we continue to detect their presence coloring
images of the mistress, a woman who is the focus of male sexual
attention and desire. She, too, is manifest as two distinct stereotypes: the goddess or woman on a pedestal and the sex object.

Mary, again, can be seen as a prototype for the woman on the
pedestal. She is the object of male reverence, of male inspiration.
She traces her origins not only to the Virgin but to Greek mythology
as well, where she figures as the Muses, the nine goddesses of the
arts and sciences. They were blessed with non-human gifts: the
ability to see into the future, to banish all grief and sorrow, and, for
a woman most telling, the ability to remain young and beautiful
forever. Early Greek writers and authors would call on the Muses
for inspiration before beginning work, and the notion of a muse or
beneficent female presence has remained with writers throughout
the ages. Notably, she is not the creator; she is the stimulus.

Beautiful woman as stimulus to make creativity has had her most
famous incarnation in Dante's Beatrice and Petrarch's Laura. Although he saw her only twice (once when he was nine and again
nine years later), Dante idealized Beatrice Portinari, the inspiration
for his literary labors. Like Dante, Petrarch found his inspiration in
a beautiful woman, Laura, but there is doubt whether this perfect

creature ever existed other than in the poet's mind. Beginning as an image of beauty, Laura gradually came to represent Christian guide and to embody human hopes and aspirations. In the phenomenon of Laura, we recognize one of the most persistent functions of the idealized woman. She becomes a mirror for man, reflecting him at twice his natural size, an image of his heroic possibilities. She serves to reflect all that is noble, all that he *imagines* he can be rather than the reality. The chivalric tradition in the Middle Ages underscores this role of the woman on the pedestal. Pledging himself to a lady, a knight would then undertake heroic feats in her name and for her honor.

We might question whether any human woman can ever embody this ideal. Surely the fact that Dante saw Beatrice only twice and that Laura may be only a figment of Petrarch's imagination should make us ask whether the role is humanly possible to fulfill. The story of Pygmalion and Galetea (made contemporary in Shaw's play *Pygmalion* and the musical *My Fair Lady*) suggests that no living woman can match a man's idealized image. Pygmalion, according to Greek legend, was disgusted with the women of his day so he crafted a beautiful statue with which he fell in love. As a fantastic fulfillment, his ideal became real, but we must recognize that that is the stuff of which only dreams and legends are made.

Men still continue to project their desires, but when they project them onto realistic women, the result is denial or disappointment. On the one hand, if a man persists in maintaining his myth of perfection — insisting that the woman embody his heroic possibility — then he denies her needs and individuality. Jean Toomer's "Fern" captures quickly the poignant fate of such a communally idealized woman: "when one is on the soil of one's ancestors, most anything can come to one . . .," but "Nothing ever came to Fern, not even I" (p. 17). On the other hand, disappointment and self-destruction may be the fate of the idealizing consciousness. Cheated out of an investment in a self-image mirrored in a woman, a man may find his existence become sordid and mean. He will, of course, blame the woman for his failure. That tendency to blame reduces the apparent distance between the goddess and the sex object and makes the step down from the pedestal to the gutter a short one. For what man no longer idealizes, he often reviles.

The image of the Southern Belle seems to belong to both spheres — woman on a pedestal and woman as sex object — and, because it belongs to both, dramatizes the relationship between them. Tennessee Williams' Blanche Dubois from *A Streetcar Named Desire* is a classic Southern Belle. But the queenliness of her behavior, her *noblesse oblige* — "I have always depended on the kindness of strangers" — gradually licenses her brother-in-law, Stanley, who rapes her in the climax of the play (p. 196). One implication of this scenario is, of course, that the goddess role is just an act; at bottom Blanche wants what other women want. Poignantly, there is truth in this recognition, but a truth that must transcend cruel and limiting stereotypes. Blanche does want human love, not the tiresome exchange of one self-denying role for another.

The Southern Belle, as I've suggested, may participate in both images — woman on a pedestal and woman as sex object — or she may be rigidly confined to the first role and find her alter ego in the black slave girl who becomes her husband's mistress and sex object. Linda Brent's nineteenth-century slave narrative details the dichotomy under which women of both races suffered: the white woman relegated to spirituality, the black one to sexuality, neither a fully human creature of body and soul.

Where the woman on the pedestal is worshipped for a spiritual beauty of which her physical beauty is but an outward manifestation, the sex object possesses physical pulchritude without the complications, for a man, of spirituality. She is the object of desire or lust. Eve is her ancestress — woman as snare and author of man's corruption. Woman seen as sexual snare or bait tends to absolve men of culpability. She has tempted him with wiles he cannot resist. A most cruel manifestation of this logic in contemporary society lies in the tendency to blame the *victim* of rape rather than the attacker. It is also present in the restrictions on women's dress in Iran and Arabic countries.

The figure of John Keats's "La Belle Dame Sans Merci" provides a transition from the woman on the pedestal and reveals the relationship between that image and the image of the sex object. In Keats's poem, a knight is "alone and palely loitering," the victim of seduction by a "Lady in the meads,/Full beautiful, a fairy's child" (p. 201). This supernatural creature, the object of his adoration, has enchanted him, and his thralldom threatens his death. She is not a pure creature but a destructive temptress.

The notion of man's slavery to a woman's beauty is common in literature and has memorable Biblical sources. The slavery emperils his life and, if he is a leader, the safety of his community. In the story of Samson and Delilah, the mighty hero of ancient Israel meets his downfall through love of the beautiful Delilah, who, learning that his strength lies in his hair, has him shorn while he sleeps. Another Biblical hero, David, king of a united Israel, covets the beautiful Bathsheba, and his adultery with her leads to his punishment, to his son Absalom's rebellion, and ultimately to the trouble between North and South Israel.

One of the most famous portraits of the sex object in literature is Shakespeare's Cleopatra. Shakespeare, of course, was drawing on earlier literary versions of the story, such as those of Virgil and Horace, in which the Queen of the Nile is represented as an Oriental temptress. Shakespeare's play opens with the disgusted words of Philo, who marks Antony's diminishment: "transformed/Into a strumpet's fool," whose captain's heart "is become the bellows and the fan/To cool a gypsy's lust" (p. 1173).

In contemporary representations, the strongest images we have of the sex object derive from film and magazine. The star system emphasizes female pulchritude and, as a powerful visual medium, films can present sexual images easily. The sexual object—unlike other images we have examined—is largely a visual phenomenon. An interior view of the woman—rather than enhancing our appreciation—tends rather to detract because it reminds the viewer that the object cannot simply be appropriated. Marilyn Monroe's life expresses the tragic consequences of a woman trapped by the sexual image.

Magazines, like films, thrive on glossy pictures, and *Playboy* is only one of a number of publications which pander to our society's tendency to reduce female beauty and sexuality to a marketable commodity. And, as any woman who has walked by the proverbial construction site knows, she may, at any moment, herself become the sex object.

OLD MAIDS AND OTHER OUTCASTS

The old maid, we all remember from the popular and enduring card game, was what nobody wanted to be. Great strategem was employed in arranging cards, facial muscles were carefully adjusted to forbid any betraying glance. Finally, of course, the poor old maid was so bent and wrinkled with the exercise of trying to disguise her as something else that the whole pack had to be retired.

The stereotypical old maid is a pathetic creature. She is alone not by choice but because she has not been chosen. She lacks beauty, charm, and distinction.

But this image of the woman alone is perhaps a relatively recent one — as recent as the rise of the nuclear family and marriage for love. If we search in the Bible, myth, and fairy tale for images of single women, we find at the negative end of the spectrum the sorceress or witch. But other images are strikingly positive. Greek myth presents the goddesses, such as Athena, the goddess of warfare and wisdom, worshipped as patroness of arts and crafts. She never married and was called Pallas (Maiden) or Parthenos (Virgin). Or Artemis, the goddess of childbirth, hunting, and the moon, reputed for her virginity, demanded that all of her followers remain pure as well.

The Bible presents memorable images in Judith and Jael. Judith saved the Jewish people, who were under attack by the Assyrian general Holofernes. She used her beauty to seduce him and, while he slept, cut off his head. Jael exhibited equal heroism in driving a spike through her enemy's head.

History gives us the remarkable instances of Joan of Arc, savior of France, and Elizabeth I, the Virgin Queen of England. Why, we must ask, is our literature not peopled with such distinguished and heroic images? Elizabeth and Joan do make appearances, but never become models for or types of single womanhood. They become isolated instances, while the norm remains negative, a laughable figure.

I've suggested that we might look for the source of the negative image in particular social changes of the eighteenth century that saw the rise of industrial capitalism and protestantism in England.[4] The new emphasis on individualism, encouraged by both historical events, made marriage for love the norm. Industrialism capitalism also required that the family as economic unit be replaced with the phenomenon of the single wage earner. For the first time, unmarried women in a household were financial burdens, not contributors to an ongoing cottage industry. We can trace the change in the single woman's status through changes in the denotation and connotations of the word "spinster." The word originally meant a member of the laudable industry of female manufacturers, a person who spun. Now, of course, we use it to mean an unmarried woman, a waspish creature who is best avoided.

This creature has many memorable literary representations. We might think of Charles Dickens's Miss Havisham, wooed by an already married man for her money, and then jilted on her wedding day. This character from *Great Expectations* has tried to stop time at the moment of her betrayal and wears her faded wedding dress while her cake moulders in the corner. She has adopted a beautiful young girl as an instrument of revenge upon men and urges her continually to "break their hearts."

Mark Twain's Miss Watson from *Huckleberry Finn* is less eccentric and therefore a truer picture of the stereotype. Although Huck is almost persuaded to accept civilization by the Widow Douglas, Miss Watson, "a tolerable slim old maid, with goggles on" (p. 2) undoes her good work: "Sometimes the widow would take me one side and talk about Providence in a way to make a body's mouth water; but maybe next day Miss Watson would take hold and knock it all down again" (p. 10). Miss Watson's mean spirited and narrow vision of life seems to be a consequence of her maidenhood, an unnatural state for women.

Kate Chopin's recently discovered novel from 1899, *The Awakening*, presents this image with somewhat more sympathy. Her spinster, Mlle. Reisz, is a talented pianist, an artist. Yet because she has devoted her life to art, because she has remained unmarried, she is seen by most of the characters as a ridiculous figure, eccentric and irascible. She cautions the protagonist that the "person who would soar above the level plain of tradition and prejudice" must have strong wings (p. 82). The price of her artistic distinction is social ostracism.

Women writers have tended to be more sympathetic to the old maid, recognizing in her singleness a choice rather than a submission to necessity. Mary E. Wilkins Freeman has given us a remarkable portrait of the woman alone in her nineteenth-century story "A New England Nun." Engaged to marry a man, who has been absent for fourteen years seeking his fortune, Louisa Ellis finds on his return that she has come to prize her solitary state. She accidentally discovers that her fiance's feelings have also changed and is able diplomatically to break off the engagement: "she felt like a queen who, after fearing lest her domain be wrested away from her, sees it firmly insured in her possession" (p. 124). Doris Lessing's protagonist in "Our Friend Judith" is a descendant of Louisa Ellis. More contemporary, she enjoys her sexual liaisons but likes to wake up in the morning "alone and her own person" (Ferguson, p. 371).

These positive images of the single life from women writers help readers to realize that the other roles offered women often demand a large price, loss of identity — a submersion of oneself in husband or children. It is surprising that the images of single women have been so negative because recent psychological studies suggest that the group showing greatest psychic happiness is married men; single women are second, single men third, and married women last. But we might say that perhaps it is not surprising that the images of single life for women have been so negative; women need to be encouraged to enter into a state that has proved detrimental to their happiness but has provided the cornerstone to men's.

This section is entitled "Old Maids and Other Outcasts" to enable us to consider fallen women, another group ostracized by society. The fallen woman has memorable representations. Thomas Hardy's *Tess of the D'Urbervilles* has recently been translated to the screen in Roman Polanski's *Tess*. Beautiful, innocent, and pure (Hardy gave his novel the subtitle "A Pure Woman Faithfully Presented"), Tess early falls into a sexual liaison that brands her for life and becomes the source of her tragedy. Charles Dickens's Lady Dedlock from *Bleak House* is relentlessly hounded by the sinister Tulkinghorn, her only crime that she bore an illegitimate child. She falls from her dignified position as wife of a lord to the condition of wounded, hunted outcast, dying at the gates to the pauper's graveyard.

But fallen women do not always receive punishment. Although George Eliot's Hetty Sorrel from *Adam Bede* suffers gravely for her illicit liaison with the local squire, she is actually punished, not for sexual incontinence, but for child murder. Other fallen women in George Eliot's novels, perhaps surprisingly, find a community of support. *Romola* and *Daniel Deronda* present male characters who have produced several children with their mistresses. They meet punishment in their untimely deaths while their wives succor their mistresses, forming a redemptive community of concern.

Although even minor violations of patriarchy's code of female purity could render a white woman outcast, women of color have always struggled with the double jeopardy of race and gender. Race has intersected with gender to produce crippling images of inadequacy and inferiority. Assumptions that *all* women are creatures of impulse and emotion, creatures who lack restraint — assumptions that stem from Christian hierarchical thinking which assigns woman a place beneath man, only slightly above animals — have made a white woman's purity seem both suspect and precarious. When race is added to the equation, patriarchal logic has concluded that the woman of color is inherently fallen and exists largely as a vehicle for his lusts, an idea succinctly expressed in Faulkner's *Absaslom, Absalom!*: "the other sex is separated into three sharp divisions, separated (two of them) by a chasm which could be crossed but one time and in but one direction — ladies, women, females — the virgins whom gentlemen someday married, the courtesans to whom they went while on sabbaticals to the cities, the slave girls and women upon whom that first caste rested" (p. 109). The cruelty of this patriarchal logic had an impact on all women but nowhere more viciously than on the lives of black women.

We have seen in this section specific ways in which women writers have reinterpreted demeaning stereotypes of women. As we continue our analysis, we shall look exclusively at the tradition of women writers and shall explore images of women as they emerge in women's writing.

THE FEMALE TRADITION IN LITERATURE

In the past decade, significant work by feminist critics has led to the definition of a female tradition in literature. Elaine Showalter has defined this critical body as *gynocritics*, feminist criticism concerned with *"woman as writer—*with woman as the producer of textual meaning, with the history, themes, genres, and structures of literature by women" (p. 128). Showalter distinguishes gynocritics from the feminist critique, which is concerned with *"woman as reader—*with woman as the consumer of male-produced literature, and with the ways in which the hypothesis of a female reader changes our apprehension of a given text, awakening us to the significance of its sexual codes" (p. 128). The first group of images we discussed in this essay belonged to the feminist critique. That is, the stereotypes of women we explored were usually products of male writers and patriarchal assumptions, at least initially, although women writers have also reinterpreted the stereotypes, as we saw.

Gynocritics gives us a new set of images because it focuses on the terms and metaphors through which women have imagined their own being and becoming within the constraints of patriarchy. This section of the essay will, therefore, concentrate on female *Bildung*, or female fictions of development, and on female being or female images for female existence.

In my discussion of these images I must refer continually to the groundbreaking studies of contemporary feminist critics. These new images have had to be uncovered, largely by female critics developing new theoretical emphases. As more women have entered the field of English literature and become established in English and Letters—56% of new Ph.D.s in 1985-86[5]—more attention has been given to women's literature, to defining its themes and traditions. One major culmination of this effort has been *The Norton Anthology of Literature by Women*, edited by Sandra Gilbert and Susan Gubar.

Often the woman's story, the woman's nature, is encoded in the text, functioning as subtext to the dominant text that gives apparent support to patriarchal institutions and assumptions. Those images, and their recognition, therefore, have by no means had the general currency of the first set of images we examined, images which belong to a patriarchal mythology of women. The new images are more difficult to grasp because they are less culturally familiar—we don't recognize them readily because we have all been raised in a patriarchy. Because these new images are not "stereotypical," they are also less easy to categorize. I shall, therefore, organize my discussion around the insights of particular critics who have made perceptible new images and patterns.

Female Bildung

According to Elizabeth Abel, Marianne Hirsch, and Elizabeth Langland, editors of *The Voyage In: Fictions of Female Development*, what has been seen as *human* development is, in fact, *male* development. The novel of a child's development to maturity is called the *Bildungsroman*; it should encompass the growth of both young men and young women, with their distinctively different patterns. But in both sociological and psychological terms, male experience has been the norm. Critics of the child's adjustment to society and its representation in literature have focused on a process accessible only to males: "even the broadest definitions of the *Bildungsroman* presuppose a range of social options available only to men. Only male development is marked by a determined exploration of a social milieu . . ." (p. 7). Women who explored their milieu so determinedly would find themselves ostracized from rather than integrated into the society. Social convention, which we have seen represented in patriarchal images of women, demanded that women remain secluded at home, passive, submissive, and dependent. As a result of different social expectations for girls and boys, we find that novels of female development "typically substitute inner concentration for active accommodation, rebellion, or withdrawal" (p. 8).

As a result of women's limited freedom to explore society, the female protagonist has often sought her definition in nature rather than in society. Female quest novels, particularly recent ones, often place their protagonists in a natural environment. For example, Margaret Atwood's *Surfacing* is a classic novel detailing a spiritual quest. It takes place within the remote reaches of Canada where the heroine, who undergoes a process of stripping away all the layers of civilization, finally discovers an authentic core which will potentially enable her to rejoin an inimical society. But the conclusion to the novel offers only a *possibility*, not a dramatized reality. The threat remains that the protagonist's retreat into her self allows no reemergence that can accommodate social life.

All "confinement to inner life, no matter how enriching, threatens a loss of public activity; it enforces an isolation that may culminate in death," as it does in Kate Chopin's *The Awakening* where Edna Pontellier "succumbs to the lure of a spiritual landscape," walks into the sea and drowns (Abel, p. 8). Virginia Woolf's Rachel Vinrace in *The Voyage Out*, George Eliot's Maggie Tulliver in *The Mill on the Floss* both find in death their only outlet. Death or even suicide in novels by women writers is thus reinterpreted as a gesture of affirmation, a refusal to submit to society's dictates. Of course, we must always feel the poignant irony of a fate which demands self-destruction as a mode of self-assertion and self-definition.

Recent feminist psychoanalytic theory has helped to explain some of the "apparent incongruities embedded in female plots — allegiances that repeatedly lead to death, for example" (Abel, p. 9). Drawing from the school of object relations, feminist theories posit the mother-daughter bond as the definitive relationship in female development. Emphasizing continuity over separation, this bond encourages girls to define themselves in relation to others rather than as autonomous and rigid egos: "A distinctive female 'I' implies a distinctive value system and unorthodox developmental goals, defined in terms of community and empathy rather than achievement and autonomy" (Abel, p. 10).

Stories of female development emphasize relation, context, and responsibility to others. These ideas will emerge as prominent narrative themes and significantly shape the images of women. At the same time they will dictate new narrative forms to chronicle that development. On the one hand, the narrative may dramatize a continuous development from childhood to maturity (as does the male *Bildungsroman*), but that growth toward autonomy will incorporate the past and the protagonist will remain anchored in relationships with others. On the other hand, women's development is often "delayed by inadequate education until adulthood," a delay that generates "the second prevailing pattern of female growth in fiction: the awakening" (p. 11). In this paradigm, the woman is already married and begins to grow only after that traditional female fulfillment has been achieved. For this reason "the novel of awakening is often a novel of adultery" (p. 12). The image of woman as adulteress is of an individual on a quest for self-discovery and autonomy, a quest which involved breaking from marital authority.

As the developmental plot is revised in literature by women, new images of women emerge. One of the most significant is the image of women as friends, which finds its enlarged representation in the image of the sustaining female community. In *A Room of One's Own*, Virginia Woolf recounts the experience of encountering the words, "Chloe liked Olivia." She remarks, "Do not start. Do not blush. Let us admit in the privacy of our own society that these things sometimes happen. Sometimes women do like women" (p. 86). It strikes Woolf that these words signal an immense change. Previously women have been seen "almost without exception . . . in their relation to men. . . . And how small a part of a woman's life is that" (p. 86). We should recognize that the stereotypical images we discussed earlier — wife, mistress, old maid (the possible exception is the mother) — postulate a woman's relationship to a man. We add great richness and complexity to our repertoire when women are seen in relation to one another — as daughters, sisters, companions, and confidantes. These relationships transform the developmental patterns for women. Because women are "more psychologically embedded in relationships," their development is often shared with other women, "who assume equal status as protagonists" (Abel, p. 12). In Louisa May Alcott's *Little Women*, the four March girls participate in and enable each other's growth. In Woolf's *Mrs. Dalloway*, Clarissa Dalloway returns imaginatively to her early love of Sally Seton; *To the Lighthouse* dramatizes Lilly Briscoe's need to resolve through art the challenge posed by Mrs. Ramsay.

Some of the most vivid contemporary representations of female friendship have come from black women writers. Doubly oppressed — racially as well as sexually — black women characters find a refuge and context for growth in the bonds they force with each other. In Toni Morrison's *Sula*, Sula and Nell stimulate self-recognition in each other, a recognition poignantly complete only at Sula's death when Nell cries, "We was girls together . . . O Lord, Sula. . . . girl, girl, girlgirlgirl" (p. 174). Alice Walker's *The Color Purple* presents a sustaining relationship of sisters, Celie and Nettie, a relationship that enables them to survive their stepfather's brutality and rape and to move beyond survival to self-affirmation. For Celie that process also includes her warm lesbian relationship with Shug Avery, a relationship that frees her from dependency, releases her creativity, and ultimately gives her the strength to thrive even without Shug.

Alice Walker's novel belongs in a new tradition of the lesbian novel where the old stereotype of lesbians as man haters is being replaced by the positive image of women liking women. Bonnie Zimmerman has analyzed the female community—in such novels as Verena Stefan's *Shedding*, Kate Stimpson's *Class Notes*, Doris Grumbach's *Chamber Music*, and Marge Piercy's *Small Changes* — as a positive context "in which female powers can be integrated, in which there are no limitations or compromises, in which the patriarchal, heterosexist world exacts no price" (Abel, p. 257).

Women of color have also given us powerful images of autonomous, independent, and successful women. Although from a white perspective such women may appear as victims, the most marginalized of the marginalized, within their own contexts in literature by women of color, these women emerge as puissant and magical, life-sustaining and life-affirming personages. In her essay collection *In Search of Our Mother's Gardens*, Alice Walker defines this being as "womanist": "From *womanish*. A black feminist or feminist of color. . . . Usually referring to outrageous, audacious, courageous or *willful* behavior. . . . Appreciates and prefers women's culture, women's emotional flexibility . . . and women's strength. *Loves* the Folk. Loves Herself" (p. xi). Walker sees her own art as produced by a kind of "magic," herself as "medium" to give voice to a voiceless culture. And Walker links her growing interest in black women writers with the fascination of voodoo and "authentic black witchcraft" (p. 10). Toni Morrison's *Beloved* builds its magnificent effects out of folklore and the supernatural as the main character, Sethe, exorcises her own past by dealing with the angry ghost of her Beloved baby daughter, murdered at age 2.

Native American writers, too, celebrate the supernatural, investing transformative powers in animals and locating the prowess of animals in individual women. In Opal Lee Popkes' "Zuma Chowt's Cave," the young daughter has "wild, uncombed black hair and a bloodcurdling scream. . . the agility of a mountain goat,'' and the hunting instincts of "a gray wildcat" (Fisher, p. 62). Rather than allow her to be "civilized," her mother captures a white man with whom she can breed and thus preserve her lineage and her freedom. In Indian mythology, women figure as central rather than secondary figures, and the literature reflects that powerful primacy of women in ritual.

Chicana literature has also plumbed the resources of folklore and legend to define more positive images of women. Marcela Christine Lucero-Trujillo has pointed to "the frustrations of being a woman within the sexist microcosmic Chicano world of machismo" and notes that the Chicana "has sought refuge in the image of the indigenous mother" (Fisher, p. 326). The danger is that this image becomes merely a reflection of the patriarchal expectations of women. But at its most powerful, in a story like "The Burning," by Estela Portillo Trambley, this image taps originary, pre-Christian myths and traditions to become a powerful representation of women's healing and curative and life-affirming powers, universal and seemingly magical in their application and therefore suspect to a Christian community.

This emphasis on magic and the supernatural produces a powerful sense of community, a weaving and knitting together of lives, an identification of an enduring commonness beneath the strange and alienating forces of discrimination. Aware of the disfigurations of slavery and prejudice which rupture communal and familial bonds, women of color reestablish connections and the sacred value of their traditions in their art.

The Female Self Conceived

It is, of course, somewhat arbitrary to subsume the images of women as friends and of enabling community under female Bildung. Those images belong here equally as some of the most powerful images that women writers have explored. I put them under images of female development because the relationship of one woman to another and the presence of an affirming context are instrumental, if not essential, to a woman's growth and self-realization.

In this section, I have chosen to focus on the images and metaphors through which women writers have conceived of themselves and their situation. To date, the most influential study of these images is Sandra Gilbert's and Susan Gubar's *The Madwoman in the Attic*. That important work was preceded by the groundbreaking studies of Patricia Meyer Spacks, *The Female Imagination*, Ellen Moers, *Literary Women*, and Elaine Showalter, *A Literature of Their Own*. It is impossible to summarize in this short space the riches these studies contain. I can only summarize briefly. Spacks opened up the field as a legitimate area of academic inquiry and documented persuasively throughout her book the various strategies through which women sought to preserve their integrity in an inimical society. She analyzes the images of woman as narcissistic, passive, self-indulgent, and masochistic and finds in them covert stratagems "to preserve the integrity and the self" (p. 106). Spacks concludes with an observation that has shaped much recent criticism: "women dominate their own experience by imagining it, giving it form, writing about it. Their imaginative versions of themselves as supporters of the social structure, guardians of the species, possessors of wisdom unavailable to men — versions derived partly from the arrogance of anger — in effect re-create the 'mighty female deity'" (pp. 13-14).

Ellen Moers's study has led to significant revisions in our understanding of female imagery and motifs. She notes the prevalence of mirrors in literature by women, literal and metaphoric mirrors: "From infancy, indeed from the moment of birth, the looks of a girl are examined with ruthless scrutiny by all around her, especially by women, crucially by her own mother," equally crucially, we might add, by herself as she scrutinizes her image in the glass (p. 149). Moers's reinterpretation of the Gothic marks one of her most exciting contributions to an understanding of female motifs. She interprets Mary Shelley's *Frankenstein* as a birth myth: "*Frankenstein* was most original in its dramatization of dangerous oppositions through the struggle of a creator with monstrous creations. The sources of this Gothic conception . . . were surely the anxieties of a woman who, as daughter, mistress, and mother, was a bearer of death" (p. 191). Frankenstein, the monster, is thus an inner landscape given concrete representation. Moers also defines a new liberation for heroines in the Gothic novel, a liberation represented by Gothic conventions and the Gothic castle: "For Mrs. Radcliffe, the Gothic novel as a device to send maidens on distant and exciting journeys without offending the proprieties . . . And indoors . . . her heroines can scuttle miles along corridors, descend into dungeons, and explore secret chambers without a chaperone, because the Gothic castle, however much in ruins, is still an indoor and therefore freely female space" (pp. 370, 372).

Moers concludes with a chapter on metaphor that identifies many of the central metaphors through which women have represented themselves and their experience. One is the kernel, "the little hard nut, the living stone"; the emphasis on "littleness" is central to women, Moers discovers, as is the use of creatures "to stand in, metaphorically, for their own sex" (p. 379). Flowers, insects, cats all figure, but most prominent is the use of birds. Birds may fly away or swoop and dive; they may nestle and bill and coo or struggle against the constraints of cages; they may be cruel as well as sweet; they may sing or be mute. Moers concludes:

> No other family of living creatures offers the poet such a variety of size and color and habitat as the birds, such a mixture of the domestically familiar and the mysteriously exotic. But it must be the extreme nature of the *contrasts* birds offer, especially the contrast between the *esse* and the *posse* implicit in their ambivalent existence, that draws from literary women a tension in the metaphor. (p. 383)

Other potent metaphors for women include the jewel-case, "female sexuality" water, associated with amniotic fluid and the beginnings of life, and breath — spirit, respiration, and inspiration (pp. 386, 400). Finally, Moers identifies two potent female landscapes — the "open, wind-swept, desolate moors . . . and the walled garden" — landscapes "charged with female privacy, and with emotions ranging from the erotic to the mystical (p. 49).

Elaine Showalter's *A Literature of Their Own* concentrates its efforts on the historical reconstruction of a female literary tradition. Unlike the previous studies we have looked at, which are ahistorical, Showalter attempts to define the stages of a woman's tradition, the movement from a *feminine* stage, a "phase of *imitation* of prevailing modes of the dominant tradition," to the *feminist* stage, stressing "*advocacy* of minority rights and values," to the *female* stage, "a phase of *self-discovery*" (p. 13). Although Showalter concentrates less on literary images, more on literary process, she has pointed in Brontë's *Jane Eyre* to potent and continuing imagery for women's growth to autonomy and integrity. Showalter identifies Bertha Mason, Rochester's mad wife, and Helen Burns, Jane's self-sacrificing friend at Lowood, as images for Jane's sexuality and spirit: "Brontë's most profound innovation . . . is the division-[of] the Victorian female psyche into its extreme components of mind and body, which she externalizes as two characters, Helen Burns and Bertha Mason" (p. 113). Both of these characters must be sacrificed in the course of the novel "to make way for Jane's fuller freedom" (p. 118).

Gilbert and Gubar discover the title to their book in this same figure of Bertha Mason, the madwoman in the attic. They explore images of the woman writer, who like her fictional sisters, confronts the mirrors of patriarchy: "Authored by a male God and by a godlike male, killed into a 'perfect' image of herself, the woman writer's self-contemplation may be said to have begun with a searching glance into the mirror of the male-inscribed literary text" (pp. 16-17). But she is unreflected: she is not author, not possessor of the pen, but the blank, "the 'pure space' of the virgin page," where the male is forever inscribing himself. Or, if an image is reflected, it is distorted:

[The woman writer] must come to terms with the images on the surface of the glass, with, . . . those mythic masks male artists have fastened over her human face both to lessen their dread of her "inconstancy" and—by identifying her with the "eternal types" they have themselves invented—to possess her more thoroughly. Specifically . . . a woman writer must examine, assimilate, and transcend the extreme images of the "angel" and "monster" which male authors have generated for her (p. 37).

Reinterpreting the images of fiend and angel as artistic stratagems by which the woman writer gives birth to herself, Gilbert and Gubar also identify themes, motifs, and metaphors which have represented women's entrapment in patriarchy. The mirror is the ultimate image of enclosure; instead of looking outward through a window, a woman is "driven inward, obsessively studying self-images as if seeking a viable self" (p. 95). This feeling of entrapment is continued in images of burial, enclosure, emprisonment, claustrophobia, paralysis. Or the woman writer may express her inability to write as disability: a crippling. Images of sickness are equally eloquent for the woman writer; she experiences a continual dis-ease with her situation, which may take the form of melancholy, headache, consuming fever, or madness. The emptiness of her lot is expressed in images of hunger or starvation. She may have a thirst, but she cannot slake it; she may be empty but unable to eat; if able to eat, she finds herself unsatisfied. No physical food can satisfy the spiritual cravings this hunger represents. She wastes and becomes anorexic.

Gilbert and Gubar also identify a powerful female landscape: the cave, a place both of imprisonment and of empowerment. It is a place where women have been "immobilized and half-blinded," but "the womb-shaped cave is also the place of female power, the *umbilicus mundi*, one of the great antechambers of the mysteries of transformation" (p. 95). The task of the woman writer is to liberate the "positive mythic possibilities" of the cave from the "cave's negative metaphoric potential" (p. 102). Gilbert and Gubar conclude their introductory chapters with this potent image because "the cave is not just the place from which the past is retrieved but the place where the future is conceived' (p. 102). It is for women a potent visionary landscape in which they can inscribe a new reality.

That new reality will, of course, generate a series of new images for women. Meanwhile, these images within the collective, creative unconscious await release. We may expect not just a reenvisioning of the old images — a process already underway — but the generation of genuinely new images for women, images that not only question but also cancel the patriarchal imprimatur and imprint women's creative potential on the world.

NOTES

1. See Dorothy Dinnerstein. Other feminists and feminist psychoanalytic critics also argue that the role of motherhood is at the root of women's oppression. See Jean Baker Miller, Adrienne Rich, and Nancy Chodorow.

2. Rich, A. (1977). Her waking. In M. A. Ferguson (Ed.). *Images of women in literature*. 2nd ed. Boston: Houghton Mifflin. I am indebted throughout this article to the pioneering work of Mary Anne Ferguson in this anthology.

3. See Deborah Gorham for a full treatment of this subject.

4. Ian Watt offers the most complete accounting to date of the social conditions that accompanied the rise of the novel. For his discussion of the word "spinster," see p. 145.

5. I am grateful to the Center for Educational Statistics, Educational Information Branch, for providing this information.

REFERENCES

Abel, E., Hirsch, M., & Langland, E. (1984). *The voyage in: Fictions of female development*. Hanover: University Press of New England.

Brontë, C. (1971). *Jane Eyre*. New York: Norton.

Chodorow, N. (1979). *The reproduction of mothering: Psychoanalysis and the sociology of gender*. Berkeley: University of California Press.

Chopin, K. (1976). *The awakening*. New York: Norton.

Dinnerstein, D. (1976). *The mermaid and the minotaur: Sexual arrangements and human malaise*. New York: Harper and Row.

Ferguson, M. A. (Ed.). (1986). *Images of women in literature*. Boston: Houghton-Mifflin.

Forster, E. M. (1921). *Howards End*. New York: Random House.

Freeman, M. E. W. (1983). *Selected stories of Mary E. Wilkins Freeman*. New York: Norton.

Gilbert, S., & Gubar, S. (1979). *The madwoman in the attic: The woman writer and the nineteenth century literary imagination*. New Haven: Yale University Press.

Gorham, D. (1982). *The Victorian girl and the feminine ideal*. Bloomington: Indiana University Press.

Jong, E. (1973). *Fear of flying*. New York: New American Library.

Keats, J., (1959). *Selected poems and letters*. Boston: Houghton Mifflin.

Masciello, L. M. (1982). *The Lilith archetype in the fiction of four writers*. Unpublished master's thesis, University of Florida, Gainesville, Florida.

Miller, J. B. (1976). *Toward a new psychology of women*. Boston: Beacon Press.

Moers, E. (1977). *Literary women: The great writers*. Garden City, NY: Doubleday.

Morrison, T. (1970). *The bluest eye*. New York: Washington Square Press.

Morrison, T. (1973). *Sula*. New York: New American Library.
Olsen, T. (1956). *Tell me a riddle*. New York: Dell Publishing Co.
Rich, A. (1976). *Of woman born: Motherhood as experience and institution*. New York: Harper & Row.
Shakespeare, W. (1969). *William Shakespeare: The complete works*. Baltimore: Penguin.
Showalter, E. (Ed.). (1985). *Feminist criticism: Essays on women, literature, and theory*. New York: Pantheon.
Showalter, E. (1977). *A literature of their own: British women novelists from Brontë to Lessing*. Princeton: Princeton University Press.
Spacks, P. M. (1975). *The female imagination*. New York: Avon.
Twain, M. (1948). *The adventures of Huckleberry Finn*. New York: Holt, Rinehart and Winston.
Watt, I. (1957). *The rise of the novel*. Berkeley: University of California Press.
Woolf, V. (1942). *Death of the moth and other essays*. New York: Harcourt Brace Jovanovich.
Woolf, V. (1929). *A room of one's own*. New York: Harcourt Brace Jovanovich.

ANTHOLOGIES OF LITERATURE BY WOMEN

Bankier, J. & Lashgari, D. (1983). Women poets of the world. London: Macmillan.
Barnstone, A., & Barnstone, W. (Eds.). (1980). *A book of women poets from antiquity to now*. New York: Schocken Books.
Bataille, G., & Sands, K. (Eds.). (1984). *American Indian women: Telling their lives*. Lincoln: University of Nebraska Press.
Bernikow, L. (Ed.). (1974). *The world split open: Four centuries of women poets in English and American*. New York: Vintage.
Brant, B. (Ed.). (1984). *A gathering of spirit writing and art by North American Indian women*. Watertown, Mass.: Sinister Wisdom Books.
Coles, T., & Coles, J. H. (1979). *Women of crisis: Lives of struggle and hope*. New York: Delacorte Press.
Cosman, C., Keefe, J., & Weaver, K. (Eds.). (1979). *The penguin book of women poets*. New York: Penguin.
Covina, G., & Galan, L. (Eds.). (1975). *A lesbian reader: An Amazon quarterly anthology*. Guernville, CA: Amazon Press.
Cully, M. (Ed.). (1985). *A day at a time: Being the diary literature of American women from 1766 to the present*. Old Westbury, NY: Feminist Press.
Ferguson, M. (Ed.). (1985). *First feminists: British women writers, 1578-1799*. Bloomington: Indiana University Press.
Ferguson, M. A. (Ed.) (1986). *Images of women in literature*. Boston: Houghton Mifflin.
Fetterly, J. (Ed.). (1985). *Provisions: A reader from 19th century American women*. Bloomington: Indiana University Press.

Fisher, D. (Ed.). (1980). *The third woman: Minority women writers of the United States*. Boston: Houghton Mifflin.

France, R. (Ed.). (1979). *A century of plays by American women*. New York: Richard Rosen Press.

Gilbert, S., & Gubar, S. (Eds.). (1985). *The Norton anthology of literature by women: The tradition in English*. New York: Norton.

Goulianos, J. (Ed.). (1973). *By a woman writt: Literature from six centuries by and about women*. Baltimore: Penguin.

Hampsten, E. (1982). *Read this only to yourself: The private writings of midwestern women, 1880-1910*. Bloomington: Indiana University Press.

Hedges, E., & Wendt, I. (Eds.). (1980). *In her own image: Women working in the arts*. Old Westbury, NY: Feminist Press.

Koppelmann, S. (Ed.). (1984). *Between mothers and daughters: Stories across a generation*. Old Westbury, NY: Feminist Press.

Lifshin, L. (Ed.). (1982). *Ariadne's thread: A collection of contemporary women's journals*. New York: Harper & Row.

Mahl, M. R., & Koon, H. (Eds.). (1977). *The female spectator: English women writers before 1800*. Old Westbury, NY: Feminist Press.

Mazow, J. W. (Ed.). (1979). *The woman who lost her names: Selected writings of American Jewish women*. San Francisco: Harper & Row.

Moffatt, M. J., & Painter, C. (Eds.). (1975). *Revelations: Diaries of women*. New York: Vintage.

Moore, H. (Ed.). (1977). *The new women's theater: Ten plays by contemporary American women*. New York: Random House.

Olsen, T. (Ed.). (1984). *Mother to daughter, daughter to mother: A feminist press daybook and reader*. Old Westbury, NY: Feminist Press.

Payne, K. (Ed.). (1984). *Between ourselves: Letters between mothers and daughters, 1750-1982*. Boston: Houghton Mifflin.

Reit, A. (Ed.). (1977). *The world outside: Collected short fiction about women at work*. New York: Four Winds Press.

Shimer, D. B. (Ed.). (1982). *Rice bowl women: Writings by and about the women of China and Japan*. New York: New American Library.

Showalter, E. (Ed.). (1978). *These modern women: Autobiographical essays from the twenties*. Old Westbury, NY: Feminist Press.

Spinner, S. (Ed.). (1978). *Motherlove: Stories by women about motherhood*. New York: Dell.

Stratton, J. (1981). *Pioneer women: Voices from the Kansas frontier*. New York: Simon & Schuster.

Washburn, P. (Ed.). (1979). *Seasons of women: Song, poetry, ritual, prayer, myth, story*. New York: Harper & Row.

Washington, M. H. (Ed.). (1975). *Black-eyed Susans: Classic stories by and about black women*. New York: Doubleday.

Washington, M. H. (Ed.). (1980). *Midnight birds: Stories by contemporary black women writers*. New York: Doubleday.

Images of Women:
Views from the Discipline of History

Barbara Evans Clements

THE ORIGINS OF WOMEN'S HISTORY

Historians have only recently begun teaching and studying the history of women in a systematic way. As late as 1967 a widely used textbook in American history, *The United States* by Richard Hofstadter, William Miller, and Daniel Aaron (second edition, Prentice-Hall, 1967), devoted only two pages of its 900 to women's history. These two pages summarized the campaign for female suffrage. Other texts of the same era were rather more generous, but even they limited their treatment of U.S. women to short discussions of women in factory labor, female participation in nineteenth-century reform movements, and, of course, women's suffrage. The situation was little different in European history. An influential survey, *The European World* by Jerome Blum, Rondo Cameron, and Thomas J. Barnes (Harper & Row, 1966), included only two references to women in its index, both very brief mentions of women's suffrage. Lecturers did not discuss women with their college classes, nor were there many histories of women's experience for these lecturers to draw on, had they wished to inform themselves and their students about it.

Women were rarely included in the story of the past as historians told it. The reasons for this are neither difficult to discover nor difficult to understand. The history written by Europeans since the time of Classical Greece (fifth century B.C.) had been the written account of the doings of great men, leaders of their city-states or nations, whose decisions influenced the lives of thousands of people. This was so in part because historians believed that the rulers were the most important people in a society, but it was also so because the rulers often paid the salaries of historians, paid them to write glowing tributes to the rulers. Historical scholarship has been, in other words, a record of the politics of the elite. Since women have been excluded from direct participation in politics through most of Western history, women have been excluded from the writings of historians, as have lower-class people of both sexes.

The only exceptions to this rule were the exceptional women, the occasional powerful queen, such as Elizabeth I of England (1558-1603) or Catherine the Great of Russia (1762-1796). Since these women wielded political power, they had their historians from the first. There were also the heroines, women such as Joan of Arc or Florence Nightingale, who found their way into the written record of the past because they seemed to exemplify the best in female personality. They were self-sacrificing, humble, and devoted to a cause, much like the female Christian saints. The historians mentioned them in passing, but did not see them as significant historical actors. Nor did the historians attach much importance to one other type of woman about whom they wrote, the female oddity. Within this category fell the witches burned in the early modern period (sixteenth and seventeenth centuries), the murderesses (Lucrezia Borgia [1480-1519], the Italian noblewoman who had a penchant for poisoning), the consorts (mistresses of kings, such as Madame de Pompadour of eighteenth-century France), and the "cranks" (the activists of the nineteenth century, be they temperance crusaders, free-love advocates, revolutionary socialists, or suffragists). Historians all too often treated these women as amusing asides, comic relief from the important business of politics. Women were given serious attention only when they entered the male arena, and they were praised only when they conformed to male-approved values, either as politicians, or as embodiments of the female virtue of self-sacrifice in the service of a cause or a man. Women's position in society, their roles in the past, the effect of gender on Western societies, all of these were unanswered questions, because they were questions that were not asked.

This has been the case for generations of historians. Historians are creatures of their society, after all, and as such they reflect the values of their society far more than they shape them. In praising famous men historians were doing what the elite of their society, those who read their books, expected them to do. This was the case even among the historians in a democracy such as the U.S. By the middle of the twentieth century there were thousands of historians studying American and European history, most of them approaching their subject with assumptions that grew out of the optimism that prevailed in their country at mid-century. The U.S. past, as they portrayed it, was a story of progress toward the realization of American democratic ideals. Historians applauded the reform of those elements in their country's past which were undemocratic, such as slavery, while ignoring undemocratic elements in the present, such as the continuing discrimination against minorities and women. John D. Hicks unwittingly gave voice to this spirit in his summary of the position of women in 1955. "If equality between the races had not yet been achieved," Hicks wrote in his textbook *The American Nation*, "equality between the sexes had very nearly approached the ultimate" (third edition, Houghton Mifflin, p. 770). Americans who studied the history of Europe, Asia, or Latin America were somewhat more critical, since it is easier to be objective about other societies than it is to be objective about one's own. But even the non-Americanists criticized from within American values, which meant that they studied the elites of foreign countries and did not consider women worthy subjects.

There is one additional reason why most historians ignored the history of women until recently: so few historians themselves were women and those few women who were historians faced tremendous obstacles. In 1970 only 12 percent of the doctoral degrees awarded in history went to women, a figure that had held constant throughout the twentieth century. The women who did find college teaching jobs remained at the bottom of the academic ladder, were poorly paid, and were not encouraged to become research scholars. If they did research, they were advised to stay away from "women's subjects," because such topics were trivial and would brand the scholar studying them as intellectually mediocre. Nor was research into women's history easy to do, even if the female historian was willing to brave the condemnation of her colleagues. Libraries and archives did not catalogue materials in women's history so that they were readily accessible, research grants were not often given to women's history topics, graduate school training did not prepare one to analyze or even locate the sorts of materials (for example, census data or probate records) in which women's history is recorded. Perhaps most importantly, there were so few people working in women's history that there was no one for the aspiring historian of women to talk to. A field of study develops because there is community of scholars pursuing separate topics but sharing their insights and reading one another's work. Before the 1970s there was no such community of historians of women. There had been female historians who overcame all these obstacles and produced women's history (Mary R. Beard's *On Understanding Women* [1931] is a preeminent example), but such studies were few.

All this changed in the 1960s. American historians began to be influenced by the so-called "new social history" pioneered after World War II by a group of French historians known as the *Annales* school. In their journal *Annales* these scholars published articles that dealt with the lives of the masses of French people. Central to their work was the idea that history had been shaped not just by the decisions of the rulers, but also by the attitudes and behavior of ordinary people. Therefore if one wanted to understand the past, one had to study ordinary people. The *Annales* historians also believed that doing this rectified a wrong, because they believed that the peasants and workers of the past were just as worthy of study in their own right, as the leaders who had so often oppressed and abused them.

Such democratic ideals began to strike a responsive chord in American historians by the early 1960s. Then there came the great political and social unrest of that decade. The Civil Rights Movement to end discrimination against blacks dominated the first years of the sixties, followed by the protests against the Viet Nam War. At the same time American feminism reawakened; it had been moribund since the 1920s. These movements inspired a critical attitude toward American society in their followers, among them a number of historians who were sympathetic to civil rights and doubtful about the Viet Nam War. Such historians began to rethink their assumptions, not just about the present condition of U.S. society, but about the past as well. At the same time, graduate programs in history swelled with young people who had been influenced by the social protests around them. Among these students were larger numbers of women than ever before. By the end of the decade, some of these young people, and the professors with whom they worked, had turned their attention to women's history.

The new interest in women's history expressed itself immediately in two ways—teaching and research. Courses in women's history began to be organized in the early 1970s, at first by people working alone. Soon teachers were pooling their knowledge, sharing syllabi and reading lists through the mails and through clearing houses such as the Coordinating Committee on Women in the Historical Profession. By the mid-1970s textbooks on women's history were available, and courses were being integrated into interdisciplinary women's studies programs.

These efforts at teaching women's history depended, as does all teaching of course, on research. Often the teachers were also scholars studying women's history, and their efforts began very early in the seventies to yield results, in the form first of articles, then book-length studies. This work was initially very difficult, for the reasons discussed above. Because research libraries had not classified materials relating to women so that they were easily found, scholars had to go hunting through card catalogues for references, without much help from librarians. Scholars also had to think creatively about the sorts of sources they could use; the government documents and autobiographies of men which had traditionally served as raw material for historians did not have much to say about women. Women's historians had to explore sources earlier overlooked—the letters of schoolgirls, the diaries of middle-class farm wives, the deeds in a county courthouse, the tales of former slaves. They also had to think long and hard about questions never asked before. How did women and men relate to each other in the past, what did women contribute, how were women treated, how did they live?

THE FINDINGS OF WOMEN'S HISTORY

The first studies of women's history centered around prominent women of the past, because they were the easiest women to discover in the historical record. Women earlier relegated to obscurity were rescued and reevaluated by historians now eager to understand women's experience. Historians of women discovered female painters, academicians, scientists, and writers scattered across the last 500 years of European history, but little remembered because their accomplishments had been ignored, or belittled. The activities of whole groups of women were also reassessed. The feminists of the nineteenth century, for example, came to be seen not as cranky spinsters, but as courageous, sometimes short-sighted women of principle. Their critique of American society's treatment of women was recognized as remarkably prescient; these women had been discussing problems of marriage, divorce, equal opportunity, free love, birth control, and education with an insight that their descendents 100 years later could admire and learn from.

The study of the feminists led American historians to an examination of the considerable role women played in all the nineteenth-century reform movements in the U.S. and Europe. Rather than being purely domestic creatures concerned with family matters, nineteenth-century women had been active members of their society, deeply involved in the intellectual and social ferment of their time. Historians found that this was true of Black women as well as White, as they studied the lives of leading Black activists such as Sojourner Truth (1797?-1883) and Mary McCleod Bethune (1875-1955). Medieval historians, analyzing the considerable power held by noblewomen under feudalism, soon realized that women had been politically important long before the nineteenth century. Thus it was discovered that even by the standards of traditional historiography, oriented toward politics and the elite, women had a past.

Women's historians soon became restive with the study of elite women, however, and began to turn their attention to the masses of women. They also began to ask new questions of the past. What was life like for women of earlier times? What deeply ingrained values had determined women's position in society? How had that position changed over time, and why? Has women's historical experience been so fundamentally different from men's that there are in fact two histories, one male, the other female? And what about the differences between groups of women: how do class and race interact with gender in women's lives?

Historians of women began to ask these questions in the early 1970s. One of the first to do so was Joan Kelly, who argued in her article, "Did Women Have a Renaissance?" that the education of women and their ability to participate in the cultural life of society actually deteriorated from the late Middle Ages to the Renaissance. Men may have had a rebirth of learning and culture during the fifteenth century, Kelly wrote, but women did not. This thesis challenged the assumption that there had been steady progress in education since the Middle Ages, and argued forcefully that in this one period, the Renaissance, women's historical experience had been very different from men's. Progress for men had brought a diminution of women's status.

Pioneering studies followed quickly on Kelly's. By the mid-1980s the bibliography on women's history had grown so large that no single article such as this could adequately summarize its findings. What follows then is a brief survey of the major ideas to emerge from the study of the history of European and U.S. women. The considerable achievements of historians studying Latin American, African, and Asian women must be left unexamined.

The Patriarchy

One of the most basic issues that historians had to address when attempting to understand women's past was one of values. What values had governed the relationship of woman to man over the centuries, defined her position within the family, and carved out her role within the world beyond the family? Very quickly scholars came on the concept of patriarchy. They discovered that no matter how far back in the European past they looked, or how close to the present they came, society granted men the right to govern women. Through most of European history society had also granted some few men of the upper class the right to govern all men of the lower classes, as well as giving fathers the right to control their sons even after those sons had grown to manhood. The Romans had called these powers *patriae potestas,* the power of the father. Borrowing Roman terminology, historians of women labelled European society "patriarchal," and the cluster of values and institutional arrangements that established woman's subordination to man, "the patriarchy."

Patriarchal values endured for centuries little altered, because the basic institutional arrangements of European society changed so slowly before the nineteenth century. Throughout most of European history, from the time of the Greeks and Romans, the great majority of people were peasants living in family groups made up of several generations. They were clustered in small village communities that survived by subsistence agriculture. Everyone worked from an early age, women along with men and children with their parents. There was a division of labor by gender that allocated chores to men and women according to their relative physical strength and the demands of childbearing and nursing on women. That is to say, men did the heavy work of plowing, reaping, and milling, built houses and other structures, tended herds, and travelled when this was necessary to sell goods or hunt and fish. Women remained more closely tied to the village, where their jobs included caring for small livestock, raising vegetables, making clothes, cooking and preserving foods, fetching water, tending the sick, and of course, bearing and breast-feeding babies. The political structure was hierarchical, with power vested in a small hereditary elite, and within that elite and throughout the hierarchy, in men. From the beginnings of the Christian era, and in truth even before in Greco-Roman times, the Europeans conceptualized the world as a "chain of being," with God the Father at the top and authority extending downward through the angels and the saints into the kings, the nobles, and merchants, and last, the peasants. A woman's position was inferior to the men of her own rank, but superior to all the men and women below her. Thus the status of women, and the kind of work they did, depended on their class and their gender.

The values which legitimated the patriarchal distribution of power also defined woman's and man's nature for the Europeans. Woman was true to her nature, and therefore virtuous, when she worked hard, obeyed her parents, her husband, and her in-laws, and bore healthy children. She strayed from virtue when she failed in any of these, and most particularly when she tempted man sexually. From ancient times the Europeans believed that woman had the potential to destroy social harmony by seducing men, or by rebelling against male authority. Greek myths spoke of Pandora, who mischievously opened a box out of curiosity and let loose all the troubles of life. The Babylonians and then the Jews told of Eve, whose temptation of Adam in defiance of God's command led to mankind's expulsion from paradise. The medieval English had the myth of Guinevere and Lancelot, whose adulterous love destroyed the perfection of Camelot. All these fables expressed a deep belief that woman must fulfill her obligations or society would fall apart.

The Cult of Courtly Love

Patriarchal arrangements and beliefs endured in European society for a thousand years, and had their roots in social customs even older. Then, in the late Middle Ages, changes began in Western Europe which seemed fairly unremarkable at the time, but which in fact marked the beginning of a lengthy transformation that would ultimately undermine patriarchal authority. The signs of change appeared first among the French nobility in the twelfth and thirteenth centuries, with the development of the cult of courtly love. According to the ideals of courtly love, woman had a uniquely feminine purity and beauty. It was akin to the purity of the Virgin Mary, a kind of innate innocence, selflessness, and delicacy that men did not have, because they were more brutish by nature. A knight must dedicate himself to a female exemplar of these virtues and seek, through serving her, to civilize his own unruly nature. The cult of courtly love did not inspire men to devote themselves to their wives; in fact the poets and theoreticians of the cult argued that a man must choose a woman not his wife, presumably because medieval nobles found it difficult to idealize, or even to love their spouses. Marriages were arranged by the parents among the nobility, with little regard for the feelings of their children. Romantic love might develop among young people so united, or it might not. Courtly love allowed for the love that sprang up among those not married, and in fact some cynical historians have seen courtly love merely as one of the more elegant rationalizations of adultery.

However many affairs between nobles were justified by the cult of courtly love, it had a serious historical meaning as well. What the emergence of the cult reflected, and then promoted, was a new role for women within the cultural life of the nobility. Noblewomen had always played an important part in feudal society, as women do in any society. Within feudalism, women of the nobility could be landowners. As such, they governed immense tracts of land, and also ruled the lesser nobles, or vassals, living off that land. During their husbands' frequent absences (noblemen travelled often to satisfy their obligations to their overlords), noblewomen ran estates inhabited by hundreds of people; even when their husbands were in residence women had substantial duties connected with supervising their large households and caring for the serfs on their property. Thus a noblewoman was a powerful figure in feudal Europe, although not so powerful as her husband, and bound by patriarchal values to subordination under the men of her own class.

The cult of courtly love represented a new role for noblewomen — that of sponsor of the development of culture. Within the courts where courtly love flourished, women learned to write poetry, compose music, play instruments, and patronize talented troubadours who then sang their praises in payment. Because the cult saw women as possessed of a more delicate spirit than men, it granted them a new role — to civilize men by creating in them a sensitivity to the arts and to the more refined human emotions of tact, sensitivity to the feelings of others, restraint, and a self-denying kind of heterosexual love. This gentling down of the crude, illiterate warriors of feudal Europe paved the way for the Renaissance; by placing women at the center of the process, it assured them access to the new learning that would soon sweep over the Western European upper class.

Early Modern Europe (The Renaissance to 1750)

Beginning in fourteenth-century Italy, and then sweeping north to affect all of Western Europe by 1500, the Renaissance brought a flowering of cultural life such as Europe had not seen since Roman times. Women played a part in this self-styled "rebirth" of classical learning, serving as patronesses of the arts, as educated participants in royal courts where the arts flourished, and, in rare cases, as painters and poetesses themselves. Joan Kelly has pointed out that women were less actively involved in creating the Renaissance than they were in the creation of the courtly love tradition. This may well be true, but the custom developed during courtly love of women acting as cultural patrons continued, indeed flourished during the Renaissance.

The practice of educating the daughters of the elite received a further boost during the Protestant Reformation, which followed the Renaissance in the sixteenth century. Protestant theologians, beginning with Martin Luther and John Calvin, argued forcefully that all Christians should study the scriptures for themselves. Protestants concluded that women must be literate in order to fulfill this religious obligation, and thus education for women spread downward, from the nobility into the emerging middle class, from which came so many of the converts to Protestantism.

By the sixteenth century, other changes were occurring in Western and Central European society that were to have a profound, if somewhat gradual effect on the position of women. Strong kings (the Tudors in England, the Valois in France) emerged to consolidate centralized governments and in the process limited the power of the once all-powerful feudal nobility. The nobles fought vigorously against the kings, but eventually lost their independent political base and were forced to enter the kings' service, as commanders in their armies or bureaucrats in their governments. In these positions the nobles still had considerable power, but it was in an arena from which women were excluded. Thus the authority of the medieval noblewoman, built as it had been on her role within the family estate, dwindled in the early modern period, when power moved off the estates and into the offices of the king.

At the same time in Western Europe the family structure of the nobility, the middle class, and the peasantry was undergoing a significant evolution. Instead of living together in extended families of three generations (parents, adult children, and their children), the English and many of the French, Germans, and Scandinavians came to prefer for sons to move into their own households after marriage. Thus the two-generational, or nuclear family, was created, weakening the power fathers could exercise over adult sons. For women as well the move away from their in-laws was liberating, for it enabled daughters-in-law to escape from working under the constant supervision of their mothers-in-law.

The ability of parents to arrange their children's marriages was also eroded by this new independence being granted to the young.

Rather than choosing a bride exclusively because of her family connections (as had been common practice among the upper classes),
or her willingness to work hard (as was common among the lower),
young men began to consider also the promptings of their hearts.
Soon romantic love, based on sexual attraction and a desire for
companionship, became the preferred reason for marriage. Within
marriage the husband's authority over his wife was strong, perhaps
even stronger than in the Middle Ages, during the time of extended
family, because people felt a need to guarantee the stability of the
new family form, and chose to do so by placing women firmly
under men's control. In Protestant countries the new faith contributed to strengthening the husband by granting him the role of moral
instructor of his wife and children. But the ethos of the emerging
nuclear family also required that a husband love his wife and see in
her a companion and friend; this demand for what the writers of the
seventeenth century often called "conjugal felicity" created more
humane standards for married life by condemning such practices as
wife beating and infidelity.

Among the middle class, other changes were afoot. The growing
bourgeoisie was concentrated in the cities, where it survived by
trade and manufacturing. Middle-class women managed their
households and assisted in the family business. A few women had
owned businesses of their own in the Middle Ages, and in France
and England had belonged to the guilds that controlled most occupations. But by the early modern period women were being excluded from the guilds, and for the most part only widows continued to have the right to run their own enterprises. Middle-class
women worked alongside their husbands, selling, buying, keeping
accounts, and serving as cook and nurse to large households that
included their employees.

The great majority of women in the early modern period were
peasants. Their situation had been least changed by the Renaissance
and Reformation, the rise of centralized governments, and the development of the nuclear family. Like their predecessors in the distant past, they still farmed, kept house, and bore babies, the
rhythms of their lives attuned to the natural rhythms of the seasons.
By 1700 the standard of living of peasant women had improved, so
that they were eating better than had their medieval ancestors and

were suffering less from disease, but still they had a life expectancy of little more than 40 years. They did gruelling work, knew few luxuries, travelled rarely, and lived in constant fear of hunger and death. Only a major change in the economy of Western Europe could relieve their burdens. That change began in eighteenth-century England.

Modernization (1750 to the Present)

The eighteenth century saw the onset of a broad process of development in European society that scholars have labelled "modernization." This somewhat vague concept embraces industrialization (the shift of production into factories powered initially by steam and later electricity), urbanization (the movement of people out of the country into the cities where the factories had been built), and the accompanying rise of egalitarian political and social values. Modernization has had an enormous impact on women's lives, an impact almost too great to assess fully, particularly since modernization is still going on. Today more people than ever before are living through and coping with modernization, for in the twentieth century it has left Europe and swept across Asia and Africa.

The Enlightenment (1700s)

To understand the effects of modernization on women, one must consider its several aspects. First chronologically came the stirring of new political and social values; this occurred during the eighteenth century in the great ferment of ideas known as the Enlightenment. A product of French and British intellectuals, the Enlightenment questioned the power of the traditional authorities of Europe — the kings, the nobles, and the church — proposing instead, in the words of the U.S. Declaration of Independence, that, "All men are created equal." The individual has rights, declared the American and later the French revolutionaries, rights that society should be organized to protect. Power resided with the people, who could delegate it to leaders, but who retained the right to take that power back when the leaders abused their trust. Many upper-class Europeans rejected these radical contentions of the Enlightenment, and indeed, the radicals themselves did not really mean what they said. They did not truly consider all men equal, for they believed the black man to be innately inferior to the white. Nor did they include women in their calculations; the phrase said, "All men are created equal," and men is precisely what most of the American revolutionaries meant.

Nonetheless, the sentence had been written, equality of all in the political system — a truly radical idea given Europe's history of hierarchy and patriarchy — had been proposed, and it took very little time for a woman to raise the question of whether equality should be extended to women. In 1792 Mary Wollstonecraft, an English admirer of the French Revolution, wrote a pamphlet entitled "A Vindication of the Rights of Woman," in which she demanded equal educational and employment opportunities for her sex. Although few readers responded positively to this message at the time, the potential of the new ideas for launching an assault on patriarchal values was apparent.

The Nineteenth Century

Before the egalitarian principles that came out of the Enlightenment could be accepted as applicable to women, the other aspects of modernization had to work their influence on European and American society. In the nineteenth century, beginning in Western Europe, cities grew, education spread, railroad trains and the telegraph made communications easier, technology brought a higher standard of living, medicine made great strides in the prevention and cure of disease. The middle class burgeoned, growing rich on the profits of industry; the working class appeared, clustered around factories in urban slums. Even those left behind in the country were affected: subsistence agriculture was replaced by farming for profit, mechanized equipment and new scientific knowledge of plant and animal husbandry made the farms yield greater crops than ever before, and the food supply swelled, further improving the standard of living.

Historians of women are still trying to understand the impact of all these changes on the lives of women. It is an immensely complex process to analyze, and many distinctions must be drawn: between women of the various classes (and races in the U.S.), between the experiences of different nations with differing cultures, between Western Europe and the U.S., where modernization began, and Eastern Europe, where it came later. With a due regard for the dangers of oversimplification, we can make some sweeping generalizations about the ways in which women experienced modernization, based on the work done by those in women's history over the last decade.

What follows is heavily indebted to Louise Tilly and Joan Scott, whose study of industrialization's impact on French and British working-class women (*Women, Work, and Family*) has done a great deal to shape our understanding of the nineteenth century. Scott and Tilly were particularly interested in how modernization affected women's roles within the family, so they examined the ways in which the family itself changed. What Scott and Tilly found was that the family has changed its form, and some of its values in the modern era, and with that change has come change in the roles of women within the family. But they also found that this change has occurred fairly slowly, because in the midst of all the upheaval of industrialization, people acted to conserve such aspects of the family as they could, in order to preserve for themselves an island of stability in a world that was often confusing and frightening. Of particular relevance to women's lives was that people preserved the patriarchy's allocation of power over women to men, and continued to consider women's domestic roles as their primary obligation.

The women of Great Britain and the U.S. were the first to experience the great changes that came later, but with many of the same consequences, to women throughout Europe. Most obvious was that it became increasingly difficult for women to fulfill their domestic tasks — housework and child care — and also work outside the home. In agricultural society this had been easy; a woman strapped her baby on her back and brought it with her to the fields or to the market. In urban society children were admitted to the workplace only as employees. Women did work in the cities: peasant women newly arrived from the countryside found jobs in the factories, particularly the textile mills, or in the homes of the affluent where they were hired as servants. There were also many middle-class women who became teachers, and later in the century clerks or nurses. But the great majority of these British and American women worked at paid labor only until marriage or the birth of their first child. Thereafter, if their husbands earned enough money to support them, they retired to their homes to devote themselves to rearing children and tending to the needs of those husbands. Prosperous middle- and upper-class women did no paid labor at all, moving instead from their schooling directly into marriage and motherhood.

Of course housework was still time-consuming, but even it had changed. The availability of cheap consumer goods meant that women no longer spent considerable time preserving food or making clothes. Rather they occupied themselves with cooking, as before, with cleaning, which now took up a greater percentage of their time, and with caring for children. Child-rearing, once a fairly insignificant part of women's responsibilities, became one of their central concerns in the nineteenth century.

The Cult of True Womanhood

As women's contributions to the family changed, so too did the society's notions about women's roles within the family. There developed, first in the U.S. and Britain, a new vision of woman, which brought together elements out of the past and adapted them to the new, urban world. It has been labelled by historian Barbara Welter "The Cult of True Womanhood"; formulated in the nineteenth century, it continues to have enormous influence in the late twentieth century.

The Cult of True Womanhood proclaimed that women were naturally, innately more emotional than men, more capable of love, and more moral. They were also physically and intellectually weaker than men. Women were created gentle, submissive, and innocent; this made them unsuitable for the dog-eat-dog world of business, but made them ideal nurturers of children, and of men. They were, by God's design, men's helpmeets: they provided love and moral guidance to men; men helped them develop their rationality and supported them financially. Their natural role within the home was to create a clean, warm, secure nest to which men would return every night to soothe their nerves and within which children would grow up healthy in mind and body. Women should also provide men with sexual pleasure, but this was more a necessary evil than a good. The practitioners of the Cult of True Womanhood—writers, physicians, and clergymen—believed that the only good associated with sex was the begetting of children. Since they condemned the sex drive as one of man's basest instincts, and since they thought that women had a far weaker sex drive than did men, the followers of the Cult urged women to set men an example of self-control by showing no interest in sex.

The Cult of True Womanhood did not create a new view of woman's nature so much as it adapted the core ideas from traditional European conceptions to the nineteenth century, modernizing world. The notion of a feminine purity stemming from woman's childishness and asexuality had its roots in the courtly love tradition and the cult of the Virgin Mary. Even older was the belief that woman's principal duties were domestic. The nineteenth-century Britains and Americans who fashioned the Cult applied these traditional conceptions of woman's nature to their times, and transformed woman into a nest builder in the midst of the din and dirt of the city. They thereby raised her affective, or emotional functions within the family to a central position which they had not held in earlier eras, when woman's economic roles, particularly the production of goods for the family, had been a far more important part of her domestic labors. Now, in the city, with woman no longer spinning thread or preserving food, new work was found for her, as care-giver and refuge.

The Cult of True Womanhood was created by the British and American middle class, whose women did not customarily work for wages. The notion of woman as a weak creature on a pedestal of moral purity seemed to have little relevance to the lives of working-class or peasant women, who were still doing back-breaking labor in the mid-nineteenth century. Nor did the U.S. advocates of the Cult apply it to Native American women, Black women, or impoverished immigrant women. In her famous "Ain't I a Woman?" speech in 1851, the Black abolitionist Sojourner Truth pointed out the narrowness of the Cult by proclaiming that men had never thought it necessary to help her across puddles or into carriages. But eventually, as the century wore on, the Cult did spread downward into the working classes, and abroad to the continent of Europe. Lower-class White women throughout the European world and Black women in the U.S. were taught to value the feminine virtues that the Cult advocated. Among Black women the influence of the Cult was weakened by traditions of independence inherited from their West African ancestors and preserved under slavery. In Catholic countries and among Hispanic Americans it was weakened by the church, which refused to replace the Virgin and the nun as exemplars of moral purity with the urban housewife. Nonetheless, even among Blacks, Catholics, and Native Americans the Cult had an effect on views of women, because it was well attuned to the realities of the modern world and because it was preached by the ruling middle class. So pervasive had the Cult become by the twentieth century that as late as the 1980s sociologists in the Soviet Union described female personality in terms identical to those used by American ladies magazines 100 years before.

Feminism

It is one of history's ironies that while the Cult of True Womanhood, a set of ideas ostensibly so traditional, was enjoining most women to devote themselves to housekeeping, it was propelling others into launching an assault on patriarchal traditions. The Cult did not do this alone, however; its propositions about feminine purity had to be combined with the egalitarian political principles also in the air. Beginning in the 1840s this uneasy synthesis was undertaken by a few women in Britain and America, who asked why they should be excluded from participation in the governing of the two countries, and discriminated against in law, education, and employment. If political equality and social reform were desirable, as the Enlightenment had argued, and if women were morally superior to men, as the Cult alleged, then why should women not play a part in cleaning up their societies, just as they were cleaning up their houses? The women and men who made this argument became involved in such philanthropic activities as charity among the poor, prison reform, public education, and, particularly in the U.S., the campaign for the abolition of slavery. They also founded organizations to promote reforms for women, and thus began what would come to be called the feminist movement, the alliance of various groups seeking the abolition of discriminatory practices against women.

Feminism was strongest in the two countries where it was born, Great Britain and the U.S., and in Scandinavia. By 1920 it had made substantial gains — laws permitting married women to control their own property; formal education for women from childhood through university; new employment for women in clerical work, sales, and nursing; regulations to protect women from dangerous working conditions. Finally, in the years preceding and immediately following World War I, women gained the vote in Scandinavia, Great Britain, the U.S., Germany, and Soviet Russia.

After the suffrage battle was won, feminism as an organized movement petered out in Western Europe and the U.S. Historians of women have yet to explain this fully, but they believe that an important reason for the quiescence of feminism after 1920 was the ebbing of a sense of common purpose among feminists. Having gained the vote, they were uncertain about and divided over their future objectives. Feminism had always been predominantly a middle-class movement; by 1920 it had achieved many of its reforms. It could go no further without beginning to question the basic values of the middle-class family and the capitalist economy, and that most feminists were unwilling to do. At the same time, Western societies were reeling from the disaster of World War I and frightened by the spectacle of revolution in Russia. A deep desire for stability swept Europe and North America, a desire that expressed itself in reassertions that women belonged in the home, not out causing trouble in the world. Thus the feminists' own uncertainty and the conservative spirit of the times combined in the twenties to throw organized feminism into a disarray from which it recovered only in the 1960s.

The Twentieth Century

Women's Emancipation in the U.S.S.R.

In the twenties the center of the drive for women's emancipation seemed to move out of Western Europe and America where the movement had begun, and into Eastern Europe, specifically into the Russia just emerging from revolution. In Russia, the government established by the Bolsheviks in 1917 had no reason to fear disrupting capitalism or the middle-class family. In fact, it was committed to destroying both, and to emancipating women in the process. As

Marxist socialists, the Bolsheviks, soon to rename themselves the communists, believed that women's inequality sprang from capitalism, which required them to be economically dependent on men. The solution was to abolish capitalism; with it would be destroyed all the barriers to women's full equality. Women would then enter the labor force as men's equals. This would require a fundamental restructuring of the family, of course, but the communists welcomed this prospect too, because they believed that the family was a bastion of middle-class prejudices. With women involved fully in the paid labor force, children would be cared for by public nurseries and housekeeping chores would be handled by public services such as laundries and cafeterias. Women and men would continue to marry, of course, but they would be free to conduct their private, intimate lives without any governmental regulation or interference. Following the vision of most nineteenth-century socialists, the Russian communists presumed that under socialism people would prefer to live in large, communal apartment houses, sharing chores and friendship.

After they came to power in 1917, the communists moved swiftly to achieve their program of female emancipation. A new marriage law was written establishing no-fault divorce, regulations were issued requiring equal opportunity for women in education and employment, protective labor legislation outlawed placing women in jobs that might damage their health, generous maternity benefits were instituted, and a special Woman's Bureau of the party was created to encourage women to take advantage of their new rights, and to organize the facilities that would make this possible. The foundations for women's emancipation laid by these early measures were then built on by subsequent Soviet administrations. Affirmative action programs in the late 1920s and 1930s required that certain numbers of women be recruited and trained for skilled positions. Nurseries and day-care centers were built. Female literacy rose from an appallingly low 15 percent on the eve of the revolution to close to 100 percent by 1960.

The accomplishments of the communist regime in educating, employing, and promoting women were truly extraordinary, particularly in view of the country's backwardness and the upheavals within it caused by war, revolution, and domestic unrest. By the

1980s, the Soviet Union had compiled an admirable record of involving women in the world beyond the home. Yet it had not fully emancipated them, even by its own standards. In searching out the reasons for the shortcomings of the Communist Party one discovers once again the enduring hold of patriarchal values, age-old values that have shaped women's experience with modernization throughout the last century and continue to do so today.

The Soviet government did not abolish the nuclear family, as its ideology had once demanded. Rather it promoted a process modernization had already begun in Russia before the revolution — replacing the extended peasant family that was the norm for the majority of the population with the modern, nuclear family. When the communist government began its crash program of industrialization in the 1930s, it drew peasants by the millions out of the villages and into the factories. The people huddled in urban slums not unlike those of England 100 years before, and began the difficult process of adjusting their family structure and roles to the new world they found themselves in. Had their government remained true to its first principles, it would have urged them into communes, but the Soviet government by the 1930s had backed off its commitment to the radical restructuring of the nuclear family. It had done so because many of the communists who had joined the party since the revolution did not like socialist proposals to abolish the family; rather they wanted to replace the extended peasant family with the more modern, but still patriarchal nuclear family. Within that nuclear family they wanted woman to serve as emotional center and chief nurturer, the role prescribed for her by the Cult of True Womanhood. This became official party doctrine in the 1930s; the ideal woman of Soviet society was to be a worker with equal opportunity in the labor force, and a wife, mother, and housekeeper.

Thus in the U.S.S.R., the socialist ideology of women's emancipation, drawn originally from principles of woman's equality with man, merged with older, traditional notions of woman's differentness from man. It was a synthesis remarkably similar to that which some feminists had earlier attempted between liberalism and the Cult. The Soviet variant of this synthesis of egalitarian and patriarchal values produced a new feminine ideal, named subsequently by American feminists, the Superwoman. She was to have full political and occupational equality, without giving up any of her domestic responsibilities. The Soviet propagandists of this new version of the female saint did not ask how women were supposed to find the hours in the day to be perfect wives, mothers, and workers. Nor did they suggest that men share housework and child-care with their wives. In truth the government made only minimal efforts to undermine the patriarchal traditions that gave power within marriage to men. Furthermore, the day-care facilities and the other social services originally proposed to emancipate women from the home were slow in coming, because the government was chronically short of the funds necessary to finance their construction. Women continued to hold primary responsibility for housekeeping and childrearing, therefore, while being told they were equal by the regime.

Soviet women dealt with their burdens by reducing the number of children they had, until it became commonplace for a city-dwelling couple to have only one child. They also limited their work outside the home, as had their nineteenth-century predecessors in Western Europe. Although virtually all Soviet women were gainfully employed, they avoided high-prestige, high-paying, but also demanding jobs, remaining instead in low-status occupations such as clerical work, teaching, medicine, food preparation, and sales. Such jobs left them time after hours for their housekeeping, and for tending to the other needs of their families.

After World War II, when the Soviet Union established its influence in Eastern Europe, the Soviet model for women's emancipation was adopted there as well, with markedly similar effects on the situation of women within those nations. Patriarchal family values endured, modified by the governments' commitment to female emancipation, but that government commitment had itself been modified by the influence of patriarchal values. The end result was that the position of women in Eastern Europe by the late twentieth century was comparable to that of women in Western Europe. Modernization, whether it evolved slowly as in the West, or came quickly under government sponsorship as in the East, seemed to produce the same results for women—participation in the paid labor force, development of the nuclear family, and weakened but still powerful male control, legitimated by altered but still influential patriarchal values.

Women in the West

Western European and North American women proceeded more slowly and peacefully toward this outcome in the twentieth century. Through the middle years of the century they pursued the pattern of living established in the nineteenth. The majority were gainfully employed until they married; after that they became housewives. The European and American standard of living improved steadily from the late-nineteenth century into the mid-twentieth, bringing women more nutritious diets, longer life expectancy, and better health than ever before. Women were also better educated, most having at least primary schooling, and many having attended high school. Romantic love continued to flourish, as girls were allowed more and more freedom in courtship; by 1920 and the revolution in women's hemlines and hairdos, even women's fashions had been liberated. Divorce law remained strict, but was being reformed slowly; women were routinely granted custody of their children, thus reversing nineteenth-century practice. With the development of safe, effective methods of contraception, women could limit the number of children they bore, and thus the demands of their family lives. Furthermore, labor-saving devices such as the vacuum cleaner, the refrigerator, and the clothes washer made housework easier. In the 1930s and 1940s the nations of Western Europe, led by the Swedes and Norwegians, also pioneered the creation of social welfare programs beneficial to women, funding day-care centers and paid maternity leaves. Thus the lives of most of the women in Western Europe and America were far more pleasant in 1960 than they had been in 1800.

Perhaps it was the security created by the modernized economy that made it possible for some women, again centered in the U.S. initially, to begin a new assault on the lingering influences exercized on Western society by the Cult of True Womanhood. In the 1950s the civil rights movement, staffed as it had always been by large numbers of heroic Black women, challenged the complacency of White Americans. Once again the call for an end to racial dis-

discrimination led to a new sensitivity to gender discrimination. In the 1960s feminism reawoke, and soon made substantial accomplishments in breaking down barriers to women's employment, in encouraging women to enter the paid labor force, and in prompting governments to provide services such as day care that would make female employment possible. The New Feminism also took aim at the cultural underpinnings of woman's position, criticizing patriarchal values and questioning the allegations about woman's nature that had depended on those values, and shored them up. It is out of this critique that women's history developed as a specialty. Thus we return to the subject with which we began.

MAINSTREAMING WOMEN'S HISTORY

These are the broad outlines of the history of women in Europe and America, a history little known until the rebirth of feminism kindled an interest in it among historians. It remains only to ask what has been the effect of the new scholarship about women on history as it is taught in the schools today.

First and most noticeable, faculty now routinely include women's history in their courses. Women's history also appears in text books. Not only are the prominent women of the past dealt with in some detail, but the lives of ordinary women are frequently discussed. To cite only one example, the fifth edition of R. R. Palmer and Joel Colton's *A History of the Modern World* (Knopf, 1978) includes references to the findings of women's history and family history in its basically traditional political narrative. An even more fundamental restructuring of the survey text can be found in the truly fine work by John P. McKay, Bennett D. Hill, and John Buckler, *A History of Western Society* (third edition, Houghton Mifflin, 1983). These authors not only treat women's history extensively, they also discuss the social history of past ages, thereby giving their readers a feel for the lives of the masses of people.

A similar revision has occurred in texts in American history. One of the best examples is *A People and a Nation,* by Norton, Katzman, Escott, Chudacoff, Paterson, and Tuttle (Houghton Mifflin, 1982). These historians consider women's experience of the past and participation in it at every stage of U.S. history. It is also noteworthy that the chief author of this text, Mary Beth Norton, is a prominent historian of women.

The advances in mainstreaming women's history into the curriculum have been paralleled by a growth in the numbers of women entering the ranks of Ph.Ds in history. The percentage of women among doctoral recipients jumped from 12 percent in 1970 to 32 percent in 1983. Many of these women have secured appointments in college teaching: 83 percent of women who earned their Ph.Ds between 1970 and 1975 held faculty appointments in 1983, and it is a rare history department that does not have at least one female member. Overall women make up roughly 15 percent of full-time faculty. Women have also made gains in publishing their work, in being elected to office in professional societies, and in presenting papers at scholarly meetings. To cite an example of the increased visibility of women in the profession, in 1969 only 15 women read papers at the annual meeting of the American Historical Association (AHA), the umbrella organization for historians in the U.S. In 1984, there were 127 women on the AHA program. The position of women within the profession is also enhanced by the existence of a number of lobbying committees, chief among them the Coordinating Committee for Women in the Historical Profession, an independent association for female historians, and the Committee on Women Historians of the AHA. These organizations have played an important part in promoting equality of opportunity, as well as publicizing discriminatory practices.

Because of the efforts of the specialists in women's history, the future of the field seems fairly secure. Not only does its inclusion in survey courses and textbooks testify to its acceptability among historians, but it is supported by a professional network that should guarantee its survival. Hundreds of historians presently study women's history. There are several professional journals publishing work in the field, the most eminent among them *Signs*. The Conference Group on Women's History acts as a clearinghouse for scholars wishing to exchange information on upcoming conferences, research interests, grants available, and archival resources.

There is so much yet to be learned about women's history that the prospects for research are limited only by the imagination of historians. Thus the future of women's history and of women in the historical profession seems bright. Nagging problems do remain, however. The employment situation has improved greatly in the last decade, but today women still hold the lowest ranking appointments in college history departments. They earn lower salaries than men, even men of the same academic rank and seniority. Efforts are being made to rectify these lingering consequences of discrimination; they must continue. Female Ph.Ds also have higher rates of unemployment than do men (3.5 percent versus .8 percent in 1983), and they hold more part-time appointments (6.3 percent of female historians in 1983 were working part-time while seeking full-time work, as compared to 1.1 percent of male historians). This seems to be largely because women are more likely than men to sacrifice full-time employment to their family commitments, thus living where their husbands work and finding what jobs they can. In a time of scarcity in college teaching positions, these choices leave many women at the very bottom of the profession, loaded down with classes which they teach for minimal wages, without the regular faculty appointment that gives one access to libraries, grants, and the other support services necessary to productive research. Solutions for the problems of underemployed female Ph.Ds are difficult to find, but a start could be made if universities would provide better pay and more privileges for part-time workers.

The difficulties still faced by women's history are also a result of the inheritance of the past. Some historians persist in denying the significance of the field, declaring that it is not a scholarly specialty at all, but a politically motivated litany of feminist complaints. Others continue to denigrate all social history, and women's history in particular, as intellectually trivial. Naturally such historians do not include women's history in their lectures. Male college students avoid classes in women's history, probably for basically the same reasons. These attitudes can also influence the decisions of administrators, committees hiring new faculty or awarding grants, promotion committees, and other individuals and groups with the power to advance or retard the development of women's history. It is to be hoped that the successful work of historians of women will continue to persuade the majority of historians that this new field is a worthy addition to the study of the past, and therefore deserving of the full support of the profession. It is also to be hoped that female historians have earned a secure enough position within the profession that they can survive any future backlash against them.

FOR FURTHER READING

Bridenthal, R., & Koonz, C. (Eds.) (1977). *Becoming Visible: Women in European History* (1st ed.). Boston: Houghton Mifflin. Joan Kelly's article, "Did women have a Renaissance?" is included in this collection, pp. 137-64.

Giddings, P. (1984). *When and Where I Enter: The Impact of Black Women on Race and Sex in America*. New York: William Morrow.

Ryan, M. P. (1983). *Womanhood in America* (3rd ed.). New York: Franklin Watts.

Stone, L. (1977). *The Family, Sex and Marriage in England, 1500-1800*. New York: Harper & Row.

Tilly, L. A., & Scott, J.W. (1978). *Women, Work, and Family*. New York: Holt, Rinehart and Winston.

Welter, B. (1983). The cult of true womanhood: 1820-1860. In M. Gordon (Ed.), *The American Family in Social-Historical Perspective* (pp. 372-92). New York: St. Martin's.

REFERENCES

Beard, M.R. (1931). *On understanding women*. London: Longmans, Green and Co.

Blum, J., Cameron, R., and Barnes, T.J. (1966). *The European world*. New York: Harper & Row.

Hicks, J.D. (1955). *The American nation*. Boston: Houghton Mifflin.

Hofstadter, R., Miller, W., & Aaron, D. (1967). *The United States*. Englewood Cliffs, NJ: Prentice Hall.

Kelly, J. (1977). Did women have a Renaissance? In R. Bridenthal and C. Koonz (Eds.), *Becoming visible: Women in European history*. Boston: Houghton Mifflin.

McKay, J.P., Hill, B.D., and Buckler, J. (1983). *A history of western socialization*. Boston: Houghton Mifflin.

Norton, M.B., Katzman, D.M., Escott, D., Chudacoff, H.P., Paterson, T.G., Tuttle, W.J., & Brophy, W.J. *A people and a nation*. Boston: Houghton Mifflin.

Palmer, R.R., & Colton, J. (1978). *A history of the modern world*. New York: Knopf.

Tilly, L.A., & Scott, J.W. (1978). *Women, work, and family*. New York: Holt, Rinehart, and Winston.

Images of Women:
An Economic Perspective

Barbara S. Burnell

I. INTRODUCTION AND PURPOSE

The general purpose of this chapter is to provide a feminist perspective on and critique of the image of women as traditionally analyzed by economists. In the process of accomplishing this task, an attempt will be made to illustrate the extent to which the analytical and methodological framework used by economists has been influenced by the male-dominated profession and society within which they operate,' and to consider what effect the use of this framework has on the perception of the economic role of women.

This type of critical analysis requires a clear statement of the essential elements of a feminist perspective, both in general terms and as it relates particularly to the discipline of economics. A consideration of these elements, along with an analysis of some of the past and present difficulties associated with implementing this perspective in economic analysis, will be the focus of the remainder of this introductory section.

Section II will present a brief statistical overview of the historical and present economic status of women in the U.S. Section III will be devoted to an examination of the major economic issues that relate to the role of women in our society. It will present a fairly detailed analysis and critique of the major aspects of economic theory that have been used to analyze (or not analyze) women. This analysis will focus on the question of how appropriate traditional economic theory is for analyzing women's experience, and will investigate the relationship between the use of such theory and the status of women.

Section IV will address economic policy issues as they relate to women. The relationship between the development and testing of economic theory and the implementation of policy will be explored. In addition, the implications of traditional cultural norms and value judgments for the formulation of economic policy and its consequent effect on the role and status of women will be examined.

The concluding section will attempt to integrate and summarize the theoretical and policy issues in an effort to draw some conclusions about the extent of traditional bias in past and current economic research and policy. In addition, this section will assess the impact that feminist research has had on the discipline. This assessment will consider the ways in which traditional theoretical analyses have been modified and new theoretical frameworks developed to more accurately analyze the particular experience of women. In addition, the relationship of such research to traditional economic analysis, both in terms of publication and curriculum, will be considered.

For any discipline or area of study, a feminist perspective involves at least two key elements. The first, from both a logical and historical standpoint, consists of an examination of traditional scholarship's ignorance of the role of women and women's experience, and an attempt to rectify omissions from the existing body of knowledge in the discipline. The second addresses the more fundamental question of whether the theoretical and methodological framework of a discipline is capable of being utilized to understand women's experience. If, as in many cases, the answer to this question is negative, then a feminist perspective is required to make the necessary modifications in that framework.

Generally speaking, this definition of a feminist perspective can be applied to any discipline, but its application will vary across disciplines, according to the nature and degree of bias in existing knowledge and to particular methodological features of different disciplines. To better understand a feminist perspective on economics, it is helpful to define what economics is and what kinds of questions economists ask.

Economics can be defined as "the systematic study of the production, distribution and use of scarce resources of a society so as to satisfy the maximum number of wants. It is the study of choices among alternatives in a situation of scarcity" (Peterson, 1973,

p. 516). Economics thus analyzes the way in which scarce resources can be most efficiently allocated in order to maximize the welfare of members of society. Since the primary mechanism for allocating resources in our economy is the market system, it is perhaps not surprising that economists have focused on questions pertaining to how markets for various goods and services operate.

This market focus has resulted in neglect of many economic activities in which women have traditionally been, and continue to be, involved. The economist's definition of Gross National Product, which is used as a very rough indicator of material well-being, illustrates this point clearly. GNP is defined as the market value of all final goods and services produced in one year. Economists and others have cautioned against using GNP figures as an indicator of well-being, since it excludes many factors that affect our welfare. The important point for this discussion is that many of the factors that are excluded pertain almost exclusively to economic activity of women that is designed to increase societal welfare — housework, child care, volunteer work, and unpaid work in general. Thus, from a statistical standpoint, a large portion of women's contribution to society is ignored.

There are many other aspects of reliance on a market economy that have resulted in neglect by the economics profession of women's economic activity. As with other social scientists, the questions economists ask depend to a certain extent on the data that are available to answer them. The data that are collected are largely the by-product of market activity. Market transactions that determine prices, wages, and costs lend themselves to tabulation, while economic activity that does not result in goods and services being bought and sold does not. Thus, even when economists are interested in economic activity outside the market sphere, often the data necessary to analyze it do not exist.

Even when data to analyze the economic activity of women do exist, caution must be exercised in their use. The process of data collection and tabulation is not completely objective and value-free; in many instances, it reflects cultural norms and stereotypes. Two examples will serve to illustrate this point. First, up until a welcome change in the *1980 Census of Population*, if a household comprised a husband and wife, husbands were always designated as the head of the household, even if responses to census questionnaires indicated otherwise.[2] While this procedure was justified on grounds of statistical convenience, it clearly perpetuates the notion that men are in charge and fosters an image of women as secondary members of households and society. Second, the way in which data are classified by the Census Bureau suggests that some traditional value judgments are built into the categorization process. Data on labor force status, for example, have a heading for "employed persons" followed by a subheading for "employed females." Similarly, participation in the labor force is categorized by the presence of spouse and children of various ages for women, yet these same categories are not presented for men.

While the economists' emphasis on market activity and data limitations do suggest some problems in analyzing the economic activity of women, these problems are not insurmountable. There is some indication that women's roles are beginning to be subject to more analysis and that more data are becoming available to study non-market activity. Many of the factors that are responsible for the change relate to growing awareness and concern about the actual economic status of women, which will be considered in the next section.

II. STATISTICAL OVERVIEW

Economists are social scientists and, as such, the questions they ask are in part motivated by the society in which they live. Further, the theories they develop to explain human behavior are, whenever possible, validated or invalidated on the basis of real-world data. Thus, before we analyze and critique economists' study of women, it is helpful to give a brief statistical overview of the phenomenon of interest.

This statistical overview will serve several purposes. First, and most obviously, it will present a picture of the economic rate and status of women and how these have changed over time. Second, it will provide the basis for understanding the relationship between trends in women's economic status and the types of questions economists have addressed. Third, it will serve to sharpen understanding of some of the limitations placed on economic analysis by the data available. And finally, it will demonstrate that women's economic position, and changes in it, constitute a very complex phenomenon.

Limitations of space and the need to focus upon and critique conceptual as well as real-world issues preclude an exhaustive statistical portrait of the economic status of women. For this reason, the statistics presented here will pertain only to the U.S., although admittedly much could be learned from a comparative analysis based on data from other countries. In addition, the statistical overview is superficial in the sense that it cannot fully illustrate the complex interactions that have been responsible for the changing (or in some instances, relatively static) economic role of women or the actual experiences of individual women. In spite of these limitations, however, a brief examination of data on women is useful for purposes of establishing a context within which economic analysis is conducted and economic policies are formulated.

Among the myriad of statistical information on women, there are four types of data that will be the focus of this section. These data have been chosen because they give a fairly clear, if not complete, picture of women's role in the economy, and because they are strongly suggestive of the kinds of questions about women's changing roles that economists are, or should be, addressing. The four categories of data to be discussed pertain to the labor force participation of women, the occupational distribution of women workers, and earnings and unemployment of women workers relative to men. Although initially data on each of these will be presented independently, it is important to emphasize at the outset that they are interrelated aspects of women's market activity, and an attempt will be made to identify some of these complexities.

Perhaps the most dramatic change in the role of women in the economy has been the rapid rise in labor force participation rates in the post-World War II period. The data in Table I illustrate this trend very clearly. The most striking aspect of the data is the increase in the labor force participation of married women with young children. Single women, and divorced and widowed women, have historically had higher rates of labor force participation for reasons of economic necessity, and the same has been true for minority women, as Table I indicates. In addition, single and widowed women have typically not had the same non-market responsibilities.

TABLE 1. Labor Force Participation of Women,
by Marital Status and Presence of Children

Year	Total	Single	Married, Total	Married, Children <6	Widowed or Divorced*	Minority Women
1950	33.9%	50.5%	23.8%	11.9%	36.0%	NA
1960	37.8%	44.1%	30.5%	18.6%	37.1%	48.2%
1970	43.4%	53.0%	40.8%	30.3%	36.2%	49.5%
1975	46.4%	56.8%	44.4%	36.3%	37.7%	49.4%
1980	51.5%	61.2%	50.2%	45.0%	41.1%	53.6%
1982	52.6%	62.2%	51.8%	48.7%	42.1%	53.7%
1983	52.3%	62.6%	52.3%	49.9%	41.2%	54.2%
1984	53.2%	63.3%	53.3%	51.8%	42.0%	55.3%

*the labor force participation rates for this category are lower because they include many women past retirement age
Source: U.S. Department of Labor, Bureau of Labor Statistics

The traditional assumption about married women with children has always been that they do not need to work, nor should they give up their home responsibilities. The data in Table II clearly indicate the middle-class bias of this assumption. Table II demonstrates that women's contributions to family income are substantial, particularly among lower income classes.

The influx of women into the labor force is often used as evidence to support the claim that women's labor market position has never been better. If we look more closely at what jobs women are doing, how much they are being paid, and what their unemployment rate is as compared to men's, it becomes clear that this claim is not valid. Table III presents information on the occupational distribution of women workers in July of 1985, and for comparison purposes the same information for 1975. For each year, the first column indicates the percentage of all women workers that fall into a given occupational category, while the second column shows what percentage of workers in a given occupational category are women. Two important points emerge from an examination of the data. First, there has been relatively little change in the occupational distribution of women workers over time. Second, women are concentrated into a very small number of occupations and grossly underrepresented in others. The theoretical explanations given for this occupational segregation will be discussed in detail

TABLE II. Contributions of Married Women to Family Income, 1981

	# of Wives (1000's)	Median % of Family Income From
Total Wives with Earnings	27,697	26.7
White, Total Full-Time Workers	10,895	38.0
Family Income		
< 10,000	238	68.1
10-15,000	383	56.4
15-20,000	1088	46.5
20-25,000	1594	42.4
> 25,000	7391	34.8
Black, Total, Full-Time Workers	1104	42.2
Family Income		
< 10,000	51	(NA)
10-15,000	87	52.6
15-20,000	157	46.3
20-25,000	171	45.2
> 25,000	637	38.0

Source: Bureau of Labor Statistics

below, but it is useful to observe here that the jobs in which women are concentrated are relatively low-paying, low-status jobs, and two reasons often advanced for occupational segregation are the socialization process that teaches women that they should want to do these jobs, and lack of opportunity to enter traditionally male-dominated fields.

The fact that women are segregated into a relatively small number of occupations explains in part their low earnings relative to those of men. Table IV presents an historical picture of the median earnings of women and men full-time workers, and the ratio of women's to men's earnings. The picture is, to say the least, discouraging. Despite minor changes in the earnings gap over the time period covered in the Table, women's earnings power relative to men's has remained relatively unchanged since 1950. The picture is

TABLE III. Occupational Distribution of Women, 1975 and 1985

Occupation	1975		1985	
	% of Women Workers	% of Workers Women	% of Women Workers	% of Workers Women
Executive & Managerial	5.6	18.9	10.2	37.8
Professional & Technical	16.3	39.1	17.4	16.4
Sales	6.5	34.2	14.2	48.5
Clerical	35.4	68.6	29.9	74.4
Service	19.7	49.2	17.4	51.2
Craft	1.6	4.1	2.5	7.9
Operators & Laborers	13.1	21.9	9.1	22.8

Source: Bureau of Labor Statistics, *Employment and Earnings*, August, 1975 and August, 1985. The data are adjusted to reflect changes in the definition of occupational categories.

TABLE IV. Male-Female Earnings Differentials, 1955-1982

Year	Male	Female	Female as % of Male
1955	$ 4,252	$ 2,719	63.9
1960	5,417	3,293	60.8
1965	6,375	3,823	60.0
1970	8,966	5,323	59.4
1975	12,758	7,504	58.8
1980	18,612	11,197	60.2
1981	20,260	12,001	59.2
1982	21,077	13,014	61.7
1983	21,811	13,915	63.6
1984[a]	25,884	16,036	62.0

Source: Lloyd and Niemi, *Economics of Sex Differentials*, p. 152 for 1955-1975, U.S. Department of Commerce, Bureau of the Census for later years.
[a] data for 1984 are averages

even more discouraging for minority women. In 1970, black women's average weekly earnings were 85 percent of white women's and 52 percent of white men's. By 1985, black women's average weekly earnings were 89 percent of white women's and 60 percent of white men's (Bergmann, 1986).

Again, some of the theoretical explanations for the existence and persistence of the wage differential will be considered in more detail below, but it is worth noting that occupational segregation is certainly not entirely responsible. The data in Table V illustrate this by presenting information on the relative earnings of women and men by occupational category. Clearly, controlling for occupation by comparing women's and men's salaries within broad occupational categories does not eliminate the earnings differential. Although women fare better relative to men in some occupational categories than in others, they still earn at most 65 percent of what male workers earn.

Two tentative conclusions can be drawn from these data. First, to the extent that occupational segregation is responsible for the earnings differential, the figures in Table III do not reveal the full extent

TABLE V. Female-Male Earnings Differentials By Occupation, 1982

| | Median Earnings, Full Time Workers | | |
Occupation	Male	Female	Ratio (F/M)
Managerial & Professional	$28,373	$17,987	.63
Technical % Sales	21,400	12,574	.59
Service	14,459	8,565	.59
Farming, Forestry, & Fishing	9,093	5,348	.59
Craft	20,913	13,591	.65
Operators & Laborers	17,223	11,029	.64
Total	21,077	13,014	.62

Source: 1985 Statistical Abstracts

of such segregation. Within each general occupational category there is a hierarchy of jobs — the professional category includes both doctors and nurses, for example — and if women are clustered at the bottom of each hierarchy, this in part explains why the earnings differential exists even within occupational categories. Second, the figures suggest that, given the magnitude of the earnings differential, there must be some other factors that contribute to it; some possibilities will be discussed in more detail below.

Turning to a final comparison between women and men in the labor force, Table VI presents an historical overview of the relative unemployment rates faced by the two sexes. The picture for women is not an encouraging one. Despite some narrowing of the unemployment differential between women and men that can be attributed to cyclical fluctuations in the economy, women's unemployment rates have historically been significantly higher than men's, particularly for minority women, and some economists have argued that the long run trend is toward an increasing differential (Lloyd & Niemi, 1979).

As pointed out at the beginning of this statistical overview, these four aspects of women's labor market status are not independent of one another, and some of the important interrelationships will now be briefly considered. First, the relationship between women's occupational distribution and their relatively low earnings has already been briefly discussed; because women are crowded into a small number of occupations, their earnings are relatively low. Yet it can also be argued that the division of occupations into men's and women's jobs has helped women in the sense that it has facilitated the increase in their labor force participation. The service sector of the economy grew very rapidly during the period being considered here, and it can be argued that the growth in demand for women workers — in secretarial and clerical jobs, for example — allowed additional women workers to be absorbed into the economy.

Women's unemployment is also related to trends in their labor force participation and their occupational distribution. Part of the reason for women's higher unemployment is that, at any given time, the proportion of the labor force composed of re-entrants or new entrants is higher for women than it is for men. This is particularly true in periods of rapid increases in women's labor force participation. If, as is usually the case, it takes some time to locate a job, the women are counted in the ranks of the unemployed. In addition, since in many cases women are recent entrants, they have less seniority than male workers and will be first to be unemployed if firms are forced to fire workers.

Women's occupational distribution also has an impact on their unemployment relative to men's, but in this case the effect is a positive one. As the data illustrate, women are much more likely to be employed in the service-oriented sectors of the economy. While these jobs tend to be lower-paying, they also tend to be more immune to cyclical fluctuations in the economy. In recessionary times, it is the heavy industry sectors of the economy, where women are not as likely to be employed, that get hit hardest with unemployment. This explains the fact that the differential between women's and men's unemployment rates is not constant over time.

Having briefly examined the data on women in the labor force, what can be concluded about women's economic role? There are many things that this statistical portrait can tell us, but also some things that it cannot. First, the statistics presented are based on average characteristics, and therefore cannot adequately represent differences in women's experiences that are attributable to race and class bias. Second, as noted above, it ignores the significant economic contribution made by women outside the paid labor force, as it is based purely on market statistics. We will see, however, as the analysis progresses, that there are some important relationships between this non-market activity and the labor force profile of women. Third, the data do not tell us much about the potential economic contribution of women. Since they are based only on women in the labor force, they do not incorporate skills, talents, and educational qualifications of women who, voluntarily or otherwise, are not part of that labor force.

The data clearly indicate that women have historically occupied a secondary economic status, and that for the most part they continue to do so. Despite the dramatic increases in labor force participation which many observers have been quick to cite as evidence of improvement in women's status, many problems persist. The occupational distribution of women has changed very little over time despite the influx of women into the labor force. Similarly, there has been little change, and even by some measures deterioration, in the relative earnings and unemployment position of women and men. This is true in spite of the fact that women are becoming increasingly involved in and attached to the labor force, in terms of continuity and length of labor force participation.

III. ANALYSIS AND CRITIQUE OF ECONOMIC METHODOLOGY

The discussion in the previous section of women's economic position leads naturally to a consideration of the way in which economists have studied women: what aspects of the situation they have chosen to analyze, and the methodology they have employed to do so. The definition of economics cited previously and the data presented in the last section suggest that the aspects of women's economic behavior economists have chosen to analyze have been market-oriented. Up until the mid-1960s this was the case, but it need not be.

To see that economic analysis can be applied to non-market activity, it is perhaps useful to give an alternative definition of economics. Sawhill said that, ". . . an economic problem exists whenever resources that have multiple and competing uses are scarce. Scarcity requires *choice*, and choices are best guided by comparing the costs and benefits of all the possible alternatives. Once one has defined 'resources' and 'costs and benefits' broadly enough, there is almost no area of human behavior to which the economic paradigm cannot be applied" (Sawhill, 1977, p. 121).

This general definition of economics has resulted in its application to many aspects of behavior not typically thought to be the purview of the economist. Tullock and McKenzie ". . . talk about family life, child rearing, dying, sex, crime, politics . . . because we believe these are extraordinarily important areas of inquiry and that economic analysis can add much to our understanding of them" (Tullock & McKenzie, 1984, p. 4).

Thus, a more general definition of economics leads us to conclude that many types of activity that have traditionally been the domain of women — child-rearing and homework, for example — are capable of being subjected to economic analysis. In fact, there has been increasing emphasis on these non-traditional types of economic analysis over the past 15 or 20 years, beginning with the analysis of Gary Becker (1976). In these non-traditional areas, as well as in those that economists have typically worked, there is a methodology or mode of analysis that is unique to economics. It is important to understand some of the key features of this methodology and the way in which it has been employed in order to critique the economic analysis of women.

Perhaps the most important characteristic of economic methodology is the construction of models of behavior. Many students of economics complain that these models are too abstract. Yet it is the process of abstracting from the real world that makes economic analysis sufficiently rigorous to make consistent predictions about behavior in different circumstances. We will find, however, that there are certain instances in which the abstraction process renders economic analysis inadequate for analyzing certain aspects of women's behavior, and that the abstraction process itself is not a completely objective one.

Central to the process of modeling human behavior is an assumption that is common to virtually all economic analysis: the rationality of individual behavior. That is, within a set of constraints, individuals are assumed to make choices so as to maximize their well-being. While this maximizing behavior is often directed to *material* well-being (and, indeed, economists are often criticized for a preoccupation with material well-being), this is only one element of satisfaction. Increasingly, economic analysis is concerned with resources other than those to which an explicit price tag can be attached, and with factors other than material goods that contribute to well-being.

One aspect of this rational choice process needs to be carefully examined, particularly as it relates to women. Choices made in order to maximize welfare are assumed to be *free* choices, or at least choices made within a set of well-defined constraints such as income, prices determined in the market, and so forth. What needs to be more fully recognized is that the set of constraints within which decisions are made may very well be different for men and women and for different groups of women. Faulkner has argued that the assumptions of individual, rational pursuit of self-interest imply that people are, "disconnected from anything larger than self, from anything (including sex, race, and social class) that limits their ability to exercise economic freedom" (Faulkner, 1986, p. 59). Lloyd and Niemi are among the authors that recognize that women's secondary economic position is related to the fact that women do not have free choice. As they point out, "The dominant orthodox approach to labor market analysis assumes that roughly the same wide array of choices lies before each individual. . . . Although each individual engages in maximizing behavior, two people with identical preferences and non-market opportunities may well end up making completely different decisions in the labor market, because they are choosing from different sets of available alternatives" (Lloyd & Niemi, 1979, pp. 2, 3). Systematic differences in the available opportunities that are sex-based, as well as class- and race-based, need to be carefully scrutinized and the factors responsible for them need to be identified before we can say that women's secondary economic status derives from a theoretical analysis that assumes free, rational choice on their part.

This brings us to a final important aspect of economic methodology. The process of abstraction inherent in developing economic models often leads us to conclude that economic theory is objective and value-free. Predictions made on the basis of this theory, therefore, must be "right" in the sense that they are logically derived from a behavioral model. This is a fallacy that can be particularly dangerous in analysis of women's economic behavior because, as will be discussed below in more detail, it can often result in circular logic, and in economic analysis being used to justify the status quo. Tullock and McKenzie claim that, "the approach of the economist is *amoral*. Economics is not so much concerned with what *should be*. . . . Our analysis is devoid (as much as possible) of our own personal values. . . . We are interested in gaining an understanding of the behavior of others, *given their values*" (last emphasis mine) (Tullock & McKenzie, 1984, p. 7). The danger in this claim is that values, either of the researcher or society at large, may become embedded in a supposedly positive, as opposed to normative, economic analysis. It then becomes very difficult to use the results to understand the role played by values in determining women's economic status. In addition, the embedding of values in "objective" theory makes it difficult to use the resulting knowledge as a tool for social change. Sawhill (1977) and others have identified this last issue as an important element of feminist scholarship.

The discussion so far has been confined to general characteristics of economic methodology and features of it which bear particularly close scrutiny when economic analysis is applied to women. A far better understanding of these issues can be developed by analyzing and critically evaluating specific economic theories from a feminist perspective. There are many possible examples that could be used here. The ones chosen will hopefully facilitate a greater understanding of the statistical overview presented in the previous section, as well as provide a foundation for economic policies to be discussed in the next section. Finally, these examples have been chosen with the hope that they will serve to most clearly illustrate problems with current analysis and prospects for change.

A good place to begin is with analysis of the determinants of labor force participation. The dramatic rise in women's labor force participation documented earlier provided an impetus for economists' interest in this topic, from both a theoretical and empirical standpoint. Initial attempts to fit women's experience into the traditional analysis proved interesting and stimulated the development of new theories. The economist's standard approach to analyzing labor force participation decisions was to view it as a choice between income and leisure time. In choosing a given level of participation in the labor force, an individual gains an income, but only at the cost of sacrificing leisure time. Conversely, the cost associated with consuming additional leisure is the income foregone by not working. The decision made by a particular individual depends on his or her preference and on the costs involved, with the cost of leisure determined by the wage rate the individual can command in the market.

Testing with actual data on male workers provided empirical support for the theory.[3] Empirical analysis of women's labor force participation decisions did not, however, seem to fit the theory. Evidence on women forced a reconsideration of the traditional analysis, and it was found to not adequately model women's experience in two important respects. First, the choice between labor and leisure is modeled as a continuous phenomenon, with the decision being the number of hours to work. This is not the same as the discontinuous decision of whether to work (i.e., join the labor force) or not. Yet it is this latter decision that so many additional women were making from the 1960s on. This realization resulted in more attention being paid to those factors—for example, an increase in wages—that would cause women to shift their decision from no market work to participation in the labor force. It is interesting to note that, even in recent analysis, one such factor that has been focused on is "other"—i.e., husbands'—income. This factor is one that is not usually systematically included in the analysis of men's labor force participation decisions.

A more fundamental problem with the analysis is that the two-way choice it considers simply does not accurately describe the situation for many women. First of all, many women really *have* no choice as to whether or not to participate in the labor force regardless of the wage they will be paid—their economic survival depends on it. Second, even for women who can make a choice, they have traditionally had to make a three-way choice between market work, leisure, and work done in the home. Thus, an accurate model of women's decision-making needs to consider not only how preferences and wage rates affect the trade-off between market work and leisure, but also the trade-offs involving non-market work as well. When traditional theory is extended to account for this more complex decision-making process, the actual data on women workers tends to support the theory.[4]

The recognition that a large portion of women's time is spent in productive yet unpaid work fostered the development of a whole new area of economic analysis beginning with the work of Gary Becker (1965) in the mid-1960s. This work comes under the heading of what is usually called "New Home Economics," and refers to economic analysis of women's non-market activity and the allocation of resources within family units. The development of the New Home Economics clearly illustrates the wide applicability of economic analysis. It represents an exciting but somewhat disturbing element in the discipline. It is exciting because its emphasis on non-market activity means that women, who were not extensively considered in much of traditional analysis, are the explicit focus of a great deal of this work.

Such analysis is disturbing for two reasons. First, non-economists, and some economists, are uncomfortable with analyses of marriage, child-rearing, and divorce that attempt to interpret the choices involved in terms of costs and benefits. This is not a serious problem as long as one recognizes that economists, like other social scientists who have studied the same things, analyze the issues from a certain perspective and do not claim to provide a complete understanding of the underlying behavior.

A second and more fundamental problem is that it is in the sphere of non-market activity that the effects of sex roles and traditional values are so pervasive. As some examples will clearly illustrate, it is very easy to accept as given certain "objective" factors that are very much determined by traditional sex roles. When these factors are built into the analytical framework, the theory predicts a logical division of household responsibilities.

As an example, consider the path-breaking analysis of the allocation of time by Gary Becker. The theory is complex and difficult to summarize, but its major thesis is the time of household members is the major constraint on maximizing behavior. People derive satisfaction from consuming what Becker calls commodities, which require time inputs to (1) earn income to buy market goods that become a part of the commodities, (2) transform market goods into consumable commodities (e.g., a home-cooked meal), and (3) actually consume them. The allocation of time that maximizes the household's satisfaction depends on the value of the individual's time and how productive they are at various tasks. Thus, if we accept as given that men make more money in the marketplace and that women are more productive at household tasks, the logical outcome of the theory is that it predicts this division of labor.

This type of analysis has been extended by Becker and others to explain household formation (i.e., marriage), child-rearing, and specialization within the family.[5] Space limitations preclude an extensive discussion of this work, but a few of its salient features are worth mentioning to illustrate some of the important conclusions and some problems with the analysis.

First, with respect to marriage, economic analysis of household formation has predicted that people with similar preferences will marry. This is certainly consistent with what other social scientists have found, but the process by which economists reach this conclusion and its implications are very different. According to Tullock and McKenzie (1984), "This means that he will seek to minimize the cost incurred through marriage and the family. If he marries someone that agrees with him, the cost associated with arriving at the marriage contract is less than otherwise. There is not as great a need for (implicit) bargaining. If he marries someone who agrees with him as to what the family should do, what kinds of recreation they should have, and the number and way in which children should be reared, then the cost of having to give up friends and goods that suit his preferences will be minimized" (p. 79).

An additional characteristic of the marriage contract that is generally not considered by other social scientists arises from the economic perspective that marriage is a process which generates gains from trade and specialization. The economic theory of marriage postulates that marriage is more likely to occur among individuals whose relative productivities in various tasks differ the most (Santos, 1975). If this is the case, then the gains from marrying, specializing in the task at which one is relatively more productive, and "trading" the resulting output are maximized.

This emphasis on specialization and its effect on increasing efficiency and welfare is a natural one for economists, but in the context of marriage and household production it needs to be scrutinized very carefully. Otherwise, the theory can be used to legitimize and perpetuate the secondary economic status of women. As an example of the way in which this is done consider the following: "If the decision facing the family is the allocation of members' time between work internal to the home and work external to the home and if the family is interested in minimizing the cost of goods produced in the home, then it should use that labor with the lowest value outside of the home. . . . Much of what we observe in household relationships may very often be the result of a conscious, rational choice on the part of the couples. Clearly, women do tend to earn less in the market . . . either because they are victims of discrimination or because they are less productive. *Given this, which is not something individual households can do much about*, it is reasonable to expect households to delegate many responsibilities, such as child care, to wives" (emphasis mine) (Tullock & McKenzie, 1984, p. 78).

According to this view, then, there is nothing wrong with the traditional division of household responsibilities; in fact, such a division makes sense given that it maximizes the family's welfare. There are several problems with this conclusion from a feminist viewpoint, however. First, it emphasizes the family unit, not the individual, and does not address the question of the satisfaction of women themselves. Second, it does not consider the consequences of this specialization, particularly as the nature of the relationship and household unit changes. Finally, it takes as *given* the assumption that women are paid less and/or are less productive outside the home, without questioning its legitimacy or underlying causes, and without considering the possible interrelationship between lower pay for women and the traditional division of labor.

This issue of lower pay for women in market work brings us to the last topic for discussion in this section: economic analysis of sex differences in earnings and occupations. This is a very difficult subject to treat adequately in the space of a few pages, but some major highlights of alternative theories and problems with them can be considered.

The theoretical and empirical work in this area begins with two observations. First, women, even after controlling for hours of work, are paid significantly less than men. Second, women have a very different occupational distribution than do men. These two observations are clearly not independent of one another, although the precise nature of the relationship between them is still the subject of considerable study.

There are two general categories of theories used to explain the disadvantageous labor market status of women. First, the human capital approach argues that women are paid less because they are less productive, and that they hold the jobs they do as a matter of *choice*. That is, women anticipate (correctly or not) less attachment to the labor force because of household responsibilities and childbearing and raising. As a result, they invest less in education and training that would make them more productive workers, simply because the expected payoff is low. Further, when women choose occupations, according to human capital theory, they will make the choice on the basis of which occupations have the lowest penalties for dropping out of the labor force. Lower earnings and occupational segregation are thus a result of voluntary choice, whereby women make their labor market decisions by comparing present and future costs and benefits of various courses of action.

There is a certain logic to this argument, but there are also some serious problems with it. The most fundamental one relates to the interdependence between market and non-market decisions. As Ferber and Teiman point out, "it becomes clear that there is considerable circular reasoning involved when traditional economists justify woman's specializing in homemaking by pointing to her lower earnings in the labor market, and explain her lower earnings in the labor market by pointing to her absorption in homemaking" (Ferber & Teiman, 1981, p. 134). In addition, there is increasing evidence that the occupational distribution of women is not consistent with what human capital theory would predict.[6] The same evidence also indicates that sex differences in occupational distributions do not explain all of the earnings differential. Further, if human capital theory is an accurate analysis of women's earnings and occupational choice, we would expect that women's earnings would be increasing relative to men's and their occupational distributions becoming more similar to men's as their commitment to the labor force grows. Yet neither of these phenomena have occurred. Finally, the human capital theory emphasizes the concept of free choice too heavily. While it cannot be denied that women, like men, choose types and levels of education as well as jobs and careers, it must be recognized that these choices are often made within a different set of societal and labor market constraints than those that face men.

The emphasis on constraints characterizes the second group of theories developed to explain sex differences in earnings and occupations. These theories hypothesize that it is inequality of opportunity that is responsible for women's lower pay and occupational segregation. Unequal opportunities may exist either because of overt discrimination on the basis of sex and race in the labor market, or because of institutional features of the labor market that dichotomize it into primary and secondary sectors.

Overt discrimination occurs when women and men are treated

differently for employment purposes even though both are equally productive. The source of this behavior is prejudice against women and minorities, either on the part of the employer, potential co-workers, or consumers. There is some debate over whether acting on this prejudice by discriminating against women is profitable for the employer,[7] but for women workers, the effect is clear. Women will be paid less than men for essentially the same work, will be denied opportunities for training and promotions, or simply will not be hired for particular jobs.

This type of overt discriminatory behavior has been outlawed, as will be discussed in the next section, but such legislation does not change the institutional structure of the labor market and its implications for women workers. According to the dual labor market theory, the labor market is divided into two segments, primary and secondary (Lloyd & Niemi, 1979). The jobs in the primary sector are those with the potential for advancement and training and good pay, while those in the secondary sector are low-status jobs with no opportunity for advancement and low pay. The theory argues that women earn less and are segregated by occupation because they are channeled into the secondary labor market.

In terms of the end result, whether the source of inequity arises from direct discriminatory behavior or labor market institutions does not really matter; women will still be at a disadvantage because they cannot freely choose jobs, occupations, or training. The more subtle forms of discrimination implicit in the dual labor market are, however, more difficult to legislate against. Moreover, it is also very difficult to legislate away the adverse effects of past discrimination, as Lloyd and Niemi point out: "Productivity-enhancing job experience and differential access to such experience are the keys to the vicious circle of constrained opportunities in which the woman worker is still trapped. It is through the dynamic interaction of supply and demand in the labor market that patterns based on past discrimination, behavior and experiences are perpetuated. In fact, the question of whether individual choice on the supply side or employer discrimination on the demand side came first in a particular case is actually almost irrelevant, because the circular process, once set in motion, . . . is extremely difficult to short-circuit at any point" (Lloyd & Niemi, 1979, p. 12).

There has been a great deal of empirical study of sex discrimination in the labor market, but its interpretation is the source of considerable controversy. Several aspects of this research are relevant to this analysis. First, most analysis has attempted to quantify discrimination as the portion of the wage gap that remains even after controlling for factors that would be expected to cause women to earn less. Virtually no studies have succeeded in explaining away the wage gap by using factors such as differences in education and training.[8] Second, the evidence that women and men make decisions in the context of different labor market environments is fairly well documented. Education and job experience have different effects on men's earnings than on women's, indicating that if equally productive women had the same opportunities as men, their earnings would be higher.

Finally, studies that have been relatively successful at explaining the wage differential have been those that focus on narrow occupational groups or incorporate detailed occupational breakdowns as explanatory factors. It cannot be claimed that these studies are truly successful unless they attempt to address the question of the unequal occupational distribution as well. In fact, the problem with studies of sex discrimination and the source of a great deal of the controversy over their interpretation is based on the question of what factors legitimately constitute *objective* productivity differences between women and men. Many economists have argued that the occupational distribution does not qualify as such a factor, but based on the discussion in this section, it is apparent that *many* of the factors—e.g., education—which these studies regard as resulting from free choice are affected by discriminatory forces.

In general, this overview and critique of the use of economic methodology to analyze the market and non-market behavior of women leads us to several conclusions. First, as a feminist perspective on almost any discipline would suggest, it is important to focus on the similarities *and* differences between women and men. It is difficult but important to try to strike the appropriate balance between the two. Some of the examples discussed here illustrate this clearly. Traditional economic theory did not adequately explain women's experience because it did not address important differences between men and women—for example, the fact that women typically had to allocate time between market work, home work, and leisure, while for men the choice was between market work and leisure. Once these differences were recognized and incorporated into economic models, a better understanding of women's behavior became possible.

On the other hand, it is extremely important not to assume that these differences are immutable and unchanging. If it is accepted at the outset of the formulation of a theory that women's specialization in home production and lower pay are *givens*, then the logical outcome of the theory will be that this is an efficient mode of organizing behavior. If these assumptions are not challenged, or if economic differences between men and women are viewed as inevitable, then economic theory gets into the same vicious circle that Lloyd and Niemi use to describe women's secondary economic status. Further, this kind of theory will be a mechanism for legitimizing this status, rather than a force for constructive change.

IV. ECONOMIC POLICY AND THE STATUS OF WOMEN

The review and critique of economic theory in the previous section is interesting in its own right; it is intellectually challenging to critique a body of knowledge and way of thinking from a perspective not often taken by economists. A critical analysis of the theory is also of obvious importance from a policy perspective, since the theories are empirically tested and used as the basis for formulating policy that affects women.

Government policy is not formulated in a vacuum; if there are biases against women in society in general, or if specific theories are based on assumptions that are not objective, then economic policy will reflect these biases. Further, even though government policy can be used as an instrument of social change, in the realm of economic policy it is often the case that policy changes lag behind changes in attitudes and in economic and social institutions. Thus, an economic policy which was once well-suited to an earlier time may now have an adverse effect upon women if there has been a significant change in women's economic behavior.

There are many instances of bias and outmoded assumptions in government policy as it affects women in the U.S., and only a few will be considered here. The discussion will illustrate that, whether a particular policy is designed specifically to impact on women or not, biases inherent in it and opposition to changing it often have an adverse effect on women's economic status.

Two areas of government policy that affect virtually all members of society are the income tax system and the social security system. It can easily be determined that both programs have an adverse effect on women, and that the adverse effects result from the fact that programs are based upon an outdated and middle-class biased concept of the family. Both programs assume a "traditional" family with a wage-earning husband, homemaker wife, and dependent children. It is clear that this is no longer an accurate portrayal of the typical American household, and for many never has been; it is equally clear that policies which are based on this notion can have a negative impact on those that do not fit the mold.

The income tax system has an adverse effect on married women for two reasons. First, the unit of taxation is the family, and second, the tax system is progressive — that is, it taxes a larger percentage of the income from higher income families. What this means is that married women who are considering participating in the labor force face a higher rate of taxation. If her income and employment are regarded as secondary in the family unit, which is often the case, she will be paying taxes at the *highest* rate that applies to her husband's income. Since labor force participation decisions are motivated in part by wage rates, and the high tax rates effectively reduce wages, the system constitutes a potentially serious disincentive for married women to participate in the labor force.[9]

The bias toward the traditional family inherent in the system can also be seen by examining what happens to tax liability when individuals marry. Because the system is progressive, two individuals who marry and continue working may find that their tax liability increases simply as a result of marriage. This so-called marriage tax can be substantial in some cases — up to several thousand dollars a year for high-income couples. Moreover, the penalty is more severe the more equally split the earnings are.[10] It may seem paradoxical that a government policy that is based on the ideal of the family actually penalizes family formation, but the example clearly illustrates the traditional family bias.

It must be pointed out, to be fair to the government, that the increasing importance of the two-earner family has initiated a policy response. In 1981, when the income tax system was more progressive than it now is, legislation was passed to provide for a two-earner deduction to become fully effective by 1983. The law allowed for a tax deduction of 10 percent of the income of the lower-earning spouse up to a maximum of $3,000. The legislation was clearly intended to respond to claims of unfair tax treatment of married working couples by reducing their tax liability. While the policy has certainly helped, it has not eliminated the marriage penalty.

Unfortunately, in the new tax reform legislation, the two-earner deduction has been discontinued. The rationale given is that under the new tax system, tax rates are not as progressive; therefore the marriage penalty is less severe. While there is some truth to this argument, it is still based on the assumption that a woman's earnings are low relative to a man's, and that her earnings will not push the family into a higher tax bracket.

Similar kinds of disincentive and inequity effects exist in the impact of the social security system on women. Again, the problems occur largely because the system is based on what is now an outmoded view of the family—a wage earning husband and dependent wife. The retirement benefits received under social security are based on the concept of dependent or spouse benefits. A retired couple collects benefits based upon a worker's payments into the system plus 50 percent of the worker's benefits. Thus a woman who has never worked outside the home is still able to collect benefits based on her husband's record—a feature of the system applauded by some as recognition of the homemaker's economic contribution to the family.

The problem occurs for women who work outside the home. Upon retirement, they are eligible for spouse benefits or benefits based on their own earning records, but not both. Given the fact that women earn significantly less than men, and that historically their labor force participation has not been continuous, it is often the case that a woman's own benefits are not significantly better, and sometimes even worse, than her dependent benefits. This means that a married woman paying into the system receives little if anything back for those payments. As well as being inequitable, this situation creates disincentive effects for women; they realize that their wages will be reduced by social security taxes, for which they will receive little compensation in the future.

The impact of these two programs has so far been discussed in the context of effects on labor force participation. Yet, given the interconnections between market and non-market activity, the income tax and social security systems have implications for the non-market sphere as well. Since the programs are based upon a very traditional conception of ideal family structure and result in disincentives for women's participation in the labor force, their impact is to further perpetuate the traditional sex division of labor. The programs as they currently operate result in a systematic undervaluation by women—and society—of the perception of their market contributions.

The impact of government welfare policy on women in poverty has also been adverse, and this can be traced to the fact that policy is again based on the traditional notion of ideal family structure.

It is widely acknowledged that the poverty problem in the U.S. has become increasingly women's problem. In 1985, there were 33.1 million people living below the poverty line in the U.S., up from 24.1 million in 1969. Of those in poverty in 1985, 7.8 million were white children, 4.1 were black children, and 16.4 million people—almost half—were living in households headed by women (*Statistical Abstract*, 1986).

While the "feminization of poverty" is a widely recognized phenomenon, less attention has been focused on the root of the problem and constructive and humane solutions. Moreover, while existing welfare policy has been criticized, there have been no fundamental changes in AFDC, the major cash benefit program, since its inception.

The welfare system is based on the outdated concept that women who are mothers should not hold paid jobs outside the home. Thus, when fathers are absent, the welfare system essentially results in the government playing a surrogate father role in a financed sense, providing low-income single mothers with cash benefits, food stamps, medical care, and, in some cases, subsidized housing. The government's replacement of the traditional male breadwinner's role thus tends to perpetuate the notion of female dependency.

Some critics of welfare policy have argued that our present system has made it more difficult for women to break out of the cycle of poverty and welfare dependency and has had the effect of increasing the incidence of poverty among households headed by women. There is some truth to these arguments, but their implications for women and for welfare policy reform need to be carefully scrutinized, for if they are not, they can be used to blame the victims — the women themselves — and to reform the system in ways that make women even worse off than they are under the present system.

There is no doubt that our welfare system does represent a welfare trap for many of the women who participate in its programs. However, the nature of the trap must be made clear. Welfare benefits are not even sufficient to provide a poverty-line standard of living in many cases, yet they are often preferable to other alternatives. For one thing, cash benefits are often not significantly less than what a woman could earn at a minimum wage job; this is particularly important given the erratic and undependable nature of such employment. Perhaps more important are the non-cash benefits for which welfare mothers are eligible — food stamps and medical benefits — which provide a significant increase in living standards. When a single mother compares these benefits, however inadequate, with the income that can be earned in a low-paying job, after taking into consideration the uncertainty of such employment, child care, transportation and clothing costs, and the loss of time that can be devoted to non-market responsibilities, remaining on welfare often appears to be the lesser of two evils. Making this choice is often reinforced by difficultly in certifying one's eligibility for welfare programs, and by the reduction in welfare benefits that accompany any paid employment.[11]

While most of these problems with the system are widely acknowledged, there has been no significant attempt to reform its basic nature, nor have there been concerted efforts by policy-makers to force a higher level of support from absent fathers as an alternative to welfare dependency. Even a fundamental reform of the system would not, however, address one crucial issue: no welfare program can truly solve women's poverty problems. It can only attempt to relieve some of the symptoms and improve to a small extent the material quality of life. Solutions to the problem itself require recognition that women with children no longer fit into the traditional mold of the dependent housewife, and that what women in poverty really need are labor force opportunities that provide them with adequate incomes with which to support their families. This leads us to the question of what government policy has accomplished in terms of combating discrimination and equalizing labor market opportunities. Answers to this question represent perhaps the most controversial aspect of government policy as it relates to women, and the controversy can be expected to persist. Although government policy affecting women's employment has a fairly long history, most of the early legislation was of a protectionist nature; it was not until the early 1960s that government policy was formulated with equal pay and equal opportunity as explicit goals. The appropriate form for such legislation, its effectiveness in improving the labor market status of women, and the direction for future policy all depend to an extent upon the theories of labor market behavior to which one subscribes.

The first major piece of legislation affecting women's employment directly was the Equal Pay Act of 1963. The Act "requires that employees performing equal work be paid equal wages regardless of sex" (Wallace, 1976, p. 125). The impact of the law in terms of decreasing the wage gap between men and women is likely to have been very small, simply because men and women so infrequently perform the same jobs. The purpose of the law is clearly to outlaw overt discrimination, but there are so many aspects of discrimination in other areas of employment and so many institutional barriers in the labor market that are not addressed by the Equal Pay Act that it is not likely that it would go very far in terms of eliminating wage differences.

This narrow focus is largely avoided in the Civil Rights Act of 1964. Title VII of the Act makes it illegal "for an employer covered by the law to (1) fail or refuse to hire or discharge any individual or otherwise to discriminate against any individual with respect to his compensation terms, conditions or privileges of employment . . . or (2) to limit, segregate, or classify his employees in any way which would deprive or tend to deprive any individual of employment opportunity or otherwise adversely affect his status as an employee" (Lloyd & Niemi, 1979, p. 289). Clearly, many more types of discriminatory behavior are covered by this legislation. Probably more important, the law stresses equality of *opportunity*, not just equal treatment for individuals whose productivity and position may be affected by unequal opportunity.

Theoretically, this legislation should address the secondary economic status of women arising from the institutional division of the labor market into primary and secondary sectors, as well as the problems arising from women acquiring less human capital as a result of unequal opportunity. Title VII does not simply prohibit wage discrimination, it also makes it illegal to deny access to jobs or training on the basis of sex alone.

As a practical matter, of course, eliminating these sources of inequality in the labor market is considerably more difficult. Initial enforcement of the legislation showed that it was ambiguous with respect to when employers could legitimately use sex as a basis for excluding people from certain labor market opportunities. This ambiguity resulted in decisions that make it very difficult to use sex — for example, sex differences in *average* labor market characteristics — as a basis for job assignment or other employment decisions. However, enforcement problems remain; it is a very costly process to accuse an employer of sex discrimination and get the claim settled, and the way in which this is presently being done increases the cost still further.

Even if we could assume the practical problems away, however, it is doubtful that the legislation described so far would eliminate the labor market differences between women and men. In an otherwise ideal world, aggressive enforcement of and complete compliance with the laws would not solve the problem because the laws do not confront the cumulative, dynamic impact of discrimination and labor market institutions on women's labor market status. Such legislation prohibits discrimination solely on the basis of sex *today* and in the future, but it does not make it illegal to make employment decisions on the basis of objective individual data on productivity, even if that productivity is based on past and continuing subtle forms of discrimination.

This is, at least in part, the rationale for affirmative action legislation. As it relates to women, the history of affirmative action policy dates back to 1968 and an executive order signed by President Johnson. The order requires that all firms doing business with the federal government refrain from discriminatory employment practices, and "take affirmative action to ensure that applicants are employed, and that employees are treated during their employment without regard to their race, color, religion, sex or national origin" (Warren, 1980, p. 11).

As stated, such a policy appears to be innocuous, and one which would not arouse much controversy. Yet, affirmative action is a controversial issue, primarily because many contend that it implies preferential treatment at best and reverse discrimination at worst. In fact, this view has some basis in the law, since in 1971 it was ordered that employers "determine if women and minorities are underemployed and set numerical *goals* and timetables by job classification and organization unit to correct any deficiencies" (Lloyd & Niemi, 1979, p. 290). Whether or not this constitutes reverse discrimination depends greatly on the way in which it is accomplished, which is an issue that will be returned to shortly.

In terms of the previous theoretical analysis of labor markets, the practical and conceptual consequences of affirmative action policies are clear. Such policies are intended to compensate certain groups for the injustices of past discrimination by opening up previously white male-dominated fields to women and minorities. These past injustices are manifested in supply and demand conditions in various labor markets which have been affected by discrimination and denial of equal opportunity. Affirmative action policies represent an attempt to restore a greater degree of competitiveness to labor markets—that is, to move the demand for women workers and the supply of women workers to where they would be if it were not for the effects of past discrimination. Put in these terms the theoretical rationale for affirmative action is clear, both in terms of fairness, and in terms of the most productive use of resources.

Why, then, does the controversy over affirmative action persist? Partly, it is a result of the way in which policies are implemented, and of the implications of implementation procedures for the qualifications of individuals hired. The goals and timetables required by affirmative action are often interpreted (correctly in some cases, incorrectly in others) as *quotas* — that is, reserving a certain number of job or promotion slots for the disadvantaged group. The use of quotas is often interpreted as inequitable (giving less-qualified people preference over more-qualified people) and inefficient (lowering standards required to perform certain jobs). Opponents of affirmative action argue that "quotas imply that women and minorities are not as well qualified, that they are unable to compete on their merits" (Warren, 1980, p. 13). Both of these criticisms, however, rest on the faulty assumptions that (1) affirmative action *requires* reverse discrimination and quotas, which it does not, and that (2) previous legislation has rendered labor markets free of discrimination so that women are truly given the opportunity to compete on the basis of their own qualifications.

The controversy over affirmative action thus continues, and is likely to intensify in the very near future; in spite of Supreme Court affirmation of the concept, the Justice Department is currently involved in efforts to overturn the Executive Order that mandated it. In addition to this policy debate, there is a relatively new policy concept that is drawing increasing attention: comparable worth.

As defined by Steinberg (1984), "comparable worth concerns the issue of whether work done primarily by women and minorities is systematically undervalued because the work has been and continues to be done by women and minorities" (p. 3). A policy of comparable worth would develop a technique for assessing the worth of various jobs to an employer, assign each job a quantitative ranking, and then determine wages for each job in accordance with the rankings.

In theory, the concept of comparable worth appears to be a fairly simple and reasonable one, but despite the fact that there has been considerable debate over its philosophical, economic, and legal implications over the past several years, its status as a policy with the potential for significantly improving the economic status of women is by no means certain. There have been some legal victories for comparable worth, and some labor organizations have adopted it voluntarily, but some major legal setbacks have also occurred.

Proponents of comparable worth argue that it is not a coincidence that jobs which are held predominantly by women and minorities pay less than jobs held primarily by white men. Further, they believe that it is not true that jobs held by women are uniformly worth less from an employer's standpoint. Rather, the existence of wage differences between women and men, according to proponents, is a result of sex discrimination and stereotyping which segregates women into certain occupations and limits their opportunity to acquire human capital. Simply enforcing existing legislation will not end these differences because they will not eliminate the stereotypes or divisions in the labor market. Comparable worth is viewed as a mechanism by which some of these barriers may be lowered.

Those who oppose the concept of comparable worth do so mostly on the basis of a belief in the primacy of the market system. They argue that comparable worth is not justified or necessary and, indeed, will wreak havoc with the operation of the labor market. Opponents find no problem with the fact that women's jobs pay less than men's jobs. They argue that women enter certain occupations as a result of free, rational choice, and that if the operation of the labor market on the basis of these choices results in lower pay for women, it does not mean that women are underpaid for the work they do.

Further, opponents argue that the whole concept of job evaluation which is central to comparable worth is based on the incorrect notion that jobs have certain intrinsic value. Critics argue that "there simply is no inherent value to a job just as there is no inherent value to an ounce of gold or an acre of real estate. A thing is worth what people are willing to pay for it, and labor is no different. Compensation is a function of the supply of and demand for labor" (Gold, 1983, p. 44). On the basis of this argument, comparable worth opponents contend that widespread adoption of a plan which ties wages to job evaluations will destroy the ability of the labor market to efficiently allocate resources. They object that "comparable worth focuses on the demand side of the labor market to the exclusion of the supply side" (Gold, 1983, p. 43), and that shortages and surpluses of various types of workers will result with comparable worth, unless widespread government intervention in the labor market prevents it.

This brief discussion of opposing viewpoints on comparable worth should indicate clearly that the debate over its appropriateness as a means of raising women's economic status is not likely to subside in the near future. Comparable worth, like the other policies designed to improve women's status, must be debated and evaluated in the context of a very crucial question: is the labor market competitive?

The answer to this question is of major importance because criticisms of policy are very much dependent on the assumption that labor markets are competitive. If the assumption is faulty, then the criticism that the policies are unnecessary and unjustified and, as some authors claim, even harmful to women, are not valid. Yet some critics have based their entire argument on the assumption of a competitive market. For example, McKenzie and Tullock (1978) have argued, with respect to equal pay legislation, that "effective enforcement of the law can reduce the employment opportunities of women and expand the opportunities of men" (p. 108). Further, some critics have argued that "comparable worth may well be counterproductive for women in the long run . . . (it) will widen the earnings gap by exacerbating occupational concentration" (Gold, 1983, p. 56).

These criticisms seem to overlook two important points. First, while in general terms the supply and demand for labor in large part do determine wages, both casual observation and more sophisticated empirical evidence overwhelmingly point to the fact that women and men operate in different labor markets. As Gold (1983) points out, "You assume the labor market operates the same way for women as for men. In fact, it does not. Men are not socialized into preparing for low-paying work before they enter the labor market; men are not excluded from high-paying work once they are in the market; and men are not crowded into a small number of occupations. The value of labor may be its price in a free market, but women are not part of a free market" (p. 45).

The second point is that changes in policy and changes in the labor market are not independent. While it is true that the government cannot legislate away sexual stereotyping and prejudice, it is certainly possible that eventually a change in policy will be translated into changes in attitudes and labor market behavior.

In fact this relationship between policy and attitudes and behavior is of crucial importance to all government policy and its impact on women. If policies are based on outdated values or stereotypes, then these policies will reinforce existing attitudes and patterns of behavior, and the vicious circle referred to by so many authors to characterize women's secondary economic status will remain in motion. To break this circle therefore requires that policy be viewed as a force for constructive change. The extent to which such policy can be formulated depends upon the development of new, and critique of existing, theory and methods of testing it. The possibilities for doing this will be discussed in the concluding section of this chapter.

V. SUMMARY, CONCLUSIONS, AND PROSPECTS FOR CHANGE

The purpose of this chapter was to present the economist's image of woman and her market and non-market behavior in our society. It attempted to critique the way in which economists view and analyze women by considering the limitations of data and methodology. The types of data collected, the way in which they are interpreted, and the assumptions implicit in the development and testing of economic models were all shown to result in an image of women that is somewhat lacking in three respects. First is the relative lack of economic analysis of activities outside the market which have traditionally been performed primarily by women. Second is the fact that some economic analysis cannot adequately understand women's behavior because the tools used to model such behavior do not take into account differences between women and men. Third, assumptions that women *should* behave differently than men and that their economic behavior is motivated by different factors often get built into economic models with the result that theory can be, and often is, used to reinforce the status quo.

The relationship between economic theory and empirical testing and the formulation of policy as it affects women was also discussed. This relationship is an important one from a practical standpoint. It is also important because analysis of policy and the way in which it is justified on the basis of theory and empirical evidence often serves as a mechanism for illuminating flaws and biases in the theory itself. In addition, study of the impact of policy on women can serve as a vehicle for the development and testing of new theory and ultimately better policy.

There are two questions that remain to be answered here. First, what does the analysis tell us about the current status of economic analysis as it pertains to women, and its implications for women's economic status in society? Second, what are the prospects for change? Ideally, feminist scholarship will integrate itself with more traditional economic analysis, with the result that women no longer will be regarded as special topics or the subject of special courses. If and when this occurs, it should have several positive implications.

First, if scholarship by and about women is regarded as an integral part of economic scholarship and not as a separate body of knowledge, the new research that adequately captures the experience and perspective of all women should lead to the development of better theory and methodology. Given the link between theory and policy, this should lead to the implementation of better policy and, finally, to improved economic status for women.

With respect to the current situation, the statistical overview presented here clearly indicates that women's economic status has changed very little over the past few decades, at least in an aggregate sense. The data presented here are no doubt very discouraging, but they do serve some useful purposes. First, they point out the common misconception that women face no problems in the labor force. It is frequently the case that individual success stories of women are used to justify the belief that women are not discriminated against and that they enjoy the same economic status as men. Even a superficial examination of the data indicates that this is not true, and that there are significant problems that need to be addressed.

Further, the fact that the earnings differential and occupational distribution have proven so resistant to change in the face of changing factors that would be expected to exert an influence has stimulated the development of new theory and methodology. When the predictions of traditional theories have failed to fit economic reality, new theories and ways of testing them have been developed.

Some progress has been made. New theories and bodies of empirical evidence represent positive steps in the direction of using economic analysis to better understand women's behavior, and using the analysis as a basis for formulating policies that can improve women's economic status. Such advances have not been free of problems, however. Particularly in the area of the "New Home Economics," many economists still view such analysis as being on the fringes of the discipline, and not being "real" economics. Thus, the results of such work are often viewed with a degree of skepticism. Indeed, the same view of this work is often held by non-economists, who argue that marriage and family matters are not aspects of people's lives that should be subjected to economic analysis. While the limitations clearly do need to be recognized, it is important that these be regarded as legitimate areas of inquiry.

Further, even though this type of analysis implies that women are the topic of more economic analysis than used to be the case, the way in which such analysis is interpreted often causes some serious problems in the way women are perceived. To simply have the tools to analyze women's behavior is not sufficient; the assumptions and value judgments which govern the way they are used and the way in which the results are interpreted must also be changed. This change, if interpretation of current literature and policy discussion is any guide, has not yet occurred on a widespread basis.

The trend does seem to move, however slowly, in the right direction though. The increasing participation of women in the labor force has been accompanied by more research on women and by women. Moreover, an increasing emphasis seems to be placed on research that challenges traditional analysis.[12] Probably most important from the standpoint of the perceived legitimacy of research on women, such analysis is published in respected journals in the field.[13]

As far as curricular issues are concerned, the picture is mixed. If economic analysis of women and by women was viewed as simply economic analysis, there would be no need to have separate courses on women in the curriculum. Economics as a discipline has clearly not yet reached this stage. There are separate courses on women, and in all likelihood more now than there were ten or fifteen years ago. There are also many more textbooks on the subject than there were even five or six years ago. The compartmentalizing of women's issues in separate courses is a cause for some concern. This concern, though, needs to be weighed against the advantages that such courses provide. If an increase in the number of economics courses about women signifies a heightened awareness of women's issues and problems, and a greater recognition that these problems are not adequately considered in traditional courses, then we should over time see this reflected in traditional courses. My perception is that women are more frequently studied in courses on government policy, labor economics, and economic development. One can only hope that the trend will continue, and that it will be facilitated by more and better research by and about women.

FOOTNOTES

1. The *Statistical Abstract* indicates that, in 1982, only 14.2% of the Ph.Ds in economics were awarded to women.
2. The way in which data are classified and tabulated is described in U.S. Department of Commerce, Bureau of the Census, *1980 Census of Population*, xii.
3. See Lloyd and Niemi, chapter 2, for a discussion of this research.
4. The first major attempt to extend the decision-making model was made by Mincer, J. (1962). Labor Force Participation of Married Women: A Study of Labor Supply. In H.G. Lewis (Ed.), *Aspects of Labor Economics* (pp. 63-105). Princeton, NJ: Princeton University Press.
5. See, for example, Tullock and McKenzie, chapters 5 and 6.
6. The major work that presents a human capital perspective on women's occupational choice is Polachek, S. (1979). Occupational Segregation Among Women: Theory, Evidence and a Prognosis. In Lloyd, C., Andrews, E., & Gilroy, C. (Eds.), *Women in the Labor Market* (pp. 137-57) New York: Columbia University Press. For a critique and new empirical evidence, see England, P. (1982). The Failure of Human Capital Theory to Explain Occupational Segregation. *Journal of Human Resources, 28*, 538-70.
7. See, for example, the discussion in Gold, M.E. (1983). *A Dialogue on Comparable Worth*. New York: ILR Press, Cornell University. 21-26.
8. For a discussion and quantitative summary of the major empirical studies on sex discrimination, see Lloyd and Niemi, chapter 5.
9. Empirical analysis has supported the hypothesis that the tax system results in a significant disincentive effect for married women. See, for example, Leuthold, J. (1976). The Effect of Taxation on the Hours Worked by Married Women. *Industrial and Labor Relations Review 31*, 520-26.
10. For some numerical illustrations of the penalty based on 1978 tax law, see Gordon, N.M. (1979). Institutional Responses: The Federal Income Tax System. In R. Smith (Ed.), *The Subtle Revolution: Women at Work* (pp. 201-22). Washington: Urban Institute Press.
11. For a more detailed discussion of these issues, see Bergmann, chapter 10.

12. England's recent critique of human capital theory cited above is a good example of this.

13. Ferber and Teiman make some interesting observations about the representation of women and feminist scholarship in leading economic journals. They point out that women's scholarship is becoming more prominent, but also that women scholars fare better when journal referees do not know the sex of the author.

REFERENCES

Becker, G. (1965). A theory of the allocation of time. *Economic Journal, 75,* 493-517.

Becker, G. (1976). *The economic approach to human behavior.* Chicago: University of Chicago Press.

Bergmann, B. (1986). *The economic emergence of women.* New York: Basic Books.

England, P. (1982). The failure of human capital theory to explain occupational segregation. *Journal of Human Resources, 28,* 538-570.

Faulkner, C. (1986). The feminist challenge to economics. *Frontiers, 8,* 55-61.

Ferber, M., & Teiman, M. (1981). The oldest, the most established, the most quantitative of the social sciences — and the most dominated by men: The impact of feminism on economics. In D. Spender (Ed.), *Men's studies modified* (pp. 125-140). New York: Pergamon Press.

Gold, M.E. (1983). *A dialogue on comparable worth.* New York: ILR Press.

Gordon, N.M. (1979). Institutional responses: The federal income tax system. In R. Smith (Ed.), *The subtle revolution: Women at work* (pp. 201-222). Washington: Urban Institute Press.

Leuthold, J. (1976). The effect of taxation on the hours worked by married women. *Industrial and Labor Relations Review, 31,* 520-526.

Lloyd, C., & Niemi, B. (1979). *The economics of sex differentials.* New York: Columbia University Press.

Mincer, J. (1962). Labor force participation of married women: A study of labor supply. In H.G. Lewis (Ed.), *Aspects of labor economics* (pp. 63-105). Princeton: Princeton University Press.

Peterson, W.E. (1973). *Elements of economics.* New York: Norton.

Polachek, S. (1979). Occupational segregation among women: Theory, evidence and a prognosis. In C. Lloyd, C. Andrews, & C. Gilroy (Eds.), *Women in the labor market* (pp. 137-157). New York: Columbia University Press.

Santos, F.P. (1975). The economics of marital status. In C. Lloyd (Ed.), *Sex discrimination and the division of labor* (pp. 244-268). New York: Columbia University Press.

Sawhill, I.V. (1977). Economic perspectives on the family. *Daedalus, 106,* 115-125.

Statistical Abstract of the United States. (1986). Prepared by the Chief of the Bureau of Statistics, Treasury Department, Washington: G.P.O.

Steinberg, R.J. (1984). "A want of harmony": Perspectives on wage discrimination and comparable worth. In H. Remick (Ed.), *Comparable worth and wage discrimination* (pp. 3-27). Philadelphia: Temple University Press.

Tullock, T.G., & McKenzie, R. (1984). *The new world of economics*. Homewood, IL: Irwin.

U.S. Department of Commerce, Bureau of the Census, *1980 Census of Population*.

U.S. Department of Commerce, Bureau of the Census, *Statistical Abstract, 1984 and 1986*.

Wallace, P.A. (1976). Impact of equal opportunity laws. In J.M. Kreps (Ed.), *Women and the American economy: A look to the 1980s* (p. 125). New Jersey: Prentice-Hall.

Warren, M.A. (1980). *The nature of woman*. Inverness, CA: Edgepress.

"Men Do Not Do Housework": The Image of Women in Political Science

Gertrude A. Steuernagel

INTRODUCTION

Political science, Aristotle wrote, is the "master science." A more appropriate term might well have been the "masters' science." The "real world" of politics has traditionally been viewed as a "man's game"; and political science, until relatively recently, has accepted rather than challenged this understanding. Tragically, this has limited the development of political science as a discipline and has affected how we as citizens look at politics and conduct our political lives. Fortunately, due in part to feminist challenges, political science is currently in the process of changing itself; and, hopefully, these changes will also affect our understanding of politics and citizenship. For far too long a time, we have been satisfied with defining politics in very narrow terms. To speak of politics is to speak of government, and to study political science is to study "who gets what, why, and how." A measure of the success of the feminist challenge to political science is the extent to which we broaden our ideas of politics and citizenship.

This essay is an examination of the major feminist challenges to political science. It will deal with the images of women presented in the classical and modern traditions which inform political science as well as the feminist correctives to these images. It will also consider the future of political science and its responses to these challenges. Part One of the essay provides an overview of the images of women which have dominated political science. Part Two presents a summary of some of the key feminist challenges to these images; and finally, Part Three serves to suggest some future directions for the integration of these feminist correctives into the research agenda and the teaching curriculum of political science.

PART ONE

Political science as a discipline has always been a house with many rooms. It traditionally has prided itself on accommodating a variety of theoretical and methodological approaches to the study of political life. There are political scientists who study relationships among nation-states, political scientists who study why people vote as they do, political scientists who study how a bill becomes a law, and political scientists who study the meaning of justice. Each political scientist must select the research methodology or methodologies appropriate for the topic under study. A political scientist interested in voting behavior, for example, might engage in large-scale survey research projects, while a political scientist concerned with the meaning of justice might satisfy herself with contemplating what is involved with being a just person and performing just actions. Nevertheless, political science, like any discipline, has a core set of concepts and assumptions which serve to define its scope and methods. Discussions of justice, equality, liberty, and power, for example, have traditionally been the lot of political scientists. Thinking about politics, of course, is always affected by the particular historical period in which the individual lives. Modern political scientists have very different lives than their classical forebears, and their ideas concerning politics are affected accordingly. All in all, however, how political scientists have defined women and their proper relationship to political life has remained relatively constant over time. Modern political scientists operate according to a set of images of women which can be traced to an earlier period. Although we have discarded many of the classical ideas concerning politics and citizenship, we—for the most part—have retained an image of women and their relationship to political life which has undergone little if any alteration since the days of its inception.

Surely one of the first political thinkers was Socrates (469-399 B.C.). Although he did not write anything, his ideas have had a major influence on political thinking, in large part due to the efforts of his most famous student, Plato (427-347 B.C.). It is in Plato's most notable work, the *Republic* (1972), that one of the classical images of women emerges, an image which can be found in the work of many feminist political scientists. In the *Republic*, Plato, through the character of Socrates, argues that men and women alike may be capable of ruling as members of the elite class, the Guardians. Gender, for Socrates, is an irrelevant characteristic in terms of fitness for rule. What does matter is a person's natural ability combined with proper education and training. This, of course, was a radical idea for its time, and in the *Republic* Socrates is forced to defend his proposal. He remains firm in his conviction that only relevant characteristics should be considered when assigning functions and that gender was not relevant to ruling. In Socrates' words:

> To conclude, then, there is no occupation concerned with the management of social affairs which belongs either to woman or to man, as such. Natural gifts are to be found here and there in both creatures alike, and every occupation is open to both, so far as their natures are concerned, though woman is for all purposes the weaker. (p. 153)

Interestingly, some contemporary political philosophers have been reluctant to take Plato's ideas on women and their fitness for rule at face value. One of the foremost translators of the *Republic* and the author of an extremely influential interpretative essay on that work has argued that Plato never intended these comments to be taken seriously (Bloom, 1968). It is his contention that Plato was simply kidding when he offered this proposal and was trying to show that his mentor Socrates could outdo the comic poets, who often ridiculed him, at their own game (p. 380).

Plato's image of woman as ruler was not to prove to be very influential. Even his most famous student, Aristotle (384-322 B.C.), rejected the idea that women might serve as Guardians. Women, according to Aristotle, were inferior to men. As such, they were not fit for citizenship much less for ruling, but they did, however, have an important role to play in the life of the city. The quality of a city, according to Aristotle, was affected by the quality of its women and children. A good city required goodness in its women and children (1962, p. 54). Likewise, unruly women could contribute to the downfall into tyranny of a city (p. 244). Aristotle was concerned enough about the character of women that he even wrote about the importance of maintaining an official office designated "Controller of Women" (p. 185). Women could best contribute to the life of the city by attending to household concerns. Any "role reversal" would be disastrous and unnatural, since, as Aristotle noted, "men do not do housework" (p. 67). Husbands and wives are to control the areas appropriate to them. It is wrong for wives to concern themselves with politics and for husbands to interfere with the running of the household.

It is the inductive Aristotle rather than the deductive Plato who has had the greater influence on the development of modern political science. Aristotle's interests in natural science have been viewed as more compatible with the overall direction of political science than Plato's more metaphysical speculations. Although political science has always made room for political philosophers in the mode of Plato, the field as a whole has always felt a greater kinship for Aristotle. Not surprisingly, Aristotle's image of women has been integrated along with his scientific orientation into modern political science. Only in recent years — with the coming of the feminist challenge to political science — has the Platonic image reasserted itself. This, of course, in no way implies that feminist political scientists are Platonists. Feminist political scientists, if anything, are amazingly diverse in their political and professional orientations, and are not even of a like-mind when it comes to interpreting Plato! (Steuernagel, 1983). Still, feminist political scientists *are* unified in their challenge to the image of women which informs their discipline.

Most empirical research on women and politics is less than twenty years old. Accordingly, the image of women which informed modern political science was based almost exclusively on "conventional wisdom" (Githens, 1983, p. 471). Even the empirical research itself did not result in a consensus image. Still, it is possible to identify a generalized image of women which dominated modern political science. Women, as depicted in the literature of political science, are not as interested in politics as men. They do not vote as often; they have lower levels of political information;

and they are less likely than men to attempt to persuade others to adopt their political views. Women do not feel as politically efficacious as men, that is to say, they are not as convinced as men that what they can do will matter politically (Campbell, Converse, Miller, & Stokes, 1964, p. 259). Women, it was argued, particularly women with small children, were unable or unwilling to take the time from their private lives and devote it to politics (Campbell et al., p. 260). Furthermore, the evidence suggested that both men and women tended as children to acquire "sex role appropriate" political attitudes. In other words, girls learn that politics is for boys. The political socialization literature also suggested that girls are more favorably disposed than boys towards our political system and tend to be more fond of political leaders than boys (Hess & Torney, 1967). Boys have more political information and turn to their fathers for political advice (Greenstein, 1965). Girls, who were less interested in politics overall than boys (Hyman, 1959), were also found to be more interested in the "soft" issue of peace than the "hard" issue of the economy, a topic which interested the boys (Iglitzen, 1974).

Much of this research also drew a connection between childhood attitudes and behaviors and their adult equivalents. The little girls who were interested in peace grew up to be women who paid more attention to this kind of thing than the economy and defense. The gender gap existed for young and old alike. Indeed, the conventional wisdom also had it that women retained their girlish, personalized view of politics and looked more to candidates than issues in deciding how to vote (Jaquette, 1974, p. xx). If women are interested in politics, it tends to be in the sorts of issues that relate to their roles as wives and mothers, e.g., school board, libraries, and the like. They also tend to follow their husbands' lead in deciding which party to support.

Lest the erroneous conclusion be drawn that women were central to political science research, it is important to note that very little attention, all in all, has been paid to the issue of women and politics by modern practitioners of political science. The research that was done in political science prior to the late 1960s by and large ignored the variable of sex (Githens, 1983, p. 471). Since women were not present in great numbers among the ranks of the political elites,

defined as those who hold elected or appointed governmental offices, they were not thought to be very important to political life or
to an understanding of politics. Women, to borrow from an important work of the mid-1970s, were a "portrait of marginality" when
it came to politics (Githens & Prestage, 1977).

To summarize. When political scientists thought about women
and politics at all, they thought about women in terms appropriate
to broader social conventions Women, whom in general were conceived of as more passive and home-centered than men, were no
different when it came to politics. The Aristotelean image of
women had both its descriptive and prescriptive elements. For Aristotle, women were found in the home and belonged there by nature.
Even though modern political scientists might reject the prescriptive
element of Aristotle's image of women, they by and large accepted
the descriptive image. Political scientists were comfortable making
generalizations which simply were not consistent with or supported
by the little data they had available. As a substitute for such information they returned consistently to the image of women in their
broader culture, an image indebted to Aristotle and his ideas of
women. To the extent that political scientists did receive information on women and their political behavior, they proceeded, for the
most part, to interpret it in terms of theoretical frameworks developed in an era of pre-gender research (Githens, 1983, p. 472). Empirical research and concomitant rethinking of theory regarding
women and politics did not immediately find a place in mainstream
political science. In the period from 1976 through 1978, for example, the *American Political Science Review* — the major U.S. political science forum — contained no articles dealing specifically with
women (Carroll, 1979, p. 290). Some feminist political scientists
despaired that political science could or would be as responsive to
feminist challenges as fellow social science disciplines (Carroll,
1979, p. 305; Jaquette, 1974, p. v). Since political science historically concerned itself primarily with governmental and military institutions and the behaviors of their key actors, it appeared that
women would continue to be on the periphery of political life and
political research. Unless. . . .

PART TWO

Wilma Rule Krauss' 1974 *American Political Science Review*, essay, "Political Implications of Gender Roles," heralded the arrival of the feminist challenge to mainstream political science. The years that followed Krauss' work have witnessed a number of changes in both the feminist challenge and the discipline of political science itself. Despite the diversity and complexity of the feminist challenge, it has succeeded — at the very least — in shaking the foundations of the image of women that has informed political science. The feminist correctives to this image are numerous, and their history constitutes an important chapter in the development of political science.

Today, from the perspective of many feminist political scientists, Krauss' essay is seen as more of a symbolic than a substantive contribution to efforts to reform their discipline. Krauss succeeded in establishing the centrality of gender to the project of political science. She did not, however, go much beyond a broad hint that research on gender would involve a major challenge to our thinking about political life and research (p. 1719). Basically, Krauss emphasized that women's political behavior was consistent with their broader sex roles. Generally, women are more passive than men; and their political behavior, she noted, is simply a reflection of this. For Krauss, women would participate more actively in politics if their broader gender roles were expanded. That is to say, if we begin to expand our image of "appropriate" female behavior to include the male domain of politics, we will see increased political participation by women (p. 1710). For all intents and purposes, Krauss seemed content to retain as her own the traditional definition of politics. She gave little if any indication of linking a new understanding of women's political behavior to a broader definition of politics. "Politics," for Krauss, is maintained as a term limited to formal governmental institutions and the behavior of actors within them. She refers, for example, to occupations such as elementary school teaching, library work, and social work as "non-politically relevant feminine occupations" (p. 1708). In contrast, many feminists post-Krauss have noted that the image of women as politically passive is as linked to a faulty understanding of politics as it is to any actual behaviors exhibited (or not exhibited) by women. Current feminist correctives to political science appear in the form of challenges to rethink definitions of politics and political behavior.

Kay Boals' 1975 *Signs* essay, for example, argued for a reconceptualization of politics from competition for power "toward conceptions that are oriented to shared values and interpersonal relationships" (pp. 171-172). Any feminist scholarship, according to Boals, should perform the following three functions: "the expansion of empirical knowledge, the critique of existing theory, and the reconceptualization of core concepts" (p. 161). Political science, as she assessed it, had begun to compile more empirical information on women, but the data available were inadequate to draw any definitive conclusions about women's political behavior. In addition, the challenges that feminists were raising to the methods used by political scientists to conduct research and the conclusions based on the data they were gathering were, for Boals, indications that the second task of feminist research was beginning to come to fruition in political science.

Researchers were noting, for example, that the kinds of questionnaires used by some political scientists guaranteed that the results would reveal politically passive women. Boals cites examples from political socialization literature in which the studies themselves reinforced sex role stereotyping of politics as a male world "by their use of pronouns, choice of pictures, and direction of questions to the father's, but not the mother's relations to politics" (p. 161). She also notes the efforts of researchers to force political scientists to rethink some of the generalizations they draw from the available empirical data. Why, for example, do these researchers tend to emphasize what is negative about women's political behavior and attitudes rather than focusing on some of the positive aspects (volunteerism) or the negative aspects of male behavior (win at any cost)? (p. 169).

The third task of feminist scholarship, the generation of new paradigms, was in its infant phase — according to Boals — in respect to political science. Most important, she noted, is our adoption of a definition of politics as "any human relationship, at any level from the intrapsychic to the international, provided it can be shaped and altered by human decision and action" (p. 171).

To what extent have feminist scholars implemented Boals' suggested agenda and to what extent has political science responded to and incorporated this feminist challenge? In many ways, Boals' assessment concerning the accumulation of information on women's political behavior remains timely. Although scholars do not neglect women in their studies, the fields of political socialization and political elites—two areas targeted by Boals for further study—have over the last ten years become relatively neglected subfields of the discipline. Neither, for example, warranted a separate chapter in the widely used American Political Science Association sponsored, *Political Science: The State of the Discipline* (Finifter, 1983).

Feminist political scientists have, however, done a great deal of work in response to the second task of Boals' agenda, the critique of existing theory. Studies by Welch (1977), Shabad and Andersen (1979), and Andersen and Cook (1985) are representative of such efforts.

Welch submitted to empirical testing the widely accepted explanation that women participate politically less than men because they are socialized into passive roles. After examining the data, Welch concluded "[O]ur analysis has shown that the stereotype of the politically passive woman simply is untrue" (p. 732). Women, she contends, have lower levels of participation in some areas than men not because of beliefs they hold about their roles but because they are not as likely as men to be found among groups who do participate in politics, namely the employed and the highly educated (pp. 726-728). Gender, in other words, does not determine levels of political participation. Employed, educated people participate. Educated, employed women participate.

Studies performed subsequent to Welch's work have supported her interpretation. An examination of 1980 presidential election data, for example, revealed that education was a better predictor of vote than gender (Poole & Zeigler, 1985, p. 52). Moreover, it is also becoming clear to researchers that a sense of political efficacy, a factor which is usually linked to males and their greater levels of participation, is a function of employment and education rather than gender. Employed men and women demonstrate similar levels of political efficacy (Poole & Zeigler, pp. 137-138) as do educated men and women (Poole & Zeigler, p. 138).

Shabad and Andersen (1979) examined the "widely accepted" generalization that "women tend to personalize politics and politicians" (p. 18). Women, according to this perspective, look at candidates' personal attributes *rather* than their positions on issues. As Shabad and Andersen note, this is considered in the literature of political science to be "irrational," "apolitical," or "naive" (p. 18).

One surprising finding of their study was that this generalization could be traced to a single source, a 1954 work entitled *The Voter Decides* authored by Campbell, Gurin, and Miller (p. 18). A reexamination by Shabad and Andersen of the *Voter Decides* data did not reveal, in their estimation, large sex-differences in respect to candidate-responses and issue-responses. In other words, Shabad and Andersen found that men and women tend to evaluate candidates in a similar fashion. Women were not very likely to look more at personal qualities than issue positions when choosing candidates to support (p. 19). How then, can we explain the persistence of this myth that women personalize politics when even the major single source of empirical evidence is so inconclusive? Shabad and Andersen suggest that the myth was accepted because it was consistent with socialization studies which showed a more "personalistic" orientation to politics among girls than boys (p. 20). Interestingly, a detailed examination of the political socialization literature itself reveals little empirical support for this generalization! The evidence which does exist is often contradictory and inconclusive and, perhaps most importantly, in no way establishes a connection between childhood political socialization and adult political attitudes and behaviors.

Shabad and Andersen also call attention to the assumptions that operate in studies of women's "personalistic" approach to politics. Researchers, for example, tend to classify anything except issue stands or party identification as "irrational' (p. 21), indicating a very interesting albeit distorted notion of appropriate leadership qualities. Recent history suggests that a decision to vote or not vote for a candidate on the basis of such personal traits as honesty and compassion may not be as irrational as previously thought!

Their own examination of survey research data led Shabad and Andersen to conclude that personalism is indeed a myth. Even the archetypal example, that women were attracted during the 1960 election to John F. Kennedy's family and background, found very little support. The data showed that both men and women were attracted to these characteristics and they were attracted in the same numbers (p. 24). Women were more influenced by JFK's "personality," but what this actually meant was that they saw him as competent, trustworthy, and reliable (pp. 24-25), questionable attributes of "irrationality."

Andersen and Cook (1985) turned to an empirical investigation of women's adult political socialization. As previously noted, much of the conventional wisdom of political science assumes a connection between childhood political beliefs and their adult equivalents, but very little data exists to support this interpretation. Andersen and Cook were particularly interested in examining the effects of entering the work force on women's political participation. Much of the previous research, such as that performed by Welch, had indicated that women who work are as likely to participate as men while housewives are likely to have lower levels of political participation. Andersen and Cook wanted to clarify the relationship between entry into the work force and political participation. Earlier studies, they noted, were not able to tell us whether or not housewives who entered the work force were the same kinds of people as housewives who remained at home. In their words, "That is, those women who eventually leave the home to take up paid employment may be significantly different initially from their compatriots who stay at home, and the alleged socializing effects of work may be merely an artifact of limited data bases" (p. 606). Obviously, research such as this has important implications. Will, for example, more working women mean higher overall levels of political participation?

Andersen and Cook were not able to offer a conclusive response to this and similar questions. Their research revealed mixed feelings. In some respects, entry into the work force did produce feminist attitudes among former housewives, but this was not true for all such women on all issues (pp 616-617). Nor did going to work appear to increase the political participation of women (p. 622). As the authors are quick to note, however, their study did not permit them to say anything about the effects of long-term involvement in the work force on women's political behavior (p. 622).

What is important about this study is not so much what the researchers found but the kinds of questions they asked and how they went about trying to provide the answers. Theirs was a sophisticated research design, and they were interested in refining the findings of some of the earlier feminist studies. This signals the coming of age of the feminist challenge to political science, and is an important step towards the reconceptualization of the core concepts of the discipline.

PART THREE

To what extent have the feminist correctives to political science's image of women been integrated into the research agenda and teaching curriculum of the discipline? This is not an easy matter to assess. Political science is a changed discipline. It has responded to the feminist challenge of the early 1970s, even though it has not witnessed the large-scale paradigm changes called for by the feminists.

A review of the impact of feminist scholarship on the various subfields of political science, specifically American politics, political theory, public policy, international relations, and comparative politics, revealed a varied picture. During the period covered by the study, 1976 through 1985, there appeared to be little, if any, evidence of broad paradigmatic change within political science as a whole (Steuernagel & Quinn, 1986).

Political science no longer automatically assumes that women are apolitical. Not only are women themselves changing (more women than men, for example, voted in the 1984 presidential election), but the discipline itself has begun to alter its ways of thinking about women. Flammang's 1984 edited volume, *Political Women*, for example, builds on the feminist tenet that women have been labeled "apolitical" not so much because of their lack of political involvement but because of the places political scientists were looking for evidence of women's political participation. The authors of the articles in Flammang's book concentrate not on frequently studied national politics but on the activities of women in state and local politics. They discovered that women have made inroads into state and local political offices, inroads that have not been paralleled in national politics. They also found evidence that women are involved in a variety of political work conducted through non-governmental organizations such as rape crisis centers, the League of Women Voters, and consciousness-raising groups (Flammang, p. 10). Women, according to Flammang and her colleagues, involve themselves in state and local governments and other forms of non-governmental political participations because these are the arenas in which decisions which affect their lives are acted out. Programs which attempt to deal with the problems encountered by poor women, by battered women, by women in their roles as wives and mothers are more likely to be privately run or supported by state and local governments than by the federal government. Women participate in politics when their lives are affected by politics. To the extent that political scientists continue to study national politics at the expense of state and local politics and to ignore non-governmental political activity, they will be unable to accept anything but an apolitical image of women.

Works such as *Political Women* suggest, however, that political science is responding to the feminist challenge. The question arises, however, as to the extent to which women and politics research is being "mainstreamed" into the minds of political scientists. Has research about women actually changed how political scientists think about politics? Have political scientists incorporated an expanded definition of politics into their research designs? All of the caucuses and specialized journals in the world are only so much window-dressing for the ghetto unless they begin to influence how political scientists in general think about women and politics.

The bulk of the research surveyed in this essay has been in the fields of American politics and public policy, two areas which have been in the forefront of the feminist challenge. The field of political theory has also been responsive to feminist correctives. Okin's *Women in Western Political Thought* (1979) and Saxonhouse's *Women in the History of Political Thought* (1985) are excellent examples of this genre. Other fields of political science have been less responsive to the feminist challenge. Comparative politics and international relations continue to look at politics in a way that guarantees that women will be absent from their inquiry. Some work on women in Third World countries has been forthcoming, but such concerns have not, in any significant manner, altered the research agendas of these fields.

Ironically, even the "successes" of the feminist challenge itself have brought mixed results. Most scholars, for example, now accept the idea that "education" and "employment" are more likely to effect levels of participation than "gender." This has had the unexpected (and unwanted) consequence of reinstituting the notion that gender is not an important variable in political research. During the period 1980-1985, for example, only three articles directly concerned with women and politics have appeared in the *American Political Science Review*. Much of the current research remains confined to women's studies journals such as *Signs* or specialized journals such as *Women & Politics*.

Another potential problem has emerged among scholars of women and politics. "Sex," a biological concept, is far easier to study from an empirical perspective than "gender," a concept thick with historical meaning. Although scholars speak about "gender" when addressing theoretical problems, much of the empirical research actually involves "sex." Consequently, "gender" becomes the equivalent of "sex" and the crucial variations among women as people existing in concrete historical situations are lost. As a result, women tend to emerge from these studies as monolithic; and this, in turn, tends to obscure crucial differences that result from age, race, class, and other such factors.

Efforts are being made to address this, although problems remain. Data on black political behavior in general are scanty (Walton, 1985). Information on the political behavior of black women is even more scarce. Evidence that does exist suggests that the political behavior of black women cannot be explained by the traditional theories of political science nor by some of the feminist correctives. It appears to be the case, for example, that feelings of political estrangement are not, as we would expect, related in black women to decreased levels of voting (Baxter & Lansing, 1983, p. 91).

Feminists continue to have a view of the proper role of political science that is not universally accepted in the discipline. Feminist political scientists in general continue to press for an activist, engaged definition for their profession. The feminist challenge was strongest in the 1970s, a period in which the behavioral orientation of political science was undergoing its own challenge from a group of post-behavioral critics. Behavioralism was characterized by a neutral, value-free stance. Its emphasis was on performing "scientific" research. Any stance by a political scientist for or against a policy position was viewed as suspect and "unscientific." The post-behavioralists urged political science to be more relevant and responsive to current problems. Interestingly, much of the current research on women and politics is occurring in the field of public policy, a part of political science which remains most responsive to the post-behavioralists' call for relevant research.

The American Political Science Association has taken a lead role in attempting to integrate women and politics research into political science classes. The APSA sponsored project "Citizenship and Change: Women and American Politics," has resulted in a number of workshops and publications intended to encourage teachers of political science to "mainstream" women and politics into the traditional curriculum. Here again, "mainstreaming" has not been an unequivocal success. As one article noted, "As long as feminist questions are seen as secondary, if not trivial to the pursuit of political science as a science, mainstreaming is doomed" (Dean, Warner, & Steuernagel, 1985, p. 9).

The fate of women and politics research within the discipline is linked as much to the demographics of political science as to any other single factor. Not all female political scientists are feminists. Nonetheless, it is clear that the feminist correctives to the image of women did not begin to emerge until women joined the ranks of the profession. In 1969, the same year that the APSA established the Committee on the Status of Women and the Women's Caucus for Political Science was formed, about 8% of U.S. political scientists were women (Lynn, 1983, p. 116). In 1981, women held 11% of all full-time political science positions (Lynn, p. 118). The comparable figure for 1984 is 13% (APSA, 1985, p. 1). Women are not evenly distributed among the ranks of political scientists. According to a 1984-85 APSA survey of departments, women constitute 6% of the full professors, 14% of associate professors, 29% of assistant professors, and 29% of all instructors and lecturers (APSA, p. 1). Looked at another way, 45% of the 4,908 male political scientists hold the rank of full professor, 28% the rank of associate professor, 18% the rank of assistant professor, and 2% the rank of instructor or lecturer (APSA, p. 1). In contrast, 20% of the 734 female political scientists hold the rank of full professor, 30% the rank of associate professor, 34% the rank of assistant professor, and 5% the rank of instructor or lecturer.

Women are more likely than men to be found among the lower ranks of the academic hierarchy. There are, of course, some historical reasons for this. Women, for example, enter the profession at later stages in their lives after postponing a career to rear children, so they are less likely to establish the scholarly credentials required for promotion to full professor. Women are also more likely to accept part-time and temporary teaching assignments so as to be able to accommodate family demands on their time. This, needless to say, is not the whole of the story. Why, for example, are there over six times more male political scientists than female political scientists in this country? Why are women more likely than men to make these kinds of trade-offs between career and family? The answers to these questions transcend concerns with political science. If politics isn't for women, then political science certainly is not. Women political scientists are expected to — and often do — define themselves as women first and political scientists second; and being a woman in our culture means placing family responsibilities above career choices. It is hoped the conditions for women political scientists will change as society's attitudes about women and their proper "roles" evolve. As more women enter political science and advance to the highest ranks of the profession, they should contribute to an invigorated feminist challenge.

Ultimately, however, women will continue to be marginal to political science as long as they remain marginal to politics. In Sapiro's words:

> Women do not appear in political life as much as men do in part because they are not valued and encouraged in politics as much as men are; they do not "fit" into politics as comfortably. Women and women's issues do not appear in political

research and teaching as much as do men and the issues they consider important in part because they are not valued as much as men are; they do not "fit" into the concerns of political science as comfortably. (1983, p. 3)

REFERENCES

American Political Science Association (1985). 1984-1985 survey of departments. Washington, D.C.: American Political Science Association.

Andersen, K., & Cook, E.A. (1985). Women, work and political attitudes. *American Journal of Political Science, 29*, 606-625.

Aristotle (1962). *Politics* (T.A. Sinclair, Trans.). Middlesex, England: Penguin Books.

Baxter, S., & Lansing, M. (1983). *Women and politics*. Ann Arbor: The University of Michigan Press.

Bloom, A. (1968). *The Republic of Plato*, translated with notes and an interpretative essay. New York: Basic Books, Inc.

Boals, K. (1975). The politics of male-female relations: The functions of feminist scholarship. *Signs, 1*, 161-174.

Campbell, A., Gurin, G., & Miller, W. (1954). *The voter decides*. Evanston: Row Peterson.

Campbell, A., Converse, P.E., Miller, W.E., & Stokes, D.E. (1964). *The American voter*. New York: Wiley.

Carroll, B.A. (1979). Political science, Part I: American politics and political behavior. *Signs, 5*, 289-306.

Carroll, B.A. (1980). Political science, Part II: International politics, comparative politics, and feminist radicals. *Signs, 5*, 449-458.

Dean, K., Warner, C., & Steuernagel, T. (1985). "Mainstreaming" at Kent State University. *News for Teachers of Political Science*, Winter (44), 8-9.

Finifter, A.W. (Ed.). (1983). *Political science: The state of the discipline*. Washington, D.C.: American Political Science Association.

Flammang, J.A. (Ed.). (1984). *Political women*. Beverly Hills: Sage Publications.

Githens, M., & Prestage, J.L. (Eds.). (1977). *A Portrait of Marginality*. New York: David McKay Company, Inc.

Githens, M. (1983). The elusive paradigm: Gender, politics, and political behavior. In A.W. Finifter (Ed.), *Political science: The state of the discipline* (pp. 471-499). Washington, D.C.: American Political Science Association.

Greenstein, F. (1965). *Children and politics*. New Haven: Yale University Press.

Hess, R.D., & Torney, J.V. (1967). *The development of political attitudes in children*. Chicago: Aldine.

Hyman, H. (1959). *Political socialization*. New York: Free Press.

Iglitzen, L.B. (1974). The making of the apolitical woman: Femininity and sex-stereotyping. In J.S. Jaquette (Ed.), *Women in politics* (pp. 25-36). New York: John Wiley and Sons.

Jaquette, J.S. (Ed.). (1974). *Women in politics*. New York: John Wiley and Sons.

Krauss, W.R. (1974). Political implications of gender roles: A review of the literature. *American Political Science Review, 68,* 1706-1723.

Lynn, N.B. (1983). Self portrait: Profile of political scientists. In A.W. Finifter (Ed.), *Political science: The state of the discipline* (pp. 95-123). Washington, D.C.: American Political Science Association.

Okin, S.M. (1979). *Women in western political thought*. Princeton: Princeton University Press.

Plato (1945). *The Republic* (F.M. Cornford, Trans.). London: Oxford University Press.

Poole, K., & Zeigler, L.H. (1985). *Women, public opinion, and politics*. New York: Longman.

Sapiro, V. (1983). *The political integration of women*. Urbana: University of Illinois Press.

Saxonhouse, A.W. (1985). *Women in the history of political thought*. New York: Praeger Publishers.

Shabad, G., & Andersen, K. (1979). Candidate evaluations by men and women. *Public Opinion Quarterly, 43,* 18-35.

Steuernagel, G.A. (1983, September). *Feminist revisionists' contribution to political inquiry*. Paper presented at the meeting of the American Political Science Association, Chicago, IL.

Steuernagel, G.A., & Quinn, L.J. (1986). *Is anyone listening? Political science and the response to the feminist challenge*. Paper presented at the meeting of the American Political Science Association, Washington, D.C.

Walton, H. (1985). *Invisible politics*. Albany, NY: State University of New York Press.

Welch, S. (1977). Women as political animals. *American Journal of Political Science, 21,* 711-730.

Images of Women in Psychology

Judith Worell

If you take a look at any psychology text published over a decade ago, you will find that psychology is described as the scientific study of "man." Reading further, you will also discover that all individuals are "he" and the person's behavior is reported in terms of "his" activities and characteristics. Although women were sometimes included as subjects of study, they were examined in terms of how they were different (and usually lesser) than men. This "androcentric" view of human behavior assumed that men were the normative population and other groups were then studied to determine how they compared with male standards. How then have we moved toward a psychology of people as well as a psychology of women?

In this chapter, we will be looking at both traditional and contemporary approaches to women in psychological theory and research. The psychology of women is an emerging field of study which examines theories about women's development through the life span. Research in the psychology of women considers her status in family, academic, work, and relationship settings as well as her skills, abilities, thoughts, feelings, and behaviors across many situations. Psychologists who study women also pay particular attention to all aspects of women's physical and mental health concerns, and have been exploring how women's experience is uniquely determined by her own physiology, the cultural values and attitudes that surround her as she grows toward maturity, and the imbalance in power relations between women and men in most societies.

Unlike some traditional approaches to studying the individual, the psychology of women cannot be understood outside the sociocultural context of the world in which girls and women develop. Therefore, it is necessary to consider societal stereotypes and myths about women and men and cultural expectations for gender differences in behavior, in order to evaluate the influence of these expectations on women's psychological development. Attention to the imbalance in social, economic, and political power between women and men leads the researcher to explore the psychological impact of oppression, isolation, discrimination, and victimization on the development and well-being of women.

The three major sections of the chapter will cover (1) gender and sex-role stereotypes; (2) psychological theories of development in women's personality and characteristics; and (3) women's mental health and psychological well-being. A final section will consider future options for women's psychological development in contemporary society.

A coordinating theme in the study of the psychology of women is that the science of human behavior is not value-free. Thus, we all look at the world through our own unique lens, shaped by the personal experiences that influence our perception and evaluation of life events and the world around us. Although a science of human behavior requires that we test hypotheses and arrive at conclusions by means of carefully conducted research studies, even scientific research can be biased by the methods and procedures of the researcher. One of the unique contributions of the new psychology of women is the examination of gender bias in research and the development of guidelines and procedures to reduce this bias in research related to women's development and behavior. The results of these efforts have been the discovery of new "facts" that contradict old "facts" and new insights into the experience and lives of women as well as of men.

GENDER AND SEX-ROLE STEREOTYPES

In every culture, the impact of gender assignment on lifespan experiences is profound. The label of female or male itself provides a framework around which stereotyped expectations, role prescriptions, and life opportunities are organized. Gender stereotypes are simplified generalizations about females and males that are intended to apply to all persons within each gender group. Some of these stereotypes may be true for some individuals (e.g., men are stronger than women) but are seldom useful when understanding or describing a particular person.

Sex roles consist of organized clusters of expectations for behaviors and activities that are considered to be appropriate and desirable for either females or males (Bem, 1974; Worell, 1978). Stereotyped conceptions about what is appropriately masculine or feminine for either ourselves or others can include at least five areas of behavior: Personality traits (e.g., aggressive or gentle), family roles (e.g., breadwinner or homemaker), leisure activities (football or knitting), work roles (miner or manicurist), and personal styles and appearance (swaggering or hipswinging). Although we are more likely to expect a coal miner to play football and swagger than to knit and bake bread, this is just one more example of stereotyped thinking in action. In reality, there is very little connection between our behavior in each of these domains (Orlofsky, 1981).

Sex-Role Stereotypes in Action

How do these stereotypes affect our conceptions of the developing person? From the day of birth, parents and other adults express divergent expectations for girls and boys. In one study, both mothers and fathers of newborns described their infant daughters as smaller, softer, and less attentive than did parents of sons. Fathers rated their sons as stronger, more alert, and hardier than did fathers of daughters, despite the fact that there were no measurable differences between the two groups of babies (Rubin, Provenzano, & Luria, 1974). By the age of three years, girls and boys can identify many of the activities that are culturally stereotyped for their gender. For example, most children in a preschool sample believed that girls like to play with dolls, like to cook dinner and clean house, help mother, never hit, ask for help frequently, and will be a mother, nurse, or teacher when they grow up. In contrast, they also believed that as adults, the man will be "the boss" (Kuhn, Nash, & Bruken, 1978).

Children's stereotyped conceptions remain strong as they progress in school. In a recent study with 4-6 year olds (Albert & Porter, 1983), the majority of both girls and boys described their classmates in sex-typed terms. Girls were more likely to be seen as dependent on adults, concerned with their appearance, passive and quiet, fearful and emotional, and incompetent (e.g., can't fix things). In contrast, boys were described as more independent, active, strong, bossy, brave, and aggressive. Boys were also described as more disobedient. Similar stereotypes have been reported for older children as well (Davis, Williams, & Best, 1982). These stereotypes about appropriate gender traits carry over into elementary and high school children's preferences for occupational roles. Although social norms for women and men have changed considerably within the past decade, both girls and boys continue to prefer traditionally sex-typed roles. Girls more frequently select parenthood, nursing, teaching, and secretarial positions (Block, Denniker, & Tittle, 1981; Herzog & Bachman, 1982), few of which are mentioned by boys as desirable life choices. Cultural norms about desirable occupations seem to have been internalized by young women themselves, and these expectations may direct their life plans and opportunities.

Finally, we find similar agreement in college-age and adult populations about the characteristics of the typical woman or man. Early studies on gender stereotypes found two broad clusters of traits attributed more frequently to either women or men: A warmth-expressive cluster of traits viewed as "feminine," and an instrumental-competency cluster of characteristics seen as "masculine" (Bem, 1974; Rosenkrantz et al., 1968: Spence, Helmreich, & Stapp, 1975). Recent replications of these early stereotypes find essentially little change over time. For example, Thomas Ruble (1983) compared the ratings of the "typical" man or woman on a set of stereotyped personality traits. On 53 of the 54 traits, sex differences appeared, with both women and men viewing the typical woman as more emotional, home-oriented, kind, considerate, understanding, excitable, and devoted to others. Once more, the competency characteristics of self-confidence, independence, and decisiveness were attributed to men. How little our conceptions have changed!

Sex-Role Stereotypes on Trial

The function of stereotypes is to provide a shortcut or cue in forming judgments about other people when we have very little information about them except their gender. The convenience of these stereotypes is outweighed, however, by their disadvantages and negative impact on the self-worth of both women and men. Three adverse outcomes of sex-role stereotypes have been demonstrated: (1) They are disproportionately unfavorable to women; (2) they tend to produce self-fulfilling behaviors; and (3) they result in biased attitudes and evaluations of women.

First, studies on the social desirability of sex-typed traits have found that more masculine than feminine traits receive positive evaluations, and that, in general, masculine traits are more highly valued (Broverman et al., 1972). That is, the social value of being independent, rational, and a leader outweighs the desirability of being conforming, emotional, and submissive. There is evidence that women themselves are aware of this societal bias toward feminine-typed traits. For example, women who rate themselves higher on masculine than on feminine traits have higher self-esteem than women who describe themselves in feminine-typed terms (Spence, Helmreich, & Stapp, 1975; Whitely, 1983).

Secondly, the "self-fulfilling prophecy" suggests that people tend to behave as they believe others expect of them (Darley & Fazio, 1980; Deaux, 1984). For example, women who participated in a study on interview behavior believed they were being interviewed by either a traditional or nontraditional man. Women who interviewed with the "traditional" man paid more attention to their clothing and makeup, displayed more "feminine" behaviors, and gave more traditional answers to questions about marriage and children (Zanna & Pack, 1975). Conformity to sex-role expectations may lead to permanent changes in a person's self-concept and behavior, thus producing a self-fulfilling prophecy for the stereotype.

Finally, stereotyped expectations about women's competence, emotionality, or physical characteristics frequently result in biased evaluations and artificial barriers to women's achievement. Judgments about the performance of women and men on a variety of tasks are influenced by the belief that men are more competent in almost everything. When men succeed on a task, observers tend to attribute his success to his superior ability; when women succeed, they are more frequently seen as lucky, or having an easier task (Deaux, 1984). Further, when jobs or activities are rated for degree of difficulty or competence required, women's jobs are rated as less demanding than those regarded as men's jobs. These ratings accommodate to the stereotyped expectations that women are less competent than men. When women do succeed in difficult tasks, their success is unexpected, thereby leading observers to conclude that it must be luck and not ability (Bar-Tal, 1978).

Biased evaluations of women's potential based on preconceptions of their abilities have been used to restrict women in their occupational choices, level of job entry, and career advancement (Ruble & Ruble, 1982). Women interested in nontraditional careers in particular have found considerable resistance, based on stereotypes about what personality and physical characteristics are required for career success. Some examples of these nontraditional career opportunities include high-paying positions as well as interesting and challenging ones, from heavy equipment operator to airline pilot to university president. Research clearly demonstrates that in these male-dominated occupations, gender-based biases favor males over females in hiring, masculine over feminine characteristics in evaluating job performance, and higher expectations for males in demanding performance situations (Ruble & Ruble, 1982; Woelfel, 1981). Although some of this bias is moderated by direct on-the-job performance, women remain essentially segregated in positions offering lower pay and less status, prestige, and influence.

Sex-Role Stereotypes and Reality

Are we really what others believe us to be? Psychological research has explored the extent of similarity between a variety of stereotyped expectations and people's behavior in real situations. The literature in this area is voluminous; the reader is referred to several excellent sources for reviews of research on gender (for example: Hyde & Linn, 1986; Maccoby & Jacklin, 1974). In particular, considerable research has focused on gender contribution in areas such as achievement, aggression, altruism, cognition, competition, cooperation, conformity, emotionality, leadership, friendliness, and love. In some areas of behavior, experimental findings suggest small differences between groups of women and men, but within any particular domain there are greater differences within each gender group than there are between them.

For example, the stereotype that boys and men are more aggressive has been examined in hundreds of studies. The summary conclusions from these studies suggest that aggression is distributed across people in such a way that most people will show some aggression in some situations and that few people of either gender are either never or always aggressive. However, the average male tends to be somewhat more aggressive across situations than the average female (Hyde, 1986). The differences between a stereotyped description of gender difference and a description based on statistical and research findings is displayed in Figure I. It can be seen that a stereotype implies an all-or-none phenomenon, in which males are

Figure I:
Distribution of personality traits among women and men

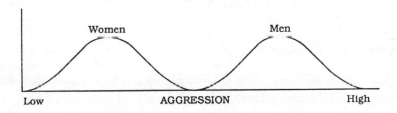

Stereotype: Men are aggressive and women are unaggressive

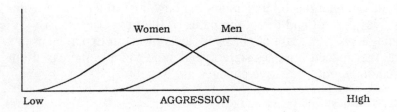

Reality: In most situations, women tend to show less aggression than men

aggressive and females are not. In reality, the two distributions of aggressive tendencies overlap considerably, so that some males are found to be less aggressive than some females. In understanding and predicting any particular aggressive act, it is more important to know the situation, the characteristics and experiences of the persons involved, the amount of provocation, and the possibilities of exposure and punishment, than it is to know the gender of the aggressor. Although hormonal influences may contribute to aggressive behavior, the small differences between gender groups suggest that it is far more fruitful to examine the conditions under which aggressive behavior is learned and maintained than to explore why men are more aggressive than women. A similar analysis is suggested for other behaviors in which some gender differences have been reported such as verbal and cognitive abilities, conformity, empathy, smiling and gazing, and preferences for football over knitting.

Summary and Implications

What do these sex-role conceptions imply for the study of women? Sex-role and gender stereotypes have been shown to be pervasive, remarkably stable over time, and generally detrimental to the well-being of women. Beliefs about the characteristics of women and men become integrated into our self-concepts and feelings of self-worth, and thus influence our expectations and goals for ourselves and others. I would suggest that we discard our working stereotypes and beliefs about how women differ from men and concentrate our energies on understanding how the influences on women's lives control and direct the paths of their experiences. By examining how the stream of our lives flows from our experiences in a world that indeed imposes stereotyped expectations, increased understanding and productive changes are possible.

THEORIES OF SEX-ROLE DEVELOPMENT

How can we explain how these gender roles and expectations are learned at such an early age by both girls and boys, and why they endure so persistently over time? Theories of human development have attempted to understand the process of sex-typing, or the mechanisms through which children develop differing thoughts, feelings, and activities in coordination with their gender. Traditional theories have emphasized the identification of the child with the same-sex parent and the consequent adoption of behaviors deemed "appropriate" for either girls or boys. In contrast, recent theories have proposed that gender-role development is flexible and continues throughout the life span, suggesting that stereotyped behaviors may represent a stage of development or a reflection of cultural expectations rather than the final outcome of personality. Accordingly, these newer theories provide contrasting views of the possibilities for women and men in contemporary society.

Traditional Theories

We can describe theories of development as traditional when they reflect four dominant themes in their conceptions of human functioning: *Androcentrism*; *gendercentrism*; *ethnocentrism*; and *heterosexism*. Androcentric theories have constructed an image of humankind based on the development of men. The male is viewed as the prototype of humanity and the female is understood only in relation to his life (Doherty, 1976). Women are added to the theory as an afterthought, resulting in a poor fit between the theory and women's real lives and experiences. Further, these theories proclaim that women are "less" than men, being less rationale, less moral, and less responsible for direction in their lives. Gendercentrism in theories is evident when separate paths of development are proposed for men and women. In these theories, gender roles are determined by biology and anatomy, thus becoming fixed and unchangeable throughout the life span. A gendercentric theory prescribes that traditional roles for women and men are the way things "ought to be."

Ethnocentrism is a core characteristic of most psychological theories that are based on observations of Anglo-European populations. Ethnocentric theories assume that the "facts" of development with regard to appearance and sequencing of behaviors and of the optimal conditions for their facilitation, are similar across all racial, national, and ethnic groups. One example of this ethnocentric view of appropriate development has been the assumption that children flourish best when in the care of a single nurturing female, the biological mother. Evidence from other cultures that extended family arrangements produce equally well-adjusted children has barely dented the American conviction that the "real" mother can provide better or optimal development when she and the preschool child are isolated in a child-care arrangement that keeps the woman at home in a non-paying, socially devalued, and frequently unstimulating occupation. Even today, most young Americans anticipating their childbearing years believe that mothers of preschool children should not work outside the home (Herzog & Bachman, 1982).

Another influence of ethnocentrism on theory development has been the neglect of cultural influences on women's roles and on the well-being of children within families where women's roles may be distinctly at variance with those of the dominant Caucasian American culture. Examples here include women's roles in Black and Hispanic families, and the impact of family arrangements in these cultures on the developing child. For Black Americans, this neglect has resulted in a disaffection of many Black women with mainstream psychology, believing that current American Psychology does not speak to the reality of their lives (Greene, 1986). For example, Black women see themselves not as the passive and submissive female of traditional psychological theory, but as more balanced, being characterized by traits of self-reliance, independence, assertiveness, and strength (Robinson, 1983). But American psychology has frequently reframed these positive assets as detrimental to the development of males in Black families, describing the "matriarchal structure" of Black families as responsible for the alienation and loss of status of Black males. The ethonocentric blinders encouraged psychologists to view the traditional Caucasian male/female dominance structures as normative, thus casting ethnic families in a deviant framework (Greene, 1986).

Finally, American Psychology has also been heterosexist in its theory and research. In all traditional theories of psychological development, heterosexual orientation is viewed as normative and desirable, and lifestyles oriented toward same-sex partners are deviant and changeworthy. One result of this heterosexist assumption about development is that Lesbian women have been ignored, denigrated, and regarded as less than normal. Although we cannot blame American Psychology for the attitudes of the entire culture, it is only recently that psychological theory and research has affirmed the "normalcy" of development and adjustment in Lesbian women (see for example Blumstein & Schwartz, 1983; Kurdek, 1987). As the results of research affirm and confirm the normative developmental course of Lesbian women, we may find psychological theory revising its assumptions.

What are these traditional images of women in psychological theory? The major example of a traditional view of women's development that reflects all four biases outlined above is that of Freud (1948, 1965). Two other theories provide embellishments to the conceptions of Freud that further restrict women's development according to traditional views and these will be briefly reviewed: Erikson's eight stages of man (sic) (1963, 1968), and Kohlberg's theories of moral development (Kohlberg, 1969, 1976). Although these theoretical views do not stand alone in their gender bias about women's development, they continue to exert an influence on the thinking of many contemporary researchers and mental health practitioners.

Freud's theory (1948, 1965) of the developmental differentiation of girls and boys was based on biological differences between them, primarily the presence of the penis in boys and the capability of women to bear children. Since this is essentially a theory of male development, we start with the experience of the boy. At around the age of three, all boys begin to lust after their mother (the Oedipal Complex) and to view their father as a competitor for her affection. Sensing his father's jealousy, the boy fears his father's retaliation in the form of emasculation (the Castration Complex), and renounces his mother as an object of complete love. In self-defense and to placate his father, the boy then *identifies* with the father, taking on his qualities and standards of "masculinity" or what it means to be a man. In this manner, the boy becomes socialized into the prevailing culture and develops a conscience and a set of moral standards (the Super Ego).

How does this identification process proceed for girls? Freud was less clear about the mechanisms responsible for sex-role development in girls, but remained committed to a genital view of identification. The little girl, observing that she does not have a penis, realizes her deficiency and blames her mother for the loss. She develops "penis envy" and a basic sense of inferiority, resolving her genital loss by transferring her affections to her father. In time she recognizes that she can own a penis only by passively accepting it from a male, and she transfers this envy into a desire to have a child (preferably a male). Her identification with her mother and with the "feminine" role develops out of her competition for the father and fear of losing the mother's love completely. Her identification is never as strong as that of the boy, however, and Freud viewed women as permanently less ethical than men, having a lesser sense of justice, and remaining more influenced by their emotions than by logical reasoning.

What is the image of women that emerges from classical Freudian theory? Women are clearly inferior to men in valued characteristics and in their biological potential for an equal role in both family and society. By nature, women are passive, emotional, masochistic (willing to accept pain in return for pleasure), narcissistic (vain and deriving pleasure from themselves), and in continual competition with other women for the sexual favors of men. Their major goals are to acquire a husband and to have his baby. When they step out of this role and move into the spheres of men, either by seeking roles other than motherhood or by showing "masculine" characteristics such as assertiveness and ambition, they are clearly afflicted by a disorder called "penis envy." Thus, the theory concludes that "anatomy is destiny" for women, and that they are doomed from early childhood by the developmental outcomes of their physical deficiencies.

In evaluating classical Freudian theory, we are faced with a curious paradox. From a scientific point of view, the theory of sex-role development presented above has had very little support in empirical research (Sherman, 1971). At the level of practical applications to human problems, however, it is still influencing the practices and assumptions of many professional mental health specialists in their transactions with women in treatment (American Psychological Association, 1975, 1978). For this latter reason, it is important to focus on the privately held images of those who treat women for mental health problems. The issue here, as we shall discuss in a later section, may be the tendency to attribute to women's personality and behaviors a quality of deviancy that is more properly a function of her underprivileged status or her socially prescribed position in life. The result of viewing women from a Freudian point of view may be to see deviance in women's "normal" behavior or in her healthy efforts to cope with her situation.

Erikson's theory of human development follows a model based on his concept of the "eight stages of man" (Erikson, 1963, 1968). According to Erikson, development proceeds throughout life according to stages in which polarities determine the formation of our personality. Each stage consists of polarities such as trust-mistrust, autonomy-shame, and industry-inferiority. Two of these stages, identity vs. diffusion, and intimacy vs. isolation, provided particular difficulty for Erikson as he attempted to understand how women's development fitted his model. In normal development, according to Erikson, the adolescent achieves a sense of personal identity, rather than "identity diffusion," by embracing a philosophy of life and commitment to a career. In the next stage of young adulthood, intimacy is achieved by relinquishing one's autonomy in the fusion of self with another and committing oneself to "affiliations and partnerships" (Erikson, 1963). Erikson questioned this life progression for women, however, and concluded that women defer their identity until "they know whom they will marry and for whom they will make a home" (1968, p. 123). A woman's identity, therefore, is not defined by career commitment, but by her commitment to the roles of wife and mother, and her search for a man to give her life meaning and direction.

Once more we see the construction of women's lives based on a theory of male development, and a restriction of women's role to her predestined biological preparation to serve in the lives of men. In addition to its androcentric bias, Erikson's theory also suffers from gendercentrism in its division of life goals between men and women to career vs. intimacy. We shall see that some contemporary theories include these life goals as equally relevant for mature identity development in both women and men. That is, a securely identified adolescent needs to develop life goals and skills that include both career planning and intimate relationships. Further, we now know that intimate relationships with both sexes are important sources of self-esteem and well being for women and men alike.

The psychological literature on disturbances in adolescent development clearly point to the need for skills in both areas of adjustment if the adolescent is to have a satisfying sense of self (Hurtig & Peterson, 1982; Kandel & Davies, 1982; Lamke, 1982a, 1982b; Worell, in press, b). The search for identity and a clear sense of self plays a major role in many theories of personality. This search is therefore of critical interest to conceptions of human development. Traditional theories have provided a continuing disservice to both women and men by patterning the quest for independent selfhood on a model developed exclusively for the lives of men.

Kohlberg's theories of sex-roles and moral development (1969, 1976) represent a third approach to traditional understandings of how women and men develop in society. Here, we shall concentrate on his theory of how individuals develop a sense of moral understanding and mature ethical judgment. Kohlberg developed his theory using the responses of young men to a set of ethical dilemmas. On the basis of their responses to hypothetical situations, he determined that some moral decisions were more advanced or mature than were others. When men and women were compared across levels of moral maturity it was found that women tended to score at a "lower" level than did men. Men solved moral dilemmas in terms of appeals to individual rights and principles of abstract justice. Women, on the other hand, tended to focus on concern and responsibility to others, emphasizing relationships, reciprocity, and interdependence (Kohlberg & Kramer, 1969). Kohlberg assumed that decisions based on the laws of society and abstract principles were more advanced morally than those based on concern for others.

In responding to Kohlberg's views, Carol Gilligan wrote an impassioned essay pleading for a recognition that women's morality speaks for the ethics of caring and attachment. As such, women are not less moral than men, but speak "in a different voice" (Gilligan, 1982). The importance of Gilligan's position is the conceptualization of women's orientation as legitimate and representative of women's lives, just as men's emphasis on justice and independence represents important facets of men's development. Why should one orientation take moral precedence over the other? Only when researchers develop theories based on the lives of women, rather than on the experience of men, says Gilligan, will we begin to understand the rich harmony that characterizes the pattern of women's lives. Recent analysis of many studies on stages of moral development have supported Gilligan's assertion that neither of the two orientations toward justice is superior to the other (Blake & Cohen, 1984). These studies also find that sex differences in moral judgment may vary with educational levels (Baumrind, 1986) or the situations presented (Rothbart, Hanley, & Alpert, 1986). Had Kohlberg developed his theory on the basis of the responses of both women and men, he might have arrived at some very different conclusions.

Summary of traditional theories: What are the problems with these traditional views of women's development? First they affirm women's position as developmentally different and as inferior to that of men, thereby supporting societal prescriptions for male dominance and privilege. Second, they tend to be internalized by women themselves, thus diminishing their self-image, their sense of self-worth, and their expectations about what and who they can become. Finally, such theories keep women locked into traditional roles and behaviors by viewing alternative lifestyles as "deviant." Women who want help in transcending their prescribed roles or who experience conflict about what they wish to become may be encouraged to retreat and to "adjust" to their situation. The resulting sense of defeat and frustration experienced by some women may lead to resignation, depression, or confusion and feelings of being deviant and "crazy."

Contemporary Theories

In contrast to traditional theories of human development that give us a picture of woman as inferior man, as wife and mother, or as moral deviant, contemporary views propose some intriguing alternatives. Why not consider the possibility that men and women can live potentially parallel lives as human beings without requirements for gender-separate pathways? Contemporary theories recognize that currently observed gender differences may reflect societal stereotyping and socialization. Given a revised approach to viewing the development of women and men, would it not be possible to enable both genders to achieve a flexible orientation free of stereotyped behaviors?

Gender-free theories view women and men as similar in psychological makeup and goals that promote growth and human potential. These theories avoid language that labels one gender as more socially desirable or valued than the other. They explain psychological differences between men and women as stemming from three major factors: (1) normal cognitive processing of incoming information to the developing child; (2) the visible organization of current social roles that provide models for children to imitate and follow; and (3) prevailing societal forces that differentially reward males and females for sex-stereotyped behaviors that ignore or punish ethnic or alternative lifestyles, and restrict opportunities for role innovation. Further, these theories provide for the possibility of developmental changes over the lifespan, enabling the individual to move toward self-modification of stereotypic behavior (Worell, 1981). A brief summary of three of these newer theories offers an optimistic view of the possibilities for a psychology of human development that conceives of both women and men as strong, caring, connected to one another, and equal.

Social Learning Theory (Bandura, 1977) challenged earlier views that gender differences are a natural result of innately determined individual development. As the title implies, social learning approaches theorize that we pattern our behavior, including our sex-roles, according to the messages we receive from the social environment. These messages take the form of models from the behavior of others, and social responses to our own behavior as we attempt to imitate these models. Social responses to our behavior can be positive (rewarding) or negative (punishing), and they gradually shape our behavior, thoughts, and feelings. Since images in the social environment are largely Caucasian, heterosexual, and gender-typed, children soon learn what behaviors are normative and will be tolerated and rewarded, and they fashion their own behavior accordingly. Parents, teachers, and peers, as well as the media (books, newspapers, T.V.) provide multiple opportunities for learning what is acceptable and "just for girls (women)" or "just for boys (men)." Crossing the boundaries of acceptable sex-typed behavior can bring disapproval from any of these socializing agents, and children soon learn to avoid behavior that will result in pain or humiliation. Boys avoid "sissy" behavior: showing emotional responses of tenderness or fear, compassion for others, and gentleness. Girls avoid being loud, aggressive, or boasting and they hide their competence under the guise of modesty. The result of this social learning process is that boys and girls appear increasingly to resemble their own gender in behavior, attitudes, aspirations, and life/career patterns.

Since the environment is complex, however, children also learn that there are exceptions to rules and that alternative possibilities exist. Social learning theory provides both the mechanisms for sex-role conformity to traditional images, as well as the possibilities for change through the provision of new models for behavior, opportunities for self-determination and skill development, and a revised system of social rewards (Blechman, 1980; Worell, 1982). Research in social learning theory has clearly demonstrated that when observed models change their sex-typed behaviors, children also revise their stereotyped expectations. Children exposed to text books in which all words and pictures about boys and girls were egalitarian were less stereotyped in their expectations about gender roles than were children exposed to traditional texts (Flerx, Fidler, & Rogers, 1976). Similarly, research on the school-age daughters of working mothers (non-traditional role for Caucasian women) shows that these girls have more flexible ideas about the roles of women and men, believing that both sexes should share equal roles in family and business settings. As each family encourages and rewards new patterns of behavior, new forms of social and interpersonal behaviors may emerge (Eron, 1980; Hoffman, 1977). Thus, the image of women that emerges from social learning theory is one of equal potential, with each individual potentially free to choose and select her own identity and destiny. But because environments interact reciprocally with individual behavior, social learning theory also reminds us that extensive changes must occur in the social environment in order for women to envisage and achieve these new images as reality.

Androgyny theory was first developed empirically by Sandra Bem (1974). Bem observed that traditional theories of personality defined healthy development in terms of "appropriate" sex-typing.

Thus, well-adjusted boys were expected to be "masculine": Aggressive, independent, and achieving, and girls were expected to be "feminine": Nurturant, passive, and compliant. It was further assumed that these characteristics were mutually exclusive, or bi-polar: That is, as masculinity increased, femininity decreased and one could not possess both sets of characteristics. Bem suggested that a healthier outcome for development would be for all individuals to display the personality characteristics expected of both women and men. Thus, both women and men should be expected to be assertive and dominant in some situations and warm and gentle in others. In contrast to the sex-typed person who shows primarily masculine or feminine characteristics, these individuals with both sets of capabilities were described as *androgynous*.

In her early work, Bem demonstrated rather convincingly that persons who described themselves as androgynous on the Bem Sex-Role Inventory (Bem, 1974) were more likely to be "flexible and adaptive" across a range of differing situations than persons who saw themselves in sex-typed terms. Androgynous males were found to exhibit higher levels of nurturant and playful behavior than masculine males (Bem, 1975) and androgynous men and women were more interpersonally responsive than were sex-typed individuals (Bem, Martyna, & Watson, 1976). When asked to perform cross-sex activities (regarded as more appropriate for the other sex), androgynous persons were less uncomfortable and made fewer stereotyped choices than did sex-typed individuals (Bem & Lenney, 1976).

As a result of these early findings, androgyny theory has been extremely popular in the psychological literature and has generated a storm of research designed to test Bem's hypothesis that androgyny is a state of being greatly to be admired. Androgyny theory assumes that access to masculine and feminine capabilities is equally advantageous to both women and men. Unfortunately, in a society in which male-typed behaviors of assertion, independence, and competition are valued more highly than nurturance and cooperation, individuals who emphasize the feminine domain in their personality styles have less to gain in social prestige and power (Kelly & Worell, 1977). Thus, both women and men who describe themselves as masculine or androgynous have higher self-esteem than those who appear as feminine-typed in their personality style (Whitely, 1983). On the surface, androgyny might seem to be more advantageous to women than it is to men.

Gender-Schema Theory. More recently, Bem has revised her theorizing to propose a gender-schema theory of development (Bem, 1981, 1983, 1985), which starts with the cognitive processing of sex-linked information from the environment. All individuals possess a natural readiness to form categories about the external world. On the basis of what they observe in a sex-typed society, children will spontaneously sort persons, attributes, and behaviors in their environment into masculine and feminine categories. These categories are then assimilated into the self-concept, forming a kind of gender identity which colors their perceptions and behaviors. Individuals become sex-typed not by the extent to which their behavior is masculine or feminine, but to the extent that they categorize the world in gender-stereotyped ways. There is some convincing research supporting the gender-schema hypothesis, demonstrating that sex-typed persons are more likely than androgynous ones to notice and recall stimulus material that is gender-typed (Frable & Bem, 1985). Thus, a predisposition to view the world in dichotomous gender terms promotes a self-fulfilling prophecy in which the world indeed appears to be organized in terms of male or female-typed activities.

Sandra Bem's (1983) solution to a gender-schematic society in which women and men both conform to societal stereotypes, is to raise "gender-aschematic" children. That is, she prescribes a set of childrearing activities designed to provide gender-free parental models. She also suggests that parents should interpret societal models for the child by means of challenges to existing stereotypes and by providing "subversive" schemata in their place. Examples of these practices would include ensuring that parents divide child-care and household roles so that children do not observe parents practicing these stereotypes, and that parents actively instruct children in non-stereotyped ways of thinking (isn't it silly that Prince Charming thinks Cinderella is helpless when she is the one who has been doing all the housework?). The image of women that arises from gender-schema theory is one of a gender-free person throughout the life-span.

Summary and Implications

Psychological theories have been divided into two groups: Those that restrict the developmental potential of women according to pre-conceived views on biological determinism, and those that provide for a fuller opportunity for human variability and change. Although we applaud and welcome the newer conceptions of women's developmental potential, it remains apparent to many researchers that our understanding of individual development continues to be compounded by sexism, discrimination, and power differentials in the social environment. In response to the limitations of current theory to adequately address the realities of women's lives, a new approach to the study of women's issues has emerged called Feminist Psychology.

FEMINIST PSYCHOLOGY

The emergence of feminist approaches to the study of human development has evolved from the combined effects of the women's movement, the increased visibility of women scholars, and the collaboration of these scholars in cooperative research and publication.

The expansion of knowledge related to issues of concern to women has been spearheaded by the organization of women within their own profession. Women in psychology have gained an increasingly influential voice. Educationally, we note that in 1984, 56% of the undergraduate degrees in psychology were awarded to women, and 50.0% of the earned doctoral degrees in psychology were represented by women. Women have gained a voice as well in their professional organizations, through coming together as separate scholarly and political groups, demonstrating competence in their professional domains, and influence on programming and resources for women. In the American Psychological Association, 36% of the members are women. Within that body, there are separate groups representing women, ethnic psychologists, and Gay and Lesbian psychologists, all of whom gain power and voice through their votes and programs. Minority women can also find representation in more specialized national groups, specifically, The Association of Women in Psychology, The Association for Black Psychologists, The National Hispanic Psychological Association, and The Asian-American Psychological Association. These gains in professional organization, however, are not matched by representation in positions of influence at the university level. In all academic settings, in comparison to men, women hold fewer positions of high rank, earn lower salaries, are less frequently represented at the administrative levels, and more frequently fail to receive tenure (Kahn & Robbins, 1985; Robbins & Kahn, 1985). Thus, opportunities to disseminate scholarly research and writing on the psychology of women is still limited by women's restricted access to the resources required to produce them.

Although individual approaches to feminist psychology vary in terms of the importance they place on key ideas and issues (for example, Henley, 1985; Parlee, 1975; Unger, 1979; Wallston, 1986), three major concepts are prominent: (1) recognition of the inequality of social and institutional power distributions, especially between women and men; (2) the integration of values into scientific study; and (3) the responsibility to advocate for change. Each of these will be briefly expanded and some applications of their thrust are offered.

1. The unequal balance of power between women and men has been called "the politics of gender" (Unger, 1979). Women are viewed as an oppressed group with limited social power to influence the direction of their lives. The key concept here is power, defined as access to desired resources and influence over others. In most cultures, the assymetry of power relationships favors the higher status male, who retains the potential for social control and influence merely as a function of his gender (Sanday, 1981). The translation of this view into human transactions has demonstrated that what have been regarded as sex differences are frequently examples of status and power differences (Unger, 1978). For example, it has been documented that males touch more than they are touched by females (Henley, 1977), they take up more public space (Henley, Hamilton, & Thorne, 1984), and in mixed-sex groups they talk more and interrupt more than women do (Swacker, 1975; West & Zimmerman, 1983). Conversely, women smile more frequently than men (Frances, 1979; Hall & Halberstadt, 1986), main-

tain a tenser position when sitting (Mehrabian, 1968), and are more likely to adjust their behavior to the personality of a male partner (Weitz, 1976). Each of these documented sex differences has been reinterpreted by feminist researchers as examples of the politics of gender, wherein male power legitimizes social initiative and dominance, while female powerlessness precipitates defensive, submissive, and ingratiating behavior. For many feminist psychologists, most interactions between the sexes are examples of the operation of power relationships, because gender and status are unequally apportioned in society.

2. The place of values in scientific study raises the question of whether science is value-free. One of the major tenets of traditional scientific study is that science is objective and unaffected by personal beliefs or bias. Feminist scholarship has amply demonstrated the many ways in which traditional research has failed to be objective by maintaining a "male" bias: Most experimenters have been male (which affects the responses of participants in experiments); more male than female persons have been the subjects of research and their responses have been generalized to all individuals (including females); the content of psychological study has frequently been biased toward male interests (aggression, achievement); and important content relating to core female experience has been largely ignored (menarche, rape, intimate relationships). The feminist position insists that values enter into the scientific endeavor in all stages of research. Thus, we state our values by the theories we select (gender-free, for example), by our choice of topic (relating to the lives and experiences of women), by our research methods which carefully examine for gender bias, and by our willingness to explore new areas of research or to reinterpret old ones (Johnson, 1978; Lott, 1985; McHugh, Koeske, & Frieze, 1981).

When earlier topics of research are re-examined from a feminist view, new "facts" emerge. For example, early research on children growing up with one parent was labeled "the effects of father absence," and was usually concerned about the male child, who was assumed to experience psychological damage as a result of "father absence." More recently, the same population has been studied from the vantage point of "single parent families." Focusing on the social and economic experiences of the single parent (90% of whom are women) provided a rich array of new "facts" about the well-being of children in single-parent homes, as well as a better understanding of the financial and social stress that might mediate the onset of problem behavior in the children (Worell, in press, a; Worell & Garret-Fulks, 1983).

A second example of reinterpretation of previous research relates to the "working mother." Earlier studies of working women focused on the well-being of the children, with the assumption that mothers who leave their children to work must (a) be bad mothers, and (b) precipitate psychological problems in their children. More recently, feminist scholars have reframed this issue, choosing instead to study "dual-career" or two-paycheck families. Within this revised context, focus is removed from the "neglectful" mother and the dynamics of the family unit are examined: Time usage, child-care, financial arrangements, mutual support, satisfaction with work, sharing of household tasks, etc. (Aldous, 1982). Now we receive a picture of the family unit in terms of overall family stress and satisfaction, not just the ill effects on the child. Notice that in both of these areas, earlier research, presumably "objective" and "scientific," resulted in massive examples of "mother-blaming" (Caplan & Hall-McCorquodale, 1985). That is, whatever the problems of the child, the immediate focus was on the care-taking behavior of the mother, assuming from a traditional stance that childrearing was her job and that she alone was responsible for the outcomes. Now we know that father participation is a critical variable in family well-being and child adjustment (Lamb, 1981; Parke, 1981). Clearly, the introduction of feminist values into the research effort has resulted in new "truths" about human behavior.

3. One of the cornerstones of feminist approaches to psychology is the responsibility to advocate for change. What does the feminist psychologist want changed? First and most important, a change in the power relations between women and men is required. For example, research on organizational settings has examined occupational sex-typing, discrimination in the workplace, sexual harassment, and gender-based barriers to women in the development and advancement of their careers. Research on families has targeted wife battering, social isolation and stress on mothers with young children, dual-career marriages, alternative child-care arrangements,

and power issues in child custody and visitation following divorce. Research on violence toward women focuses on rape and people's attributions about both the rapist and the victim, on pornography and violent images portrayed toward women in the media, and on sexually abused children, most of whom are girls. Finally, research on women's mental health and psychological well-being has taken a look at the disproportionate utilization of mental health facilities by women, the power issues between women and their male therapists, and the high prevalence rates of certain psychological problems in women such as depression, anxiety, and issues concerned with eating and weight control. For women of color, research has been concerned with the high rates of suicide in young Black women and the over-representation of nonwhite women with a psychiatric diagnosis of schizophrenia (Wilkinson, 1980). All of these issues are relevant for scientific study and all have social policy implications.

The feminist researcher is mindful of the policy considerations of the research topic and seeks to maximize human potential as a research outcome. Each of these areas calls for planned intervention, community education, and social policy aimed at remediation and prevention. An example of the mandate for social change is the rise of feminist psychotherapy and counseling. As women become more aware of their options, new forms of treatment have been developed to assist them in realizing their goals.

Summary

The development of a feminist psychology has issued a call for new ways of approaching the psychology of women. Feminist psychology has reinterpreted the relations between women and men, has introduced feminist values in the research effort, has offered a fresh view of women's mental health, and has lobbied for social awareness and public policy outcomes for research. Let us be clear here that feminist researchers consist of both women and men, and that the feminist researcher believes that both women and men will benefit from a change in the social, family, and institutional relationships between the sexes. Admittedly, not all men will respond with enthusiasm to equality of power distribution, since gain by one may be seen as a loss by the other. Kahn (1984) suggests that a fruitful avenue of research is to examine men's response to a loss in power, in order to prepare both women and men for new ways of relating.

MENTAL HEALTH AND WELL-BEING

Recent approaches to the study of personal well-being and distress have taken a fresh look at the contributions of gender and sex-role socialization to the development, expression, and treatment of psychological problems. Studies on the prevalence of psychological disturbance show some distinct differences in the kinds of problems more frequently diagnosed for women and men. Examples of these differences can be seen in Table 1. Men tend to be hospitalized more frequently for antisocial and substance abuse problems, and women have higher rates of depression, eating disorders, and anxieties (Kaplan, 1983). Feminist researchers have questioned these rates of disorders, and have pointed to biased assumptions about sex-typed behaviors that are incorporated into the standard diagnostic categories (Rosewater, 1985; Worell, 1986). Kaplan (1983) asserts that the psychiatric diagnostic categories for many disorders more commonly ascribed to women are based on male-formulated norms about healthy and "crazy" behaviors. (See the Diagnostic and Statistical Manual of the American Psychiatric Association [1986] for examples of diagnostic categories and their behavioral criteria.) In addition, she agrees with other researchers that many women have been oversocialized into traditional sex-role behaviors that become exaggerated and dysfunctional for them (Chesler, 1972).

In private and outpatient settings, however, women are clearly the primary users of mental health facilities (Russo & Sobel, 1981), contributing to the perception that women are "crazier" than men (Chesler, 1972). Furthermore, the utilization rates for women would be much higher if many of the mental health needs of women currently ignored in medical data-reporting procedures were routinely included, such as alcoholism, prescription drug addiction, rape, wife-battering, and incest. Women may also experience spe-

Table 1

Diagnoses of Behavioral Disorders Assigned More

Frequently to Either Women or Men

WOMEN	MEN
Primary degenerative dementia	Multi-infarct dementia
Depression	Alcohol hallucinosis
Cyclothymic disorder	Transsexualism
Dysthymic disorder	Paraphilias
Agoraphobia	Factitious disorder
Simple phobia	Impulse control disorder
Panic disorder	Paranoid personality disorder
Somatization disorder	Antisocial personality disorder
Psychogenic pain disorder	Compulsive personality disorder
Multiple personality	
Inhibited sexual desire	
Inhibited orgasm	
Histrionic personality disorder	
Borderline personality disorder	
Dependent personality disorder	

cial problems associated with age, race, ethnic group, or sexual orientation that are not included in these data.

How can we account for these findings? Researchers have looked to the cultural expectations for gender-differentiated roles and behaviors in attempting to understand the evidence for differential rates of psychological disorders. These expectations have influenced both the kinds of symptoms and disturbances of behavior that bring people to the attention of the mental health profession, as well as the basis for judging these behaviors as normal or deviant. Traditional gender-based expectations, as we have seen, encourage different sets of behavioral orientations in women and men. Of particular relevance to mental health issues are those behaviors that relate to passivity, helplessness, self-abasement and self-blame, dependency, nurturance and care-taking, emotional expressivity, and submissiveness. These are all behavioral traits that are culturally acceptable for women in certain situations, but may contribute both to women's higher rates of certain disorders as well as psychiatric diagnoses of emotional disturbance.

In a landmark study on existing biases in the views of mental health professionals toward women, Broverman and associates (1970) showed that these health professionals made distinctions between the healthy man and the healthy woman; the trait descriptions of the healthy man, but not the healthy woman, were similar to those for a healthy adult. However, the healthy woman was described as more submissive, more emotional, less independent, and less competitive than the healthy man. That is, the healthy woman was seen in more negative terms than the healthy man. These authors described their findings as support for a double standard of mental health, whereby good adjustment was defined in terms of conformity to sex-role standards. A more recent replication of this study with college students as respondents found that males, but not females, continued to use a double standard of mental health for women and men (Brooks-Gunn & Fisch, 1980). This double standard puts women in a paradoxical bind, caught between wanting to fulfill societal expectations for being a "good woman" and experiencing social devaluation for the same traits she has been trained to display. On the other hand, should she rebel and reject her "feminine" side, she risks censure and rejection for not being sufficiently feminine.

Models of Mental Health

The evidence for gender differences in psychological symptomology and sex-role bias in mental health standards have resulted in efforts to develop alternative models of what is healthy and optimal in human functioning. In addition to the traditional model discussed above, two alternative approaches have received attention in the research literature — masculinity as a model of effective adjustment, and androgyny. The traditional model, also viewed as a *congruence model* (Whitely, 1983) presumes that mental health and well-being are maximized when gender and sex-role functioning are matched. Healthy personal adjustment in this model is evaluated by conformity to sex-role prescriptions. The *masculinity model* proposes that masculine-typed traits of assertiveness, independence, and dominance will lead to more effective functioning because they are more highly valued in society and lead to higher rewards for the individual (Kelly & Worell, 1977). Finally, the *androgyny model* proposes that individuals with both sets of traits available to them will be more flexible and adaptive across situations and thus will experience greater psychological well-being (Bem, 1974; Gilbert, 1981; Kaplan, 1976).

In testing these competing models of personal functioning, researchers have examined two broad groups of behaviors: First, those behaviors that signal effective adjustment such as measures of self-esteem, life satisfaction, social skills and relationships, and coping with life stress; and second, dysfunctional behaviors or those that indicate psychological disturbance such as indices of depression, somatic complaints, anxiety, loneliness, substance abuse, and psychosis. In comparing these mental health indices across the three models, it is clear that the traditional model of adjustment is the least advantageous to women. That is, women who are relatively unskilled in situations requiring mastery, competence, independence, and appropriate assertiveness are likely to experience problems in coping with life stress. Women whose personal orientations conform to the sex-role congruence model show lower levels of self-esteem, more anxiety, and increased evidence of depression and social introversion (Burchardt & Serbin, 1982; Feather, 1985; Spence & Helmreich, 1978; Whitely, 1984).

Of particular interest to models of mental health is the higher incidence of depression in women with traditional sex-role orientations. Women who feel depressed show symptoms of crying, loss of appetite and sleep, pervasive sadness, feelings of helplessness and hopelessness, guilt and self-blame, suicidal thoughts, and a reduction in the level of customary activity. Theories of women's depression highlight the manner in which these symptoms fit into cultural socialization patterns. More specifically, evidence points to deficits in behavioral skills that contribute to feelings of mastery and self-competence, tendencies toward blaming themselves for perceived failure, especially in their intimate relationships, and a sense of "learned helplessness" that leaves the woman feeling she has no control over the outcomes in her life (Norman, Johnson, & Miller, 1984; Rothblum, 1983). Combining these data into a cohesive picture, we can conclude that a traditional sex-role orientation that is primarily compliant, passive, and unassertive contributes to negative personal outcomes in the lives of women.

Evidence for the two alternative models of masculinity and androgyny have suggested that both of these orientations lead to high levels of self-esteem, feelings of control and mastery, positive mood states, social competence, self-rated happiness, and resistance to depression (Burchardt & Serbin, 1982; Heilbrun, 1984; Kelly & Worell, 1977; Spence & Helmreich, 1978). Repeated research on the contributions of the expressive feminine component to these mental health indices suggests that the instrumental/assertive traits contribute more heavily to feelings of competence and self-esteem, lending support for a masculine model of psychological well-being.

Before we reject the androgyny model, however, it is wise to point out that the interpersonal/expressive traits characteristic of traditional female orientations have been shown to relate in important ways to the relational skills and attachments that make women's lives meaningful and rewarding. That is, women who are high on these expressive traits demonstrate increased empathy with others, pay more attention to the behavior of others in interpersonal interactions, and are more likely to reach out to those who are in need of social support (Bem, Martyna, & Watson, 1976; Hall & Halberstadt, 1981; Worell, Newsome, & Romano, 1984). Emphasizing only the assertive and competence modes of our personalities would certainly attenuate and neglect a core component of our female identity.

Returning to our earlier discussion on theories of women's development, it appears that these data support the androgyny model of development. Although the gender-free model is intuitively appealing and in theory it becomes a goal for all personal development, it is insufficient at this time to overcome the massive socialization of women in current society that leaves them lacking in the assertive and competency skills required for effective living. To relegate our development to a limited set of capabilities and values is to deny our fullest human potential. The androgyny model, by envisioning all persons as equally competent in achievement and affectional behaviors, provides a firm foundation for positive contributions to psychological well-being.

Feminist Therapy

New ways of addressing the problems in living that face all women have been developed in response to dissatisfaction with traditional therapies. In most traditional approaches to therapy, women were helped to "adjust" to their circumstances. Differences in power and prestige that relegated women to secondary positions, sexist behaviors of male psychotherapists, and failure to attend to the external contexts of women's lives were all issues that served as catalysts for change (Brodsky, 1981; Gilbert, 1980; Rawlings & Carter, 1977). Finally, the growing body of knowledge about the psychology of women offered important information on new directions for women's development. Although many differences exist among feminist therapists on approaches and procedures in counseling, there are certain essential guidelines that are endorsed by all feminist therapists (Worell, 1980).

Guidelines for feminist therapy:

"1. Providing an egalitarian relationship with shared responsibility between counselor and client. The client is encouraged to trust her own judgment and to arrive at her own decisions. In contrast to many traditional counseling relationships, the client is never in a one-down position of having to accept counselor interpretations of her behavior or external prescriptions for appropriate living.

2. Employing a consciousness-raising approach. Women are helped to become aware of the societal restraints on their development and opportunities. Clients are helped to differentiate between the politics of the sexist social structure and those problems over which they have realistic personal control.

3. Helping women explore a sense of their personal power and how they can use it constructively in personal, business, and political relationships.

4. Helping women to get in touch with unexpressed anger in order to combat depression and to make choices about how to use their anger constructively.

5. Helping women to redefine themselves apart from their role relationships to men, children, and home; exploring women's fears about potential role changes that may alienate spouse and children, as well as co-workers and boss.

6. Encouraging women to nurture themselves as well as caring for others, thereby raising self-confidence and self-esteem.

7. Encouraging multiple skill development to increase women's competence and productivity. This may include assertiveness training, economic and career skills, and negotiation skills with important others who resist change." (Worell, 1980, pp. 480-481).

In addition to these principles, feminist therapists are particularly sensitive to core issues in women's lives that are frequently overlooked by traditional therapists: Body image, pregnancy and childbirth, menopause and aging, incest and rape, date and wife abuse, and sexual preference. Although these principles of feminist therapy have received limited attention in the research literature, women who are seeking for new expression in their lives and who identify themselves as feminist are more satisfied with feminist therapy than with traditional psychotherapy (Maracek, Kravetz, & Finn, 1979).

DIRECTIONS FOR CHANGE

Recent changes in the economic, social, and legal position of women have brought about an upheaval in traditional values, expectations, and life goals for both women and men. As a result of these events, a new field of knowledge, the psychology of women, has emerged as a force for both exploration of women's lives and as a catalyst for change. New roles for women and men are evolving, revamped power relationships between the sexes are evident, and women are eager to gain new insights into themselves. These changes demand innovations on at least three levels: Research, consumer enlightenment, and social policy. We will discuss each of these briefly.

Research is the cornerstone without which science cannot flourish. Research in the psychology of women is proceeding into uncharted areas that would not have been addressed in the absence of a feminist psychology movement. We are learning more about women's unique experiences related to both the joys and sorrows in their lives and in doing so, we are gaining new insights into ourselves. The commitment to research on topics of relevance to women's lives is essential in expanding the frontiers of knowledge about both women and men. As women's lives become the focus of exploration, researchers have extended their investigations to questions about women of color, women in poverty, and women with nontraditional sexual orientations. Ignored and neglected populations of women are targeted for a greater understanding into the themes of their lives and the meanings that are transmitted to them as a function of their minority status. It has become clear that the psychological environments of White and Black women, for example, may be very different, and may each have to be understood in their separate contexts. As each new generation of researchers explores issues of personal relevance and value, they will uncover new truths about women and men that may change the "facts" that underline our current understandings.

Consumer enlightenment refers to the dissemination of research-based knowledge to all levels of society so that this information can be integrated into current attitudes, beliefs, and practice. Parents need new information that will enable them to raise gender-free children; teachers need information that will help them in erasing school-based discrimination procedures from their curriculum and interactions with children; the media is a prime target for dissemination of information about women's lives that will help eliminate racial and gender-based stereotypes routinely portrayed to the public; and finally, colleges and universities themselves require continual infusion of new information about the psychology of women into their coursework not only in the social sciences but in all areas that deal with human behavior.

Finally, social policy dictates the quality and direction of our lives on many fronts. Social policies may be mandated through legislation that enables or requires practices in schools, communities, and in the workplace that facilitate women's development. For example, pervasive stereotypes about women's work-related abilities and characteristics have placed severe restrictions on women's access, promotion, and compensation in employment settings. Legislation affecting sexual harassment, equity in employment practices, daycare facilities, flex-time for working families, pregnancy leaves, and affirmative action are only a few of the policy implications of our knowledge that women can be as capable and productive in the workplace as men. Social policy can be also implemented in more informal ways that recognize women's powerlessness under present regulations and that modify operating procedures accordingly. For example, integrating women into religious hierarchies allows them a voice in their own spiritual lives; eliminating the generic masculine "he" in textbooks and public media enables women to feel included as equal members of the human endeavor; establishing offices in local government agencies to collect court-mandated child support following divorce facilitates single mothers in maintaining a standard of living beyond the poverty level. All of these examples of policy implementation are relatively simple in conception and inexpensive to effect. Each policy innovation sends a message to women of today and those who follow in succeeding generations that we are valued, equal, and important. As psychological research, consumer enlightenment, and so-

cial policy work together to effect societal change, we will see a
new image of women emerging and new visions of what we are and
what we can become.

REFERENCES

Albert, A.A., & Porter, J.R. (1983). Age patterns in the development of chil-
dren's gender stereotypes. *Sex Roles, 9*, 59-68.
Aldous, J. (Ed.) (1982). *Two paychecks: Life in dual earner families*. Beverly
Hills, CA: Sage.
American Psychiatric Association (1987). *Diagnostic and statistical manual of
mental disorders* (4th ed.). Washington, D.C.
American Psychological Association (1975). Report of the Task Force on Sex
Bias and Sex-Role Stereotyping in Psychotherapeutic Practice. *American Psy-
chologist, 30*, 1165-1175.
American Psychological Association (1978). Task Force on Sex Bias and Sex-
Role Stereotyping in Psychotherapeutic Practice. Guidelines for therapy with
women. *American Psychologist, 33*, 1122-1133.
Bandura, A. (1977). *Social learning theory*. Englewood, NJ: Prentice-Hall.
Bar-Tal, D. (1978). Attributional analysis of achievement behavior. *Review of
Educational Research, 48*, 259-271.
Baumrind, D. (1986). Sex differences in moral reasoning: Responses to Walker's
(1984) conclusion that there are none. *Child Development, 57*, 511-521.
Bem, S.L. (1974). The measurement of psychological androgyny. *Journal of
Consulting and Clinical Psychology, 47*, 155-162.
Bem, S.L. (1975). Sex-role adaptability: One consequence of psychological an-
drogyny. *Journal of Personality and Social Psychology, 31*, 634-643.
Bem, S.L. (1981). Gender schema theory: A cognitive account of sex-typing.
Psychological Review, 88, 354-364.
Bem, S.L. (1983). Gender schema theory and its implications for child develop-
ment: Raising gender-schematic children in a gender-schematic society. *Signs,
8*, 598-616.
Bem, S.L. (1985). Androgyny and gender scheme theory: A conceptual and empirical integration. In T.B. Sonderegger (Ed.), *Nebraska Symposium on Moti-
vation, 1984: Psychology and Gender*. (Vol. 32), pp. 179-226. Lincoln: University of Nebraska Press.
Bem, S.L., & Lenney, E. (1976). Sex-typing and the avoidance of cross-sex
behavior. *Journal of Personality and Social Psychology, 33*, 48-54.
Bem, S.L., Martyna, W., & Watson, C. (1976). Sex-typing and androgyny: Further explorations of the expressive domain. *Journal of Personality and Social
Psychology, 34*, 1016-1023.
Blake, C., & Cohen, H. (1984). *A meta-analysis of sex difference in moral devel-
opment*. Paper presented at the annual meeting of the American Psychological
Association, Toronto, Canada.

Blechman, E.A. (1980). Behavior therapies. In A.M. Brodsky and R. Hare-Mustin (Eds.), *Women and psychotherapy: An assessment of theory and research*. NY: Guilford Press.

Block, J., Denniker, E.R., & Tittle, C.K. (1981). Perceived influences on career choices of eleventh graders: Sex, SES, and ethnic group comparisons. *Sex Roles*, 7, 895-904.

Blumstein, P., & Schwartz, P. (1983). *American couples: Money, work, sex*. NY: William Morrow.

Brodsky, A. (1981). A decade of feminist influence on psychotherapy. In E. Howell and M. Bayes (Eds.), *Women and Mental Health*. NY: Basic Books.

Brooks-Gunn, J., & Fisch, M. (1980). Psychological androgyny and college students' judgments of mental health. *Sex Roles*, 6, 575-580.

Broverman, I.K., Broverman, D.M., Clarkson, F.E., Rosenkrantz, P.S., & Vogel, S.R. (1970). Sex-role stereotypes and clinical judgements of mental health. *Journal of Consulting and Clinical Psychology*, 34, 1-7.

Broverman, I.K., Vogel, S.R., Broverman, D.M., Clarkson, F.E., & Rosenkrantz, P.S. (1972). Sex role stereotypes: A current appraisal. *Journal of Social Issues*, 28, 59-78.

Burchardt, C.J., & Serbin, L.A. (1982). Psychological androgyny and personality adjustment in college and psychiatric populations. *Sex Roles*, 8, 823-834.

Caplan, P.J., & Hall-McCorquodale, I. (1985). Mother-blaming in major clinical journals. *American Journal of Orthopsychiatry*, 33, 345-354.

Chesler, P. (1972). *Women and madness*. NY: Doubleday.

Darley, J.M., & Fazio, R.H. (1980). Expectancy confirmation processes arising in the social interaction sequence. *American Psychologists*, 35, 867-881.

Davis, S.W., Williams, J.E., & Best, D.L. (1982). Sex-trait stereotypes in the self and peer descriptions of third grade children. *Sex Roles*, 8, 315-331.

Deaux, K. (1984). From individual differences to social categories. *American Psychologist*, 39, 105-116.

Doherty, M.A. (1976). Sexual bias in personality theory. In L.W. Harmon, J.M. Birk, L.E. Fitzgerald & M.F. Tanney (Eds.), *Counseling women*. Monterey, CA: Brooks/Cole.

Erikson, E. (1963). *Childhood and society*. (2nd edition). NY: Norton.

Erikson, E. (1968). *Identity: Youth and crisis*. NY: Norton.

Eron, L.D. (1980). Prescription for reduction of aggression. *American Psychologist*, 35, 244-252.

Feather, N.T. (1985). Masculinity, femininity, self-esteem, and subclinical depression. *Sex Roles*, 12, 491-500.

Flerx, V.C., Fidler, D.S., & Rogers, R.W. (1976). Sex role stereotypes: Developmental aspects and early intervention. *Child Development*, 47, 998-1007.

Frable, D.E.S., & Bem, S.L. (1985). If you're gender aschematic, all members of the opposite sex look alike. *Journal of Personality and Social Psychology*, 47, 459-468.

Frances, S.J. (1979). Sex differences in nonverbal behavior. *Sex Roles*, 5, 519-535.

Freud, S. (1948). Some psychological consequences of the anatomical distinction between the sexes. In *Collected Papers*, Vol. 5, London: Hogarth.

Freud, S. (1965). *New introductory lectures on psychoanalysis*. NY: Norton.

Garrett, C.S., Ein, P.L., & Tremaine, L. (1977). The development of gender stereotyping of adult occupation in elementary school children. *Child Development, 48,* 507-512.

Gilbert, L.A. (1980). Feminist therapy. In A.M. Brodsky and R.T. Hare-Mustin (Eds.), *Women and psychotherapy: An assessment of research and practice.* NY: Guilford Press.

Gilbert, L.A. (1981). Toward mental health: The benefits of psychological androgyny. *Professional Psychology, 12,* 29-38.

Gilligan, C. (1982). *In a different voice: Psychological theory and women's development.* Cambridge: Harvard University Press.

Greene, B.A. (1986). When the therapist is white and the patient is black: Considerations for psychotherapy in the feminist heterosexual and Lesbian communities. In D. Lamb (Ed.), *The dynamics of feminist therapy.* NY: The Haworth Press.

Hall, J.A., & Halberstadt, A.G. (1981). Sex roles and nonverbal communication skills. *Sex Roles, 7,* 273-287.

Hall, J.A., & Halberstadt, A.G. (1986). Smiling and gazing. In J.S. Hyde & M.C. Linn (Eds.), *The psychology of gender: Advances through meta-analysis.* Baltimore: The Johns Hopkins Press.

Heilbrun, A.B. (1984). Sex-based models of androgyny: A further cognitive elaboration of competence differences. *Journal of Personality and Social Psychology, 46,* 216-229.

Henley, N. (1977). *Body politics: Power, sex and non-verbal communication.* Englewood Cliffs, NJ: Prentice-Hall.

Henley, N.M. (1985). Review essay: Psychology and gender. *Sign: Journal of Women in Culture and Society, 11,* 101-119.

Henley, N., Hamilton, M., & Thorne, B. (1984). Womanspeak and manspeak: Sex differences and sexism in communication, verbal and nonverbal. In A.G. Sargent (Ed.), *Beyond sex roles.* St. Paul: West Publishing, 2nd edition.

Herzog, A.R., & Bachman, J.G. (1982). *Sexrole attitudes among high school seniors: Views about work and family roles.* Institute for Social Research, University of Michigan.

Hoffman, L.W. (1977). Changes in family roles, socialization and sex differences. *American Psychologist, 32,* 644-657.

Hurtig, A.L., & Peterson, A.C. (1982). *The relationship of sex-role identity to ego-development and self-esteem in adolescence.* Paper presented at the annual meeting of the American Psychological Association, Washington, D.C.

Hyde, J.S. (1986). Gender differences in aggression. In J.S. Hyde & M.L. Linn (Eds.), *The psychology of gender differences: Advances through meta-analysis.* Baltimore: The Johns Hopkins University Press.

Hyde, J.S., & Linn, M.C. (Eds.) (1986). *The psychology of gender: Advances through meta-analysis.* Baltimore: Johns Hopkins University Press.

Johnson, P.B. (1978). Doing psychological research. In I.H. Frieze, J.E. Parsons, P.B. Johnson, D.N. Rublee & G. Zellman (Eds.), *Women and sex roles: A social psychological perspective*. NY: W. W. Norton.

Kahn, A. (1984). The power war: Male response to power loss under equality. *Psychology of Women Quarterly, 8*, 234-247.

Kahn, E.D., & Robbins, L. (1985). Social psychological issues in sex discrimination. *Journal of Social Issues, 41*, 135-154.

Kandel, D., & Davies, M. (1982). Epidemiology of depressive mood in adolescence. *Archives of General Psychiatry, 39*, 1205-1212.

Kaplan, A.G. (1976). Androgyny as a model of mental health for women: From theory to therapy. In A.G. Kaplan & J.B. Bean (Eds.), *Beyond sex-role stereotypes: Readings toward a psychology of androgyny*. Boston: Little, Brown.

Kaplan, M. (1983). A woman's view of DSM III. *American Psychologist, 38*, 786-792.

Kelly, J.A., & Worell, J. (1977). New formulations of sex roles and androgyny: A critical review. *Journal of Consulting and Clinical Psychology, 45*, 1101-1115.

Kohlberg, L. (1969). Stages and sequences: The cognitive-developmental approach to socialization. In D.A. Goslin (Ed)., *Handbook of socialization theory and research*. Chicago: Rand McNally.

Kohlberg, L. (1976). Moral stages and moralization. In T. Likona (Ed.), *Moral development and behavior*. NY: Holt-Rinehart.

Kohlberg, L., & Kramer, R. (1969). Continuities and discontinuities in child and adult moral development. *Human Development, 12*, 93-120.

Kuhn, D., Nash, S.C., & Brucken, L. (1978). Sex role concepts of two- and three-year olds. *Child Development, 49*, 445-451.

Kurdek, L.A. (1987). Sex-role self schema and psychological adjustment in coupled homosexual men and women. *Sex Roles, 17*, 549-562.

Lamb, M.E. (1981). *The role of the father in child development*, 2nd edition. NY: Wiley.

Lamke, K. (1982a). The impact of sex-role orientation on self-esteem in early adolescence. *Child Development, 33*, 1530-1535.

Lamke, L.K. (1982b). Adjustment and sex-role orientation in early adolescence. *Journal of Youth and Adolescence, 11*, 247-259.

Lott, B. (1985). The potential enrichment of social/personality psychology through feminist research and vice versa. *American Psychologist, 40*, 155-164.

Maccoby, E.E., & Jacklin, C.N. (1974). *The psychology of sex differences*. Stanford: Stanford University Press.

Maracek, J., Kravetz, D., & Finn, S.A. (1979). A comparison of women who enter feminist therapy and women who enter traditional therapy. *Journal of Consulting and Clinical Psychology, 47*, 734-742.

McHugh, M.C., Koeske, R.D., & Frieze, I.H. (Eds.) (1981). *Guidelines for nonsexist research*. Report of The Task Force of Division 35, American Psychological Association, Washington, D.C.

Mehrabian, A. (1968). Relationship of attitude to seated posture, orientation, and distance. *Journal of Personality and Social Psychology*, *10*, 26-30.

Norman, W.H., Johnson, B.A., & Miller, I.W., III (1984). Depression: A behavioral-cognitive approach. In E.A. Blechman (Ed.), *Behavior modification with women*. NY: Guilford Press.

Orlofsky, J.L. (1981). Relationship between sex-role attitudes and personality traits and the sex-role behavior scale—I: A new measure of masculine and feminine role behaviors and interests. *Journal of Personality and Social Psychology*, *40*, 127-140.

Parke, R. (1981). *Fathers*. Cambridge, MA: Harvard University Press.

Parlee, M.B. (1975). Review Essay: Psychology. *Signs: Journal of Women in Culture and Society*, *1*, 119-138.

Rawlings, E.I., & Carter, D.K. (Eds.) (1977). *Psychotherapy for women: Treatment toward equality*. Springfield, IL: Charles C. Thomas.

Robbins, L., & Kahn, E.D. (1985). Sex discrimination and sex equity for faculty women in the 1980's. *Journal of Social Issues*, *41*, 1-16.

Robinson (1983). Black women: A tradition of self-reliant strength. *Women & Therapy*, *2*, 135-143.

Rosenkrantz, P.S., Vogel, S.R., Bee, H., Broverman, I.K., & Broverman, D.M. (1968). Sex-role stereotypes and self-concepts in college students. *Journal of Consulting and Clinical Psychology*, *32*, 287-295.

Rosewater, L.B. (1985). Schizophrenic, borderline, or battered? In L.B. Rosewater & L.E. Walker (Eds.), *Handbook of feminist therapy: Women's issues in psychotherapy*. NY: Springer.

Rothbart, M.K., Hanley, D., & Alpert, M. (1986). Gender differences in moral reasoning. *Sex Roles*, *15*, 645-654.

Rothblum, E. (1983). Sex-role stereotypes and depression in women. In V. Franks and E. Rothblum (Eds.), *The Stereotyping of women: Its effects on mental health*. NY: Springer.

Rubin, J.Z., Provenzano, F.J., & Luria, Z. (1974). The eye of the beholder: Parent's views of sex of newborns. *American Journal of Orthopsychiatry*, *44*, 512-519.

Ruble, D.N., & Ruble, T.L. (1982). Sex stereotypes. In A.G. Miller (Ed.), *In the eye of the beholder: Contemporary issues in stereotyping*. NY: Praeger.

Ruble, T. (1983). Sex stereotypes: Issues of change in the 1970's. *Sex Roles*, *9*, 397-402.

Russo, N.F., & Sobel, B.S. (1981). Sex differences in the utilization of mental health facilities. *Professional Psychology*, *12*, 7-19.

Sanday, P.R. (1981). *Female power and male dominance: On the origins of sexual inequality*. Cambridge: Cambridge University Press.

Sherman, J.A. (1971). *On the psychology of women: A survey of empirical studies*. Springfield, IL: C. C. Thomas.

Spence, J.T., Helmreich, R., & Stapp, J. (1975). Ratings of self and peers on sex-role attributes and their relation to self-esteem and conceptions of masculinity and femininity. *Journal of Personality and Social Psychology*, *32*, 29-39.

Spence, J.T., & Helmreich, R.L. (1978). *Masculinity and femininity: Their psychological dimensions, correlates and antecedents*. Austin: University of Texas Press.

Swacker, M. (1975). The sex of the speaker as a sociolinguistic variable. In B. Thorne & N. Henley (Eds.), *Language and Sex: Difference and Dominance*. Rowley, MA: Newbury House.

Unger, R.K. (1978). The politics of gender: A review of relevant literature. In J. Sherman and F. Denmark (Eds.), *Psychology of Women: Future Directions of Research*. NY: Psychological Dimensions.

Unger, R.K. (1979). *Female and male: Psychological perspectives*. NY: Harper & Rowe.

Wallston, B.S. (1986). *What's in a name revisited: Psychology of women versus feminist psychology*. Invited address presented at the Association for Women in Psychology, Oakland, CA, March.

Weitz, S. (1976). Sex differences in nonverbal communication. *Sex Roles*, *2*, 175-184.

West, C., & Zimmerman, D.H. (1983). Small insults: A study of interruptions in cross-sex conversations between unacquainted persons. In B. Thorne, C. Kramarae, & N. Henley (Eds.), *Language, Gender, and Society*. Rowley, MA: Newbury House.

Whitely, B.E., Jr. (1983). Sex role orientation and self-esteem: A critical meta-analysis review. *Journal of Personality and Social Psychology*, *44*, 765-778.

Whitely, B.E., Jr. (1984). Sex-role orientation and psychological well-being: Two meta-analyses. *Sex Roles*, *12*, 207-225.

Wilkinson, D. (1980). Minority women: Sociocultural issues. In A. Brodsky & R. Harc-Mustin (Eds.), *Women and psychotherapy*. NY: Guilford.

Woelfel, J.C. (1981). Women in the United States Army. *Sex Roles*, *7*, 785-800.

Worell, J. (1978). Sex roles and psychological well-being: Perspectives on methodology. *Journal of Consulting and Clinical Psychology*, *46*, 777-791.

Worell, J. (1980). New directions in counseling women. *Personnel and Guidance Journal*, *58*, 477-484.

Worell, J. (1981). Life-span sex roles: Development, continuity, and change. In R.M. Lerner & N.A. Busch-Rossnagel (Eds.), *Individuals as producers of their development*. NY: Academic Press.

Worell, J. (1982). Psychological sex roles: Significance and change. In J. Worell (Ed.), *Psychological development in the elementary years*. NY: Academic Press.

Worell, J. (1988, a). Single mothers: From problems to policies. *Women & Therapy*, *7*, 3-14.

Worell, J. (in press, b). Sex roles in transition. In J. Worell & F. Danner (Eds.), *Adolescent development: Issues for education*. Academic Press.

Worell, J. (1986). *The DSM III-R: Controversies in gender bias*. Paper presented at the annual meeting of the Association for the Advancement of Behavior Therapy. Chicago, IL: November.

Worell, J., & Garret-Fulks, N.J. (1983). The resocialization of single-again women. In V. Franks & E. Rothblum (Eds.), *The stereotyping of women: Its effects on mental health*. NY: Springer.

Worell, J., Newsome, T., & Romano, P. (1984). *Patterns of nurturance in same and cross-gender close friendships*. Invited paper presented at the first Nag's Head Conference on Sex and Gender, May.

Zanna, M.P., & Pack, S.J. (1975). On the self-fulfilling nature of apparent sex differences in behavior. *Journal of Experimental Social Psychology, 11*, 583-591.

Images of Women:
Reflections from the Medical Care System

Judith E. Albino
Lisa A. Tedesco
Cheryl L. Shenkle

INTRODUCTION

Historically, the childbearing role of women set certain expectations and limits on their lives and activities which seemed inevitable and immutable. Pregnancy and lactation represented primary social survival functions which precluded extensive participation in other activities such as meeting needs for food, shelter, and safety, or later, providing income to obtain these things, as well as participation in governance. The fact that women generally have less muscle mass and physical strength than men also contributed to the development of distinct images of men and women, and to the traditional gender-based division of labor whereby men were responsible for such external and "instrumental" activities as hunting, fighting, building, and organizing society, while women stayed close to home and carried out supportive or "expressive" tasks such as food preparation and home-tending, as well as work related to child care. These patterns were virtually universal among early societies.

In the past 200 years or so, however, science and technology have provided both increasing control over reproductive functions and modification of the requirements of the childbearing and caregiving responsibilities. Clearly, in modern society these responsibilities no longer require the full and life-long dedication of women. Indeed, with the exception of childbearing itself, it can be said that these responsibilities do not necessarily require the participation of women at all. Yet the previously described division of labor continues to be practiced — if somewhat less purely than in the past, and considerable social pressure supports this practice. During the World War II years, of course, women were encouraged to take up the male factory and other work roles abandoned by soldiers sent abroad, but which were necessary to support the war effort. This was the one significant exception (quickly reversed when the men returned home) to what now appears to represent a sustained and often extraordinary effort to maintain traditional perceptions of male and female roles—particularly with respect to the division of labor. This has been evident in the slow opening of job opportunities for women and the lingering inequities in pay and status for men and women doing the same work, as well as in the individual reluctance of many men to assume domestic responsibilities.

A number of theories have been advanced to explain the unwillingness of society to give up outmoded and unfair attitudes towards women's work and life roles. These have included psychodynamic and economic, as well as social psychological, approaches to the question. It is not the goal of this chapter to explore such theories, however. Rather, our special interest lies in some of the social mechanisms through which the myth of gender-determined roles has been maintained. In particular, it is our thesis that the teaching and practice of medicine, as it is related to women and women's health issues, has served to communicate an image of woman which has unnecessarily and inappropriately limited and proscribed the work and life roles of women. While it is important to realize that the actions of the medical profession have been shaped by the larger social and economic contexts within which they occurred, they are of even greater interest precisely because they have reflected broader concerns. No doubt the picture for minority women is probably even more dismal; however, the literature scarcely addresses the combined problems of racism and sexism for women in the medical profession. With this in mind, it is our contention that all women, regardless of their cultural backgrounds, suffer from problems inherent in a medical profession heavily dominated by males. Moreover, since medicine has represented "scientific" and "expert" opinions, it has provided perhaps the single most influential instrument in the validation of social efforts to maintain anachronistic images of women, in general.

BIOLOGY AND SELF-CONCEPT

Women and men alike develop perceptions of their bodies and their physiology through social learning processes, as well as through direct experience and discovery. Mothers and fathers, siblings, and influential others in a child's life provide models for what we can expect of our bodies in terms of both appearance and performance. This represents, of course, one important aspect of gender identification and also an important part of our understanding of sex differences and, correspondingly, of the behaviors, tasks, and life roles which are appropriately assumed by men and by women. Yet adult understandings and expectations of our bodies are shaped by formal sources of knowledge as well — by the scientific and medical experts who investigate and describe human physiology, and who treat physical ailments and make recommendations for the maintenance of health. While information from these formal sources may reach the majority of the population slowly, there is no doubt of its influence on social standards over time. One narrow, but salient, example of this might be the changing public perceptions of cigarette smoking. Accepted as a mark of masculine behavior more than 100 years ago, cigarette smoking did not become "feminine" in this country until long after women gained the vote and smoking became a symbol of equality, as well as part of a new, more overt sexuality expected of women. Today, of course, smoking is increasingly seen as a sign of weakness in either sex — at least within the better informed and more affluent parts of society which place strong emphasis on healthy lifestyles and behavior. Perhaps because of what is now known about the potential effects of smoking on fetal development, we can expect that even stronger social sanctions will apply to smoking by women. While most of us would consider this type of influence on women's behaviors as a positive phenomenon, the same cannot be said for all medical recommendations which have shaped women's behavior over the years.

Historical Perspectives

One of the best accounts to date of the influence of expert advice on the lives of women can be found in *For Her Own Good*, the 1978 work by Barbara Ehrenreich and Deirdre English. This work

chronicles more than 100 years during which male-dominated professions have created and re-created women to meet the needs and
enhance the goals of men. While we recommend the Ehrenreich and
English volume in its entirety, a brief summary of some of the
points they covered provides an appropriate historical context for
our discussion of the medical care system's part in shaping images
of women and influencing women's life and work roles.

Ehrenreich and English described the rise of the psychomedical
experts of the nineteenth century as a movement which paralleled
and, indeed, was inextricably related to the suppression and even-
tual demise of female-dominated lay healing and healers which
flourished in this country's first century. The development of a
medical system based on the European models raised medical care
to the status of a commodity and, therefore, made it attractive for
the first time to men. The subsequent exclusion of women from the
practice of medicine—and eventually even from the practice of
midwifery as well—was merely one aspect of an evolving social
structure with the marketplace at its center. Much of women's traditional work had already been taken over by the industrialization of
America, allowing the possibility of a rational approach to division
of labor. Ehrenreich and English saw the romantic solution to "the
woman question" as primarily a response to the possibility this represented—that is, the possibility that women might simply join men
in the savage competition of the industrial marketplace. The greatest need of men was for a counterpoint to their own lives. As a
result, they called on science to support a view of women as delicate creatures who must be protected from the harsh realities of life
and from labor, either physical or mental.

Even as the new medical specialty of gynecology was developing, women were categorically denied admission to medical school.
Physicians maintained that too much mental work would render
them sexually debilitated and unfit for motherhood. They depicted a
continuing tension between the brain and the uterus, and maintained
that virtually all physical complaints of women were related to the
uterus. Dr. Edward Clarke went so far as to say that higher education would cause a woman's uterus to atrophy. Physicians such as
Dr. S. Weir Mitchell of Philadelphia specialized in nervous disorders of women of the affluent classes. Neurasthenia, or nervous

prostration, as it was sometimes called, was increasing dramatically among these women by the mid-nineteenth century, thus creating a new clientele for the elitist medical profession. Their treatment, other than extended bed rest and admonitions to accept their womanly roles and responsibilities, invariably focused on the sexual organs and included the application of leeches, cauterization of the cervix, or injections of a variety of substances into the uterus. Clitoridectomies were common during the 1860s, and removal of the ovaries became common toward the end of the century—all for complaints that look now for all the world like depressions related to life circumstances, perhaps the lack of meaningful activities or relationships.

While they rarely exhibited the symptoms and, at any rate, could not have afforded the treatments rendered their wealthier sisters, women of poverty also played an important role in the development of the new medical experts. They provided the "low-risk" case material on which young physicians in training could practice. After the publication of the Flexner Report in 1910, virtually every medical school which survived attached itself to a charity hospital for just this purpose. While the Flexner Report is still heralded as the single most influential event in the history of medical education, primarily because of its recommendations that medical schools should provide instruction in basic and laboratory sciences and extensive clinical practice, its position on the training of women physicians was equally influential, if less enduring. Flexner reported that he found virtually no demand for women physicians and no indication that women wanted to become physicians. Even had he not made these statements, his general recommendations for reform ensured the closing of seven out of ten female medical schools, as well as most of the so-called "irregular" schools based on the Popular Health Movement, which had generally admitted women. By the early part of this century, women had been effectively excluded from the profession which proceeded to define them as "sick" merely because of their reproductive anatomy.

The journey back from this predicament has been tortuous and still appears incomplete. Ehrenreich and English trace its route through the home economics movement, whose growth was not unrelated to changes in medical views wrought by the germ theory of disease, and the child development movement of the middle third of this century, which brought new attempts to define women's roles and responsibilities thoroughly, rigidly—and almost always by men. Even today, when there is at least superficially some commitment in society to equality of opportunity for women, social perceptions—including those of medical professionals—do not always provide women with clear or consistent feedback which allows them to make personally appropriate choices about their lives and work.

How Physicians View Women

The physician's view of women is part of the social fabric that defines the culture of medicine. Despite the increasing numbers of women accepted into medical schools, the medical profession continues to be dominated by male physicians in control of the patient environment. This control has a profound influence on the socialization of new physicians, both male and female, and on the development of attitudes toward women patients. In a review of what medical schools teach about women, Howell (1974) concluded that the gender-specific or "special" health problems of women are frequently devalued, characterized as psychological in origin, or are considered too unimportant to discuss. Demeaning jokes, made at the expense of women by male medical school faculty, also are instrumental in creating negative attitudes toward the female patient within the medical care system. In effect, medical students are learning both cognitive and behavioral responses to a new and powerful attitude object, the woman patient.

Lennane and Lennane (1973), physician researchers, investigated medical teaching and practice on the four disorders of women that are frequently described as psychogenic in origin. These were primary dysmenorrhea, nausea of pregnancy, pain in labor, and behavior disorders of infants. They reported that each of these health problems are routinely presented in textbooks and in lectures as being psychogenic in origin, even though there are no data to support such explanations. In each case, moreover, there are sound reasons for accepting an alternative explanation. For example, infant colic is a common and well-defined clinical condition occurring in normal thriving babies between one and four months of age. It has an unknown origin, and it is responsive to drug therapy, although as late as the '60s standard pediatric textbooks referred to colic as stemming from maternal conflicts with the feminine role, insecurity, and tension. The Lennanes reported that physicians were labeling mothers concerned about colic as "neurotic" or "unfeminine." They found no attempts to explain maternal tension as a normal response to the new infant's unexplained screaming and discomfort.

Moving from teaching to clinical practice, Armitage, Schneiderman, and Bass (1979) compared physicians' responses to the health complaints of men and women. From the charts of 52 married couples seeing nine male family physicians, 90 male and 91 female illness episodes were analyzed. Primary among the presenting complaints were back pain, headache, dizziness, chest pain, and fatigue. The investigators found that physician workups were more extensive overall for men than for women. This difference was also found for each individual complaint, with low back pain and headache producing the greatest differences. While the patients in this study had nearly identical numbers of physician visits for these non-sex-related complaints, the authors allowed that the study differences might be related to the general notion that women make more frequent visits than do men to their physicians, justifying the greater attention paid to male patients per visit.

For a similar study, however, Greer, Dickerson, Schneiderman, Atkins, and Bass (1986) found no significant differences between male and female patients for either content or extent of care provided for five non-sex-related complaints nor any evidence that females visited the doctor more times for any of the five complaints than did males. Greer et al. (1986) attributed their nonsignificant findings, in part, to the fact that the physicians were women as well as men and that they practiced together in partnership. In other investigations that included sex-related complaints (e.g., pregnancy, gynecological well-care), the female to male visit ratio was 1.5 to 1. When data are not presented in terms of type and purpose of visit by sex, then, it appears that women utilize physician services more than men. Whether women are trying to get well or trying to stay well with sex-specific care for preventive purposes, they seem to run the risk of having their experiences or complaints trivialized by the medical profession.

Informative processes in medical care were the focus of a federally funded study by Wallen, Waitzkin, and Stoeckle (1979). These investigators analyzed 336 tape recorded doctor-patient interactions and assessed differences in information seeking and responding for 184 male and 130 female patients. Information was offered spontaneously with equal frequency to males and females by the 34 male physicians in the study. Women patients asked significantly more questions, however, and were the recipients of a greater total number of informative statements or explanations, a finding that appears consistent with other reports that women have more interest in health matters. There was no difference for male and female patients when total time spent explaining rather than the absolute number of explanations was assessed, however. This suggests that men were receiving fewer, but fuller, explanations without asking as many questions. The physicians were also asked to respond to several questions on attitudes and beliefs about their patients. Even though women asked significantly more questions than men, physicians did not perceive women to need or want more information than men. Wallen and her associates suggest that physicians may attribute the questioning behavior of women to other motives. In addition, physicians indicated that psychological components were more important in illnesses of female patients than they were for male patients. The physicians also perceived their women patients to have significantly less favorable prognoses than their men patients. This was a particularly remarkable finding, since inspection of diagnostic categories revealed that generally the women in this sample tended to be diagnosed as physically well. These findings were consistent, too, with sex differences found for quality of physician information. The technical nature of physicians' responses was not different for male and female patients. The level of technicality for physician responses to female patients' questions was frequently mismatched, however, with the most errors occurring as responses lower in level than the questions asked. This indicates that physicians frequently "talked down" to their female patients.

Efforts of female patients to gain information and to take responsibility for their health are reconstructed by physicians to reflect women as emotionally dependent and hypochondriacal. As Wallen et al. (1979) point out, these attitudes and beliefs impair women's ability to make autonomous decisions and to select from a number of health care options. The maintenance of a male power advantage through withholding and reconstructing information reflects what Ehrenreich and English (1973) have described as the white male middle-class monopoly on medical knowledge and practice. The problem for women then is twofold: first, it involves gaining access to health care and then, gaining full benefit from health care.

Research on attitudes of patients and hospital staff's perceptions of patients shows that the consequences of being perceived as a "problem patient" included early discharge, referral for psychiatric help, neglect, or prescription of tranquilizers (Lorber, 1975). Patients who questioned, complained, or interfered with routines by requiring more time than the staff expected were defined as "problem patients." While data on staff perceptions by sex of patient were not reported, about half of the 103 surgical patients were women. Based on the findings of Wallen et al. (1979) regarding perceptions of women patients, we would expect this group to receive a disproportionate share of "problem patient" remedies.

How Physicians Treat Women

A recent report by Verbrugge (1984) analyzed a National Ambulatory Medical Care Survey for physician treatment differences of mentally distressed men and women. From office-based physician records, 1,871 mental complaint visits and 2,505 mental diagnosis visits were examined. There were no significant differences between men and women patients to present a mental symptom or to receive a mental diagnosis. However, when men complained of a mental problem, they were more likely than women to be diagnosed with a mental disorder. Physicians also tended to evaluate men's mental distress as more serious than women's. When women complained of mental symptoms they received more physical diagnoses than men. Conversely, when women complained of physical symptoms, they received more diagnoses of mental disorders.

One explanation Verbrugge (1984) offers for these findings is that men are reluctant to seek help for psychological reasons and when they do, their problems are rather acute. This prompts agreement between male patient symptom presentation and physician diagnoses. It also has been suggested that women generally present both physical and mental symptoms, in combination. Again, the medical establishment can construe these data to suggest that women patients present a set of confused symptoms, often not reporting the most salient ones to aid in diagnosis. The sensitivity women appear to have related to mind-body connection is minimized and ignored via non-concurring physician diagnoses.

While Verbrugge found that men and women received the same amount of diagnostic, therapeutic, and follow-up services, the types of services were different. Women received limited examinations, blood pressure assessments, and more drug prescriptions than men. Men received either no service at all, general examinations, or medical counseling. Follow-up care occurred with the diagnosing physician more often for women than men. Men were either sent on to another physician or received no follow-up care. When medical factors such as patient's age, seriousness of complaint, or prior illness status were controlled for, these differences between male and female patients still emerged. Two psychosocial explanations are offered by the author. Perhaps the emotionally distressed woman requests and receives more care, or maybe physicians perceive the female patient with psychological problems as "gullible and fussy," causing physicians to offer unnecessary services and follow-up appointments. At best, these data suggest that physicians view the woman patient as childlike, confused, and ill-defined, not knowing the difference between mental and physical symptoms, and in need of monitoring and guidance.

A sociolinguistic analysis conducted by West (1984) of patient-physician encounters reveals some very interesting sex differences in communication. Male physicians tended to interrupt their patients more than patients interrupted their physician. This was especially true for black patients. Interruptions were often used for control and interaction dominance. This pattern was reversed for female physicians. Female physicians were interrupted by patients as much or more than they interrupted patients. This conflicts with traditional sociological notions presented by Parsons (1951) regarding the essential nature of communication asymmetry between physician and patient. That is, physicians can only provide medical care if they have control over the patient. This is placed in motion through appropriate role taking and social expectations of behavior. The physician is to remain emotionally neutral and the patient is to be emotionally and situationally dependent. West (1984) concludes that her data suggest that gender is a "master" status variable, having more influence in this situation than the traditional power relationship between physician and patient.

Other writers have presented psychosocial explanations for patient gender and provider gender differences (Weisman and Teitelbaum, 1985; Shapiro, McGrath, & Anderson, 1983). For example, male and female physicians are perceived differently by patients in terms of their personal qualities. Women view women physicians as both technical in orientation (instrumental) and interpersonally sensitive (expressive). Male physicians were not perceived to be skillful in the expressive domain.

These results seem to coincide with other findings that indicate women physicians' attitudes are more oriented toward the social aspects of health care, with more concern for women's health issues than their male colleagues. These attitudes may explain some of the practice differences reported for male and female physicians (Weisman & Teitelbaum, 1985). One estimate indicates that male obstetrician-gynecologists see 3 patients per office hour, compared with 1.73 patient visits per hour for female obstetrician-gynecologists (Langwell, 1982). Another investigation of practice characteristics shows female obstetrician-gynecologists as having an average of 49 visits per week of 17.1 minutes average duration. This compares with 69.5 visits of 13.8 minutes for male obstetrician-gynecologists (Cypress, 1984).

Weisman and Teitlebaum (1985) suggest that both structural characteristics, such as fee for service versus clinic settings or differences in staffing, and interpersonal characteristics may explain these gender-related physician differences. The congruence of gender status and the non-trivialization of patient distress are no doubt key factors that enhance the female physician-female patient transaction. While these qualities have the potential for expression in male provider-female patient transactions, they are the exception and not the rule. The masochistic adjustment of women to the negative image of her as a patient may be coming to an end as we see the emergence of new physicians who validate and affirm the unique health care needs of women.

WOMEN AND MEDICAL EDUCATION

Women in Medical Schools

One development which has the potential for effecting change in the health care of women is the increase in the number of women entering medical school. More than 21,000 women were enrolled in 1984-85, or almost 32% of all medical school enrollees. While only 14,000 women graduated from medical school between 1930 and 1970, more than 20,000 received medical degrees between 1970 and 1980, and over 16,000 have received degrees since 1980 (Heins, 1985). Data from the American Medical Association indicate that among black physicians, the increasing proportion of women is even more appreciable. As early as 1981, women constituted 33 percent of black medical graduates; they are projected to comprise 20 to 30 percent of all physicians by the year 2000 (Epps, 1986). However, the number of female graduates seems to be leveling off with annual increases of only one or two percent in the last five years.

Three major factors have influenced changes in female admissions to medical schools. First, federal antidiscriminatory legislation was enacted. Title IX of the Higher Education Act Amendments of 1972, as well as regulations issued in promulgation of the Public Health Service Act of 1975, outlawed sex discrimination in medical school admissions. The second major factor was the adoption of a resolution on equal opportunity by the Assembly of the Association of American Medical Colleges in November 1970. Finally, the feminist movement stimulated changes in women's attitudes and aspirations (Heins, 1985). While the first two of these factors served to lower formal barriers to medical education for women, the social support and encouragement for women to pursue careers in the male-dominated medical profession may have been the single most significant factor in increasing female applications.

For blacks in particular, the tremendous increase in the number of women medical school enrollees also represents a relative decrease in the size of the black male medical school applicants. With the breakdown of racial barriers, many young black men who once would have chosen medicine as a career are aspiring to other lucrative occupations. Other explanations, such as the problems in medical practice, competition, and lack of adequate support systems have also contributed to the reduction in available black male medical school students and the subsequent increase in the number of well prepared black women taking their place (Epps, 1986).

Clearly, many of the women entering medicine today have been inspired by the women's health movement. Although there are as yet no data to confirm this, Dr. Naomi Bluestone has observed that women students appear to have a personal commitment to the health problems of women and realize that a degree in medicine is a power base from which to work toward change (Bluestone, 1978). Based on her conversations and interviews with female medical students, Bluestone reports that these women are more vocal in protecting themselves against the sexist remarks and slurs characteristic of the male-dominated medical profession. They are also aware of the loneliness and depression experienced by women of a previous generation and are forming support networks to counter this (Bluestone, 1978). Other researchers have noted that the blatant sexist remarks made by male professors have diminished greatly, as they have become more conscious of the female presence (Heins, 1985).

Nevertheless, medical schools are still primarily a male domain to which women must adapt if they are to succeed. Although facilities are now provided for women interns and residents (they no longer have to use the nurses' locker rooms), women still must negotiate space for themselves in other ways. Institutional practices are designed for the male biological clock, for example. Arranging time for childbearing within the rigorous medical training schedule is extremely difficult. In fact, a woman can easily earn the animosity of her male colleagues by asking for alterations in her call schedule, hours, or assignments because of childcare responsibilities. Such requests may be interpreted as a woman taking advantage of her sex (Adelman, 1983).

In the past, women medical students often simply decided not to get married or not to have children. Current pressures, however, are for women both to pursue careers and to have children, and new conflicts are created for women who wish to have children before they are 30. The concerns of marriage and a family occur at a time when professional careers are most demanding, with clinical rotations that demand long hours away from home and often with very little sleep. Even for women who remain single, there are stresses and role conflicts. Integration of the feminine self-concept with the physician's role is not an easy task. While male medical students can identify with other male physicians and maintain consistency with their own masculine identification, the paucity of female role models makes it difficult for women medical students to maintain a feminine identity in a male-dominated world.

One of the functions of medical school, and indeed of any professional school, is socialization into a profession—that is, communicating to aspiring professionals the roles, values, attitudes, and expectations that are a part of one's professional career. In medical school, and afterwards, this socialization occurs in both formally structured and informal settings. Women medical students, however, often have been excluded from informal social gatherings and study groups where much of this socialization occurs (Smith, Lancaster, & Fleming, 1984). The informal support provided by a role model or mentor is also vitally important to socialization within one's future career. Students learn how to function within the profession by identifying with successful role models. These mentors can help enhance the student's visibility and find opportunities for research, training, and practice arrangements. A recent study showed that the most important factor in the professional attainment of female physicians was the prestige of the hospital of residency, and mentors help provide access to these programs (Bobula, 1980). The paucity of black female role models and mentors and the lack of social networks becomes an even greater impediment for black women physicians being trained in predominantly white institutions (Epps, 1986).

In general, the problem of female role models is exacerbated because there are so few women at the top in medical academia. While women represented one out of every four faculty members hired between 1975 and 1978, they comprised only 5% of full professors, 13% of associate professors, and 20% of assistant professors (Heins, 1985). "In 1981, the latest year for which data are available, there were 7,500 women faculty members and it is estimated that in 1983 women constituted 17% of all medical school faculty" (Heins, 1985, p. 47). The largest numbers of women faculty are in pediatrics, internal medicine, psychiatry, and anesthesiology. The fewest are in orthopedic surgery. Between 1975 and 1981, however, the percentage of women increased in every department except pharmacology and neurology.

There is some evidence that women are increasingly being chosen to head medical school departments, although their total numbers remain small. In 1978, 33 out of 2,400 chairs were women. In 1983, the number had risen to 61. The largest number of women chairs are in pediatrics, and no women currently chair any of the surgical departments (Heins, 1985). There are no women deans of medical schools today, although Leah Lowenstein, who died in 1984, held that post at Jefferson Medical College in Philadelphia for a short time in 1982. There are 60 women at the rank of associate dean today, and this represents a four-fold increase since 1974 (Braslow & Heins, 1981). Women have not, however, made significant inroads in organized medicine as only five women are members of the House of Delegates of the American Medical Association (Members, 1984).

While there still are relatively few women at the top, women physicians are obviously important to women's health care. According to the National Medical Ambulatory Care Survey of 1977, 71.5% of the patients of women general practitioners and internists were women, compared with 60% in the practices of male physicians. Furthermore, female general practitioners and internists average 21% black and minority patients in their practices, compared with 9% for male physicians. The location of women in underserved areas may account for this difference (Nadelson, 1983).

The practice locations of women sometimes are due to discrimination on the part of male physicians who choose not to hire women (Brown & Klein, 1982). They may also reflect a preference of women for salaried positions in institutional practice in clinics, hospitals, schools, or industry rather than in private practice. Some women physicians choose such careers because they offer more regular hours and minimize the pressures of competition, thereby allowing them to more easily combine job and family. On the other hand, women physicians may be preferred by some medical administrators who believe that women are more likely than men to accept relatively low salaries, or that women wish to avoid management responsibilities. Available data clearly reveal that women physicians are overrepresented in specialties with lower mean incomes. The average 1982 net income of male physicians was $102,000, while it was only $65,200 for women (Heins, 1985).

Until role expectations and attitudes change, women physicians will continue to lag behind their male colleagues in many ways. As Marcia Angell, M.D. characterized this dilemma, "Women trade career advancement for time to raise their families" (Angell, 1982). Regardless of their level of professional commitment, women often maintain responsibility for managing the household and caring for children. In a survey of lifestyles and stresses of women and men in medicine, 54.8% of the men physicians answered "wife" when asked who was responsible for child care, while only 6.3% of the women physicians answered that their husbands were responsible for child care. Fifty percent of the women reported they had full-time household help while only 9.7% of the men had these arrangements. Furthermore, 58% of these women, but only 38% of the men, reported experiencing conflicts related to the demands of work and family (Nadelson, Notman, & Lowenstein, 1979). For black women physicians, role conflicts are not as apparent. Specifically, black women physicians are satisfied with their careers and in harmony with their dual roles. Epps (1986) attributes the above finding to the fact that minority women have traditionally been in the labor force and thus have had practice integrating the work and family roles. Women physicians, in general, will not be able to make the kinds of contributions they are qualified to make without real changes in the organization of medicine, or in the organization of family styles and responsibilities. It is unlikely, however, that family structure and roles will change for physicians, until the profession itself changes enough to permit alternative family patterns.

Estimates based on current trends suggest that women will continue to represent only about 30 to 35% of physicians. Women interested in changing the images and the care of women within the health care system, therefore, will continue to face a harsh challenge in working to improve the medical education of both men and women, in ways that allow for more positive and realistic attitudes toward women patients.

Women and the Medical Curriculum

One specific attempt to change the content and structure of medical education is represented by the use of gynecologic teaching associates (GTA's) to teach breast and pelvic exams. In one such program, developed at the University of Iowa Medical School in 1972, women educators are trained to act as both instructors and patients for these examinations. They emphasize technical skills, anatomical information, and attitude, including sensitivity to the woman patient's feelings and attitudes. The approach of the GTA workshop is to regard the patient as a partner in her care (Wallis, 1984). This challenges the traditional approach in which medical students were taught to be dominant, assertive, and to expect passivity from their patients. By 1980, about 75 U.S. medical schools had GTA programs, and 82% of the schools rated the teaching associate method as "extremely effective" (Wallis, 1984). Evaluations of the TA programs indicate that respect of medical students for their patients increases and students become more proficient and are more gentle in conducting the examinations (Wallis, Tardiff, & Deane, 1984).

Another positive change in the way medicine is being taught is the emphasis on women's studies at some medical schools. At the Indiana University School of Medicine, the Department of Psychiatry integrates an attitudinal and cognitive focus to women's studies. Although there are no separate courses on women, the orientation of all departmental courses is a biopsychosocial approach to patients. The courses move from a focus on the patient's illness to an understanding of their attitudes toward the patient and a greater understanding of themselves as professionals and human beings. In addition, course material on stress and the physician includes specific information about the evolution of the woman student's self-concept (Roeske, 1983).

The incorporation of women's studies into medical school curricula and the use of TA programs reflects the influence of the women's movement on medical education. As women and men with this social and educational orientation graduate from medical schools and become faculty members, medical school curricula may become less sexist. Institutional practices may also change as more women and men begin to demand and to utilize part-time internships and to insist on alternatives to the rigorous on-call schedules. Perhaps some day internships and residencies will not be crash courses in "macho behavior," as one woman surgeon labeled her experience (Adelman, 1983).

FEMINIST CORRECTIVES

Alternative Health Care

The women's health movement had its roots both in the women's liberation movement and the consumer movement, and was largely a response to the paternalistic, authoritarian manner in which many male physicians treated female patients. In addition, women were beginning to lose faith in the medical profession's competence and commitment to safe and effective care. For instance, in the late 1960s and early 1970s DES was still prescribed as a "morning after" contraceptive pill despite the fact that it was found to cause vaginal cancer in women whose mothers took DES during pregnancy. Radical mastectomy was long considered the preferred treatment for breast cancer despite its disfiguring effects and the lack of any proof that it was more effective than less traumatic procedures in preventing recurrence. Modern childbirth practices were designed more for the convenience of the physician than for the health of the mother and fetus (Ruzek, 1980). Women began to question the male monopoly of medical information and practice which rendered them submissive and robbed them of control over their bodies.

Even many women who did not share the political goals of the women's movement shared the movement's concern for women's control of their health. An underlying assumption of the women's health movement was that women lose control of their bodies out of ignorance. To combat this ignorance, women formed consciousness-raising and self-help groups and courses throughout the country to teach women about their bodies, their reproductive processes, nutrition, and general health care. Women also taught one another how to conduct breast and pelvic self examinations.

One of the earliest women's health groups was the Boston Women's Health Book Collective started in 1969. The Collective began when a group of women met to discuss women and their bodies. Each woman wrote a paper on some aspect of women's health, and these papers were used to give courses to women in churches, schools, and homes. Eventually, the papers were bound together into a publication, *Our Bodies, Ourselves*, which in 1984 was revised and expanded into a 647-page book.

Since 1969, women have formed at least 1,000 women's health organizations, more than 25 alternative women's clinics, and numerous small self-help groups (Corea, 1977). In Los Angeles, the Feminist Women's Health Center pioneered the "participatory clinic" in which six women come for their appointment at the same time. After meeting with a female physician for about two hours, the women complete and discuss their medical forms and the reason for their visit. Then with the help of the physician and the nurses, the women examine each other. They perform the breast and pelvic exams and complete the lab tests for each other. Through this experience the women learn more about their bodies and how to care for them (Corea, 1977).

This type of collaboration between female physicians and women's health activists is of fairly recent origin. In the early days of the women's health movement there was some suspicion of female physicians. In the first edition of *Our Bodies, Ourselves*, women were warned not to choose a physician solely on the basis of sex. Female physicians were regarded as "honorary males" and not to be trusted (Walsh, 1979).

This negative attitude toward all physicians — male and female — was a reflection of the women's health movement's emphasis on deinstitutionalization of health care. Many believed that women could only challenge the male monopoly of basic medical information by teaching each other. Consulting with physicians, even female ones, was seen as cooperation or collusion with the enemy.

The women's health movement, however, quickly extended its base, developing differing perspectives and engaging in a variety of activities aimed at improving the health care of women. Some women's health organizations have been active politically to help change the health care delivery system. In California the Coalition for the Medical Rights of Women has filed petitions and lawsuits to hold drug companies, doctors, and the state government accountable to women health consumers. Its first action in 1974 was to petition the California Department of Health for new regulations on IUD's which would require adequate premarket testing. As the result of the Coalition's action, the Health Department approved new regulations in 1976 (Corea, 1977).

The increase in female midwife deliveries is another example of the women's health movement's changes in the health care of women. For centuries women birthed at home attended by lay midwives. It was only when men-midwives, as the early obstetricians were called, wished to establish obstetrics as a medical specialty, that childbirth was redefined (Scully, 1980; Wertz, 1983). Instead of a natural process, childbirth became a surgical specialty complete with "scientific instruments," such as forceps, to aid in the delivery. As men with their latest technological discovery established control over childbirth, the practice of midwifery declined, and midwives were left to attend primarily poor and immigrant women.

Today as women have become discouraged and skeptical of the latest technological advances, they are returning to the pre-obstetrical model. By the late 1970s, the United States was experiencing a rebirth of midwifery. As the appeal of home birth and midwifery spread, certified nurse-midwives and a few physicians began to support out-of-hospital delivery. Most physicians, however, still supported hospital delivery, although they sometimes allowed modifications which provided a more homelike atmosphere (Ruzek, 1980).

In California, where lay midwifery has received widespread attention, the number of midwives and out-of-hospital births has increased steadily since early 1970. It was estimated that there were 400-500 practicing lay midwives in California in 1979. As of 1981 certified nurse-midwives may practice in 43 states and the District of Columbia, although lay midwifery is legal in only 20 states (Throne & Hanson, 1981).

Obstetricians initially resisted nurse-midwives by using such tactics as harassment, refusal to assist if complications arose, and in some cases, legal prosecution. Despite these efforts, midwife-controlled birth centers and home births have persisted. In fact, with the declining birth rate and empty maternity beds, many hospitals and doctors began to adopt some of the practices of the birthing centers, such as allowing fathers in the delivery room, homelike birthing rooms, sibling visitations, and early release of new mothers and infants (Ruzek, 1980).

While the adoption of these changes may represent improvements in the health care of women, they can also be viewed as cooptation. Although progressive and humanistic, these changes do not directly challenge the male domination of the health care delivery system, since control of medicine is still in the hands of men. Cooptation in one area may reduce discontent and thereby decrease the impetus for change in other health care areas. For these reasons, such partial solutions continue to be opposed by many feminists.

Feminist Therapy

Feminist therapy grew out of the consciousness-raising aspect of the women's movement which encouraged women to become aware of their social oppression attributable to traditional sex roles. In the context of the development of other self-help approaches, women in consciousness-raising groups shared their problems and concerns with each other. The assumption of these groups was that the social environment plays a major role in the problems of the individual. By providing women with a forum to discuss aspects of their lives that they previously had been unable to share with significant others, the consciousness-raising groups fulfilled a psychotherapeutic function (Brodsky, 1981). Within these groups, a woman's distress could be regarded not as an indication of psychopathology, but as an adaptative response to an unhealthy environment (Howell, 1981).

This emphasis on sexism in the social structure along with other concepts of consciousness-raising were incorporated into the basic tenets of feminist therapy. Although feminists were instrumental in providing a psychotherapeutic function via consciousness-raising, a great deal of progress also has occurred in terms of providing direct psychotherapeutic services (Brodsky, 1981). For example, rape crisis centers established to treat and counsel rape victims have been very successful. Recognition that the rape victim is, in fact, a victim rather than a seducer has resulted in the development of support systems for them which have helped many women deal with this emotionally damaging occurrence. The elimination, in many states, of rules of evidence requiring corroborating testimony and the identification of differing degrees of rape are other examples of changes initiated by the feminist movement. Rape crisis centers, which have helped women cope with the social stigma of being a rape victim, have also taken a political action role in achieving these other changes.

It was through working with rape victims and other women who rejected professional psychological care that women in the professions often became aware of how their work roles could reflect and again reconstruct the oppression of women in society. As a result, the Association for Women in Psychology was formed in 1968 and presentations on the psychology of women began appearing at American Psychological Association conventions and in the scientific literature.

The need to de-masculinize mental health practices and psychotherapy for women was brought to psychology's attention in a landmark study by Broverman (1970) and her colleagues. Male and female psychologists, psychiatrists, and social workers actively involved in clinical settings were asked to judge qualities that describe a mentally healthy male, female, or ideal adult. The finding revealed a strong match between the healthy male qualities and ideal healthy adult qualities. The mentally healthy woman, however, was described very differently, with adjectives that characterized her as more submissive, less independent, less competitive, less aggressive, more emotional, more concerned with personal appearance, less objective, less adventuresome, less interested in scientific subjects, and so on. Broverman and her colleagues asserted that this was, indeed, an irregular description of a mature adult person. Yet, the mentally healthy woman apparently was seen as emotional, illogical, submissive, and intellectually superficial by both male and female therapists. Clinicians working with these stereotypes and biases against women are contributing to what Ehrenreich and English have called the "masochistic adjustment" (1978).

In mental health settings, as in physical health settings, women have struggled with the conflicts of "role appropriate" behavior based on sex stereotypes. Women's options were limited. They could model their behavior on the mature adult (or male) profile, with the result that their femaleness might be questioned or they might be considered deviant. On the other hand, women could act like sex-role prescribes and surrender full opportunity for social expression. Broverman and her associates urged their clinician colleagues to become aware of these stereotypes and to work to correct them.

Research such as Broverman's appears to have paved the way for the development of feminist mental health therapies. Howell (1981) outlines the impact of feminism on psychotherapy in terms of a societal focus. Mental health and mental illness of women need to be explained through the transactions of women in their social environments. How the environment shapes and is shaped by women is an important dialectic common in feminist approaches to psychotherapy. Brodsky (1981) and others (Hawley & Sanford, 1984; Hare-Mustin, 1981; Goz, 1981) have described how traditional psychotherapy relationships and outcomes have been altered with the shift of focus provided by the women's movement of the 1960s and early 1970s. Family therapy to re-define work roles within the home, pregnancy termination counseling, and therapies aimed at rape, incest, and sexual violence problems are some specific interventions directed at the unique needs of women clients.

Whether the psychotherapist is male or female, feminist approaches to problems presented in these areas have a common theme. This theme involves the identification and use of personal strengths (Hawley & Sanford, 1984). Generally, the therapist is aware of status or power differences that exist in their relationship with their clients. Mental well-being is usually defined within the relevant social, economic, and political contexts. While all women therapists are not feminist in orientation, it may be equally incorrect to assume that no male therapists are feminist. Hawley and Sanford

(1984) urge women to remember that a feminist approach to psychotherapy is an attitude, and not a professional label.

The Task Force on Sex Bias of the American Psychological Association began collecting data in 1974 from women psychologists and developed a set of guidelines for therapy with women (Guidelines, 1978). The guidelines endorse the use of: (1) APA standards for ethical practice (2) concepts of feminist counseling, and (3) avoiding sexist language and contact between therapist and client. The basic concepts of feminist counseling include: (1) the establishment of an egalitarian relationship between the therapist and the client; (2) a consciousness-raising approach to differentiate between the sexist social structure and individual problems the woman can control; (3) developing a sense of personal power and the ability to use anger constructively; (4) developing a self-identity that encompasses role changes; (5) encouraging women to care and nurture themselves, thereby increasing their self-confidence; and (6) encouraging skill development to enhance one's competence (Worell, 1981). Utilizing these concepts of feminist counseling, an enlightened therapist, male or female, can help change the oppressive consequences of stereotyped sex-roles and expectations.

A FINAL COMMENT

A primary theme of this chapter has been that health care practitioners and practices in this country have invented and promoted images of women as weak and incompetent, both physically and mentally. Historically, women have been treated as ill because of natural physiological processes which simply differed from those of men. As men gained control of health care, moreover, they judged women to be basically dependent and incapable of understanding and participating in decisions about their own health and health care. While we have cited many recent improvements in both health care and medical education, negative stereotypes of women continue to be deeply rooted in the values and attitudes of some components of the health care system. We have yet to overcome the inexcusable practice of unnecessary hysterectomies imposed on so many women (Scully, 1980). The patently false assumptions regarding both menstruation and menopause that reduced women to less than human status in the nineteenth century (Smith-Rosenberg & Rosenberg, 1984) continue to influence, albeit more subtly, the diagnoses and treatment of women's health problems today. Rothman (1979) points out that menopause often still is referred to as a "disease" in the medical literature. Many practitioners also continue to assume an association between psychological and/or psychosomatic symptomatology and menopause, although research demonstrates no such relationship (Notman, 1981).

It is neither fair, nor completely accurate, of course, to hold the health care establishment singularly responsible for negative and dysfunctional attitudes toward women. Medicine — and our health care system in the broader sense — are created by social norms and values as much as they contribute to them. Bullough and Bullough (1973) described this in their excellent volume on attitudes toward women, *The Subordinate Sex*. They demonstrated the fact that, throughout history and in virtually all cultures, both Eastern and Western, men have defined the roles of women, and these roles have been articulated and enforced through whatever systems and institutions were available to those respective societies. Similarly, our health care system today is just one institution which both addresses and responds to social issues. It is our contention, however, that physicians and others working in health care have a special responsibility with respect to the development of attitudes toward women. In our society, medicine and related disciplines have been granted a proprietary role with respect to issues of normal human development, as well as concerns related to illness and disability. This role of expert extends quite naturally into a very broad range of issues regarding how we live our lives, and the "doctor's advice" is heeded more readily and taken more seriously than that of almost anyone else. For a number of reasons, this is especially true for women.

Women's lives are inevitably and inextricably tied to the health care system. Most women will spend far more time interacting with health care providers than will their male peers. This is true because medicine has claimed the normal hormonal and reproduction-related functions of women for its purview. It is also true because women continue to accept primary responsibility for the care of children and, later in life, for the care of aging and ill relatives, including their spouses and other male-age peers whom they continue to outlive. There is much at risk in all of these matters, and women must find a way to access and learn from health care providers — for the sake of those they love and care for, as well as for themselves. This means, of course, that the power relationship in the doctor-patient relationship is especially salient for women. Consequently, women can be expected to be particularly vulnerable to the attitudes expressed by physicians and unduly influenced by them in developing their own self-images. The optimistic side of this picture, of course, is that an enlightened health care system can contribute enormously to the development of new and more positive images of women.

Changes in the medical care establishment brought about by the women's movement have been primarily attitudinal. As women have become more informed health care consumers, the attitudes of physicians have begun to change. Women are demanding and, in many cases, receiving more information and respect from medical care professionals. These changes in the way services are delivered, as well as the challenge to the male-dominated hierarchical structure imposed by the growth of alternative health care systems, are legacies of the women's movement. Only when women began taking control of their own health care did the medical profession begin to respond with positive changes. When women turned away from institutionalized medicine and began consulting with each other and establishing their own systems, the medical establishment took note. Just as the feminist movement in the nineteenth century resulted in the establishment of women's medical colleges and the promotion of women healers, the women's movement of the 1960s and 1970s changed the aspirations and expectations of women. Women today are better informed, better organized, and more vocal. It is our belief that the changes brought about by the current feminist movement will continue to exert a positive influence in changing the health care of women.

REFERENCES

Adelman, S. (1983). The female surgeon. In J.P. Collan (Ed.), *The physician: A professional under stress* (pp. 279-293). Norwalk, CT: Appleton-Century-Crofts.

Angell, M. (1982). Juggling the personal and professional life. *Journal of the American Medical Women's Association, 37,* 64-68

Armitage, K.J., Schneiderman, L.J., & Bass, R.A. (1979). Response of physicians to medical complaints in men and women. *Journal of the American Medical Association, 241*(20), 2186-2187.

Bluestone, N.R. (1978). The future impact of women physicians on American medicine. *American Journal of Public Health, 68*(8), 760-763.

Bobula, J.D. (1980). Work patterns, practice characteristics, and incomes of male and female physicians. *Journal of Medical Education, 55,* 826-833.

Braslow, J., & Heins, M. (1981). Women in medical education: A decade of change. *New England Journal of Medicine, 304,* 1129-1135.

Brodsky, A.M. (1981). A decade of feminist influence on psychotherapy. In E. Howell & M. Bayes (Eds.), *Women and mental health* (pp. 607-619). New York: Basic Books.

Broverman, I.K., Broverman, D.M., Clarkson, F.E., Rosenkrantz, P.S., & Vogel, S.R. (1970). Sex-role stereotyping and clinical judgments of mental health. *Journal of Consulting and Clinical Psychology, 34,* 1-7.

Brown, S-L., & Klein, R.H. (1982). Women-power in the medical hierarchy. *Journal of the American Medical Women's Association, 37*(6), 155-164.

Bullough, V.L., & Bullough, B. (1973). *The subordinate sex.* Urbana: University of Illinois Press.

Corea, G. (1977). *The hidden malpractice: How American medicine treats women as patients and professionals.* Garden City, NY: Anchor Press.

Cypress, B.K. (1984). *Patterns of ambulatory care in obstetrics and gynecology.* Vital and Health Statistics, Series 13, No. 76. Hyattsville, MD: U.S. Department of Health and Human Services.

Ehrenreich, B., & English, D. (1978). *For her own good: 150 years of the experts advice to women.* Garden City, NY: Anchor Press.

Epps, R. (1986). The black woman physician—Perspectives and priorities. *Journal of the National Medical Association, 78*(5), 375-381.

Goz, R. (1981). Women patients and women therapists: Some issues that come up in psychotherapy. In E. Howell & M. Bayes (Eds.), *Women and mental health* (pp. 514-533). New York: Basic Books.

Greer, S., Dickerson, V., Schneiderman, L.J., Atkins, C., & Bass, R. (1986). Responses of male and female physicians to medical complaints in male and female patients. *The Journal of Family Practice, 23*(1), 49-53.

Guidelines for therapy with women: APA task force on sex bias and sex role stereotyping in psychotherapeutic practice (1978). *American Psychologist, 33*(12), 1122-1123.

Hare-Mustin, R.T. (1981). A feminist approach to family therapy. In E. Howell & M. Bayes (Eds.), *Women and mental health* (pp. 553-571). New York: Basic Books.

Hawley, N.P., & Sanford, W. (1984). Psychotherapy. In *The new our bodies, ourselves*: The Boston Women's Health Book Collective (pp. 73-76). New York: Simon & Schuster.

Heins, M. (1985). Update: Women in medicine. *Journal of the American Medical Women's Association*, 40(2), 43-50.

Howell, E. (1981). Psychotherapy with women clients: The impact of feminism. In E. Howell & M. Bayes (Eds.), *Women and mental health* (pp. 509-513). New York: Basic Books.

Howell, M.C. (1974). What medical schools teach about women. *New England Journal of Medicine, 291*, 304-306.

Langwell, K.M. (1982). Factors affecting the incomes of men and women physicians: Further exploration. *Journal of Human Resources, 17*, 175-261.

Lennane, K.J., & Lennane, R.J. (1973). Alleged psychogenic disorders in women — A possible manifestation of sexual prejudice. *New England Journal of Medicine, 288*(6), 288-292.

Lorber, J. (1975). Good patients and problem patients: Conformity and deviance in a general hospital. *Journal of Health and Social Behavior, 16*, 213-225.

Members of the House of Delegates (1984). *Journal of the American Medical Association, 252*(13), 1702-1709.

Nadelson, C. (1983). The women physician: Past, present and future. In J.P. Callan (Ed.), *The physician: A professional under stress* (pp. 261-276). Norwalk, CT: Appleton-Century-Crofts.

Nadelson, C.C., Notman, M.T., & Lowenstein, P. (1979). The practice patterns, lifestyles and stresses of women and men entering medicine. *Journal of the American Medical Women's Association, 34*(11), 400-406.

Notman, M.T. (1981). Midlife concerns of women: Implications of the menopause. In E. Howell & M. Bayes (Eds.), *Women and mental health* (pp. 385-394). New York: Basic Books.

Parsons, T. (1951). *The social system*. New York: The Free Press.

Roeske, N.C.A. (1983). Women's studies in medical education. *Journal of Medical Education, 58*, 611-618.

Rothman, B.K. (1979). Women, health, and medicine. In J. Freeman (Ed.), *Women: A feminist perspective* (pp. 27-40). Palo Alto, CA: Mayfield.

Ruzek, S.B. (1980). Medical response to women's health activities: Conflict, accommodation and cooptation. In J. A. Roth (Ed.), *Research in the sociology of health care* (pp. 335-354). Greenwich, CT: Jai Press.

Scully, D. (1980). *Men who control women's health: The miseducation of obstetricians-gynecologists*. Boston: Houghton-Mifflin.

Shapiro, J., McGrath, E., & Anderson, R.C. (1983). Patients', medical students', and physicians' perceptions of male and female physicians. *Perceptual and Motor Skills, 56*, 179-190.

Smith, I.K., Lancaster, C.J., & Fleming, G.A. (1984). Medical students' feelings related to isolation and school environment. *Journal of the American Medical Women's Association*, *39*(5), 159-162.

Smith-Rosenberg, C., & Rosenberg, C. (1984). The female animal: Medical and biological views of woman and her role in nineteenth-century America. In J.W. Leavitt (Ed.), *Women and health in America* (pp. 12-27). Madison, WI: University of Wisconsin Press.

Throne, L.J., & Hanson, L.P. (1981). Midwifery laws in the United States. *Women & Health*, *6*(314), 7-26.

Verbrugge, L.M. (1984). How physicians treat mentally distressed men and women. *Social Science and Medicine*, *18*(1), 1-9.

Wallen, J., Waitzkin, H., & Stoeckle, J.D. (1979). Physician stereotypes about female health and illness. *Women & Health*, *4*(2), 135-146.

Wallis, L.A. (1984). A quiet revolution. *Journal of the American Medical Women's Association*, *39*(2), 34-35.

Wallis, A., Tardiff, K., & Deane, K. (1984). Changes in students' attitudes following a pelvic teaching associate program. *Journal of the American Medical Women's Association*, *39*(2), 46-48.

Walsh, M.R. (1979). The rediscovery of the need for a feminist medical education. *Harvard Educational Review*, *49*(4), 447-466.

Weisman, C.S., & Teitelbaum, M.A. (1985). Physician gender and the physician-patient relationship: Recent evidence and relevant questions. *Social Science and Medicine*, *20*(11), 1119-1127.

Wertz, D.C. (1983). What birth has done for doctors: A historical view. *Women & Health*, *8*(1), 7-24.

West, C. (1984). *Routine complications*. Bloomington: Indiana University Press.

Worell, J. (1981). New directions in counseling women. In E. Howell & M. Bayes (Eds.), *Women & mental health* (pp. 620-637). New York: Basic Books.

Directory of Curriculum Integration Resources

LIBRARY RESOURCES IN WOMEN'S STUDIES

For valuable discussions on how to use the card catalog and finding books on women's issues, consult:

Searing, S.E. (1985). *Introduction to library research in women's studies*. Boulder: Westview Press.

Lynn, N.B., Matasar, A.B., & Rosenberg, M.B. (1974). *Research guide in women's studies*. Morristown, NJ: General Learning Press.

Indexes and abstracts that can be used to locate articles, documents, and papers in serials, books, and collected works about women's issues include the following:

Women's Studies Abstracts
Alternative Press Index
Psychological Abstracts
Sociological Abstracts
Dissertation Abstracts International
Masters' Abstracts
Social Science Index
Monthly Catalog of U.S. Government Publications
Modern Language Association Bibliography
Contemporary Literary Criticism

Sample listing of journals devoted to women's issues:

Chrysalis: A Magazine of Women's Culture
SIGNS
Ms.
Feminist Studies Quarterly
Sex Roles

Women and Literature
Women and Environment
Psychology of Women Quarterly
Women and Performance
Women & Health
International Feminist Studies Quarterly
Women and Aging
Women & Politics
Women's Studies Quarterly
Women and Work
Quest: A Feminist Quarterly
Journal of Black Psychology
Journal of Cross-Cultural Psychology
Journal of Social Issues
Gender and Society
Journal of Women and Music
Feminist Art Journal
Journal of Black Studies
Women & Therapy
Journal of Gay & Lesbian Psychology
Journal of Feminist Family Therapy
Journal of the American Medical Women's Association
The Western Journal of Black Studies
The New England Journal of Black Studies
SAGE

Monographs distributed by the National Institute of Education, U.S. Department of Health, Education, and Welfare, Washington, DC 20208:

The effectiveness of women's studies teaching.
Women's studies as a catalyst for faculty development.
The impact of women's studies on the campus and the discipline.
The involvement of minority women in women's studies.
Women's studies in the community college.
Re-entry women involved in women's studies.
The relationship between women's studies, career development
    and vocational choice.
Women's studies graduates.

ORGANIZATIONS CONCERNED WITH WOMEN IN THE ACADEMY

National Women's Studies Association
University of Maryland
203 Behavioral and Social Sciences Building
College Park, MD 20742

National Organization for Women
425 13th St. NW
Suite 723
Washington, DC 20004

National Network of Minority Women in Science
Association for the Advancement of Science
1776 Massachusetts Ave., NW
Washington, DC 20036

National Institute for Women of Color
1712 N St. NW
Washington, DC 20036

Federation of Organizations for Professional Women
1825 Connecticut Avenue, NW
Suite 403
Washington, DC 20009

Association of Black Women in Higher Education
30 Limmerick Dr.
Albany, NY 12204

American Association of Community and Junior Colleges
Center for Women's Opportunities
One Dupont Circle, NW
Suite 140
Washington, DC 20036

American Association of University Professors
Committee on the Status of Women
One Dupont Circle, NW
Suite 500
Washington, DC 20036

Center for the Study, Education, and Advancement of Women
University of California, Berkeley
Building T-9; Room 112
Berkeley, CA 94720

Working Women United Institute
593 Park Avenue
New York, NY 10021

Project on the Status and Education of Women
1818 R Street, NW
Washington, DC 20009

Adult Educational Association of the USA
810 18th St. NW
Washington, DC 20006

Hispanic American Career Educational Resources, Inc.
115 West 30 St.
Room 900
New York, NY 10001

National Institute of Education
Minorities and Women's Programs
1200 19th St. NW
Washington, DC 20208

National University Continuing Education Association
Division of Women's Education
One Dupont Circle
Suite 360
Washington, DC 20036

American Educational Research Association
Special Interest Group on Research on Women and Education
1230 17 St. NW
Washington, DC 20036

American Psychological Association
1200 17th St. NW
Washington, DC 20036

SAMPLE AUDIO-VISUAL MATERIAL

She's nobody's baby: American woman in the 20th Century
MTI, Inc.
3710 Commercial Avenue
Northbrook, IL 60062

Women in management: Threat or opportunity?
CRM/McGraw Hill Films
McGraw Hill Book Company
Delmar, CA 92014

Back to school, back to work
American Personnel and Guidance Film Department
1607 New Hampshire Avenue, NW
Washington, DC 20009

Careers and babics
Polymorph Films
118 South St.
Boston, MA 02111

Who remembers mama?
New Day Films
22 Riverview Dr.
Wayne, NJ 07470

The power pinch: Sexual harassment in the workplace
MTI, Inc.
3710 Commercial Avenue
Northbrook, IL 60062

Black women
National Educational Television
2715 Packard Road
Ann Arbor, MI 48104

Permanent wave
Third World Newsreel
335 West 38th St.
New York, NY 10018

You are the game: Sexual harassment on campus
Indiana University
Audio Visual Center
Bloomington, IN 47405

Your right to fight: Stopping sexual harassment on campus
University of Albany, State University of New York
Affirmative Action
Administration 301
Albany, NY 12222

The Willmar 8
California Newsreel
630 Natoma St.
San Francisco, CA 94103

SAMPLE REFERENCES ON THE TRANSLATION OF WOMEN'S STUDIES INTO EDUCATIONAL PRAXIS

Bunch, C., & Pollack, S. (Eds.) (1983). *Learning our way: Essays in feminist education*. Trumansburg, NY: The Crossing Press.

Carmen, E., & Driver, F. (1982). Teaching women's studies: Values in conflict. *Psychology of Women Quarterly*, *7*, 81-95.

Clarey, J., Hutchins, J., Powers, V., & Thiem, L. (1985). Feminist education: Transforming the research seminar. *Journal of Thought*, *20*, 147-161.

Conway, J. (1974). Coeducation and women's studies: Two approaches to the question of women's place in the contemporary university. *Daedalus*, *103*, 239-249.

DeFour, D.C., & Paludi, M.A. (1988, March). Integrating the scholarship on women of color and ethnicity into the psychology of women course. Workshop presented at the Association for Women in Psychology, Bethesda, MD.

Faunce, P. (1985). Teaching feminist therapies: Integrating feminist therapy, pedagogy, and scholarship. In L.B. Rosewater & L.E.A. Walker (Eds.), *Handbook of feminist therapy: Women's issues in psychotherapy*. New York: Springer.

Howe, F. (1976). Women's studies in the high schools. *Women's Studies Newsletter*, *4*, 4.

James, S. (1985). Teaching about women in the arts. *Journal of Thought*, *20*, 243-249.

Lord, S.B. (1982). Teaching the psychology of women: Examination of a teaching-learning model. *Psychology of Women Quarterly*, *7*, 71-80.

Maglin, N. (1979, Spring). What is feminist teaching? Paper presented at the Meeting of the New York State Women's Association, Portland, NY.

Manner, F. (1985). Pedagogics for the gender balanced classroom. *Journal of Thought*, *20*, 48-64.

Mumford, L.S. (1985). "Why do we have to read all this old stuff?" Conflict in the feminist theory classroom. *Journal of Thought*, *20*, 88-96.

Paludi, M.A. (1989). *Exploring/teaching the psychology of women: A manual of resources*. Albany, NY: State University of New York Press.

Ross, J., & Holbrook, J. (1985). The Taycheedah experience: Teaching women's studies in a women's prison. *Journal of Thought*, *20*, 97-105.

Rosser, S.V. (1985). Introductory biology: Approaches to feminist transformation in course content and teaching practice. *Journal of Thought*, *20*, 205-217.

Rothenberg, P. (1985). Teaching about racism and sexism: A case history. *Journal of Thought*, *20*, 122-136.

Russell, M. (1976). Black-eyed blues connections: Teaching black women. *Women's Studies Newsletter*, *4*, 7-8.

Schniedewind, N. (1985). Cooperative structured learning: Implications for feminist pedagogy. *Journal of Thought*, *20*, 48-64.

Stinemann, E. (1979). *Women's studies: A recommended core bibliography*. Littleton, CO: Libraries Unlimited.

CENTERS FOR RESEARCH OF WOMEN: UNIVERSITY AFFILIATED

A complete list of centers for research on women has been compiled by the National Council for Research on Women; for more information contact the National Council for Research on Women, 47-49 East 65th St., New York, NY 10021. The *Women's Studies Quarterly* (Feminist Press) prints a list describing women's research centers each spring. The Women's Research and Education Institute publishes *A Directory of Selected Women's Research and Policy Centers*. This is available from WREI, 204 Fourth St. SE, Washington, DC 20003.

Name	University	Address
Southwest Institute for Research on Women	University of Arizona	Modern Languages 269 Tucson, AZ 85721
Pembroke Center for Teaching and Research on Women	Brown University	Box 1958 Providence, RI 02912
Center for the Study Education, and Advancement of Women	University of California, Berkeley	Room 112 Building T-9 Berkeley, CA 94720
Women's Resources and Research Center	University of California, Davis	10 Lower Freeborn Hall Davis, CA 95616
Center for the Study of Women	University of California, Los Angeles	236 A Kinsey Hall Los Angeles, CA 90064
Higher Education Research Institute	University of California, Los Angeles	Grad. School of Educ. 405 Hilgard Ave. Los Angeles, CA 90024
Center for Women's Studies Research and Resources Institute	University of Cincinnati	Room 150 McMicken Hall Mall Location 164 Cincinnati, OH 45221
Center for the Study of Women and Society	CUNY Graduate School and University Center	33 West 42nd St. New York, NY 10036

Institute for Women and Work	Cornell University	New York State School of Industrial and Labor Relations 15 East 26th St. New York, NY 10010
Women's Studies Research Center	Duke University University of N. Carolina	119 East Duke Building Durham, NC 27708
The Women's Studies Program and Policy Center	George Washington University	Stuart Hall Room 203 Washington, DC 20052
Higher Education Resource Services, New England	Wellesley College	Cheever House Wellesley, MA 02181
Higher Education Resource Services, Mid-America	Colorado Women's College Campus, University of Denver	Denver, CO 80220
Higher Education Resource Services, West	University of Utah	Women's Resource Center 293 Olpin Union Salt Lake City, UT 84112
Center for Research on Women	Memphis State University	College of Arts & Sciences Memphis, TN 38152
Center for Continuing Education of Women	University of Michigan	350 South Thayer St. Ann Arbor, MI 48109
Center of Advanced Feminist Studies	University of Minnesota	492 Ford Hall 224 Church St. SE Minneapolis, MN 55455
Center for Women in Government	State University of New York at Albany	Draper Hall Room 302 1400 Washington Ave. Albany, NY 12222

Center for the Study of Women in Society	University of Oregon	Room 636 Prince Lucien Campbell Hall College of Arts & Sciences Eugene, OR 97403
Center for Rural Women	Pennsylvania State University	College of Agriculture 201 Agricultural Admin. Bldg. University Park, PA 16802
Alice Paul Center for the Study of Women	University of Pennsylvania	106 Logan Hall, CN Philadelphia, PA 19104
Mary Ingraham Bunting Institute	Radcliffe College	10 Garden St. Cambridge, MA 02138
The Henry Murray Research Center	Radcliffe College	77 Brattle St. Cambridge, MA 02138
The Arthur and Elizabeth Schlesinger Library	Radcliffe College	10 Garden St. Cambridge, MA 02138
Center for the American Woman and Politics	Rutgers University	Eagleton Institute of Politics New Brunswick, NJ 08903
Institute for Research on Women	Rutgers University	Douglass College New Brunswick, NJ 08903
Project on Women and Social Change	Smith College	138 Elm St. Northampton, MA 01063
Program for the Study of Women and Men in Society	University of Southern California	Taper Hall 331M Los Angeles, CA 90089
Women's Resource and Research Center	Spelman College	Box 362 Atlanta, GA 30314
Center for Research on Women	Stanford University	Serra House, Serra St. Stanford, CA 94305

Northwest Center for Research on Women	University of Washington	Cunningham Hall AJ-50 Seattle, WA 98195
Center for Research on Women	Wellesley College	828 Washington St. Wellesley, MA 02181
Women's Studies Program and Research Center	University of Wisconsin, Madison	209 North Brooks St. Madison, WI 53715

CENTERS FOR RESEARCH ON WOMEN: NON-UNIVERSITY AFFILIATED

Center	Address
American Council on Education	One Dupont Circle, NW Washington, DC 20036
Association of American Colleges Project on the Status and Education of Women	1818 R Street, NW Washington, DC 20009
Business and Professional Women's Foundation	2012 Massachusetts Ave., NW Washington, DC 20036
Center for Women Policy Studies	2000 P Street, NW Suite 508 Washington, DC 20036
Equity Policy Center	4818 Drummond Avenue Chevy Chase, MD 20815
The Institute for Research in History	1133 Broadway Suite 923 New York, NY 10010
International Center for Research on Women	1717 Massachusetts Ave., NW Suite 501 Washington, DC 20036
National Association for Women Deans, Administrators, and Counselors	1325 18th St., NW Suite 210 Washington, DC 20036

Project on Equal Education
   Rights

1413 K Street, NW
9th Floor
Washington, DC 20005

Program of Policy Research on
   Women and Families Urban
   Institute

2100 M St., NW
Washington, DC 20037

Women's Interart Center

549 W. 52nd St.
New York, NY 10019

The Women's Research and
   Education Institute,
   Congressional Caucus
   for Women's Issues

204 Fourth St., SE
Washington, DC 20003

Index